Information Security Management Principles

An ISEB Certificate

The British Computer Society

BCS is the leading professional body for the IT industry. With members in over 100 countries, BCS is the professional and learned society in the field of computers and information systems.

The BCS is responsible for setting standards for the IT profession. It is also leading the change in public perception and appreciation of the economic and social importance of professionally managed IT projects and programmes. In this capacity, the society advises, informs and persuades industry and government on successful IT implementation.

IT is affecting every part of our lives and that is why the BCS is determined to promote IT as the profession of the 21st century.

Joining BCS

BCS qualifications, products and services are designed with your career plans in mind. We not only provide essential recognition through professional qualifications but also offer many other useful benefits to our members at every level.

BCS Membership demonstrates your commitment to professional development. It helps to set you apart from other IT practitioners and provides industry recognition of your skills and experience. Employers and customers increasingly require proof of professional qualifications and competence. Professional membership confirms your competence and integrity and sets an independent standard that people can trust. Professional Membership (MBCS) is the pathway to Chartered IT Professional (CITP) Status.

www.bcs.org/membership

Further Information

Further information about BCS can be obtained from: The British Computer Society, First Floor, Block D, North Star House, North Star Avenue, Swindon SN2 1FA, UK.

Telephone: 0845 300 4417 (UK only) or + 44 (0)1793 417 424 (overseas)

Contact: www.bcs.org/contact

Information Security Management Principles
An ISEB Certificate

Andy Taylor (Editor)

David Alexander

Amanda Finch

David Sutton

 BCS

The British Computer Society
Publishing and Information Products
First Floor, Block D
North Star House
North Star Avenue
Swindon
SN2 1FA
UK

www.bcs.org

ISBN 978-1-902505-90-9

British Cataloguing in Publication Data.
A CIP catalogue record for this book is available at the British Library.

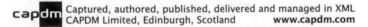 Captured, authored, published, delivered and managed in XML
CAPDM Limited, Edinburgh, Scotland   **www.capdm.com**

Printed at Antony Rowe.

Contents

List of Figures and Tables

Authors

Andy Taylor, after initially teaching in secondary schools, has been involved with information assurance for over 20 years starting when he served in the Royal Navy in several posts as security officer. He had responsibility for all classified and cryptographic materials in both warships and shore establishments at times helping to maintain the effectiveness of the nuclear deterrent. After leaving the Royal Navy he chose a further career in consultancy and was instrumental in achieving one of the first accreditations for a management consultancy against the information security standard ISO17799 (now ISO27001).

As one of the earliest members of the CESG Listed Advisor Scheme (CLAS) approved by Government Communications Headquarters (GCHQ), he has provided information assurance advice to a wide variety of organisations in the public and private sectors including the Health Service, Home Office, utility regulators, the Prison and Probation Services and web developers. He has developed and delivered a number of specialist security briefings to help educate users in the effective use of information in a secure manner and has been lecturing to all new staff in the Treasury Solicitors for over seven years. He was recently a team leader for the group revising the Government's Information Assurance policy. He has a passionate interest in maintaining the highest standards of information assurance and helping others to gain expertise in it.

David Alexander is Technical Solutions Director of Vistorm Professional Services and specialises in information security architectures, information assurance and governance. He has 10 years experience as an information security practitioner and consultant. In that time he has worked on a wide range of commercial, central government and defence projects. David started his career as an Officer in the RAF, learning the need for information security at the outset of his working life. He has been involved in IT for over 20 years, the first 10 as a Software Engineer, Operations Manager, Project Manager and IT Consultant before he changed sides from 'poacher to gamekeeper' and became an Information Security Practitioner. He has been a CLAS consultant for six years and was one of the first 50 people in the world accredited as Lead Auditor for what is now ISO27001. David is a member of the Institute for Information Security Professionals, a Chartered IT Professional, a Fellow of the British Computer Society and a committee member of their Information Security Special Interest Group.

Amanda Finch has specialised in Information Security management since 1991 when she helped establish the function within Marks & Spencer. As Security Manager, she has been at the heart of shaping information security within the company, and has developed an extensive understanding of the commercial sector and its particular security needs. Amanda is engaged in all aspects of Information Security Management and takes a pragmatic approach to the application of security controls to meet business objectives. As an active contributor within the industry Amanda is particularly interested in raising levels of education and in gaining recognition for the discipline as a recognised profession and is involved with the principal organisations to encourage this. Amanda has a Masters degree in Information Security and holds full membership of the Institute of Information Security Professionals (IISP). In 2007 she was awarded European Chief Information Security Officer of the year by *Secure Computing* magazine.

David Sutton's career in the information technology and telecommunication industries spans more than 40 years and includes computing, voice and data networking, fibre optics, radio transmission and information security.

He joined Cellnet (now Telefónica O2 UK Limited) in 1993, where he is responsible for the continuity and restoration of the core cellular networks.

He represents O2 at the national level tripartite forum known as the Electronic Communications Infrastructure Resilience and Response Group (EC-RRG), and in December 2005 gave evidence to the Greater London Authority enquiry into the mobile telecoms impact of the London bombings.

David delivers lectures on risk management, business continuity and disaster recovery at Coventry University and the Royal Holloway University of London from which he holds an MSc in Information Security, and also on mobile telecoms on Communications courses at the Cabinet Office Emergency Planning College at Easingwold near York.

He is a member of the Institution of Engineering and Technology, a Certified Information Systems Security Professional (CISSP) and a Specialist member of the Business Continuity Institute.

Acknowledgements

The authors would like to acknowledge the contributions made by Karen Webb and Stef Venn of ISEB for bringing them together, providing good lunches and generally trying to keep them in order to enable the examinations to be developed effectively which in turn enabled this book to be written. Also, thanks to Ed Brown for the cartoons.

Abbreviations

AES	Advanced Encryption Standard
ANSI	American National Standards Institute
BCP	Business Continuity Plan
BCS	British Computer Society
BIA	Business Impact Analysis
BS	British Standard
CA	Certification Authority
CBT	Computer-Based Training
CC	Common Criteria
CCRA	Common Criteria Recognition Arrangement
CCT	CSIA Claims Tested
CCTV	Closed-Circuit Television
CESG	Communications-Electronics Security Group
CIO	Chief Information Officer
CISMP	Certificate in Information Security Management Principles
CISO	Chief Information Security Officer
CLEF	Commercial Licensed Evaluation Facility
CMM	Capability Maturity Model
COSO	Committee of Sponsoring Organizations of the Treadway Commission
CPNI	Centre for the Protection of National Infrastructure
CSIA	Central Sponsor for Information Assurance
CTCPEC	Canadian Trusted Computer Product Evaluation Criteria
DES	Data Encryption Standard
DHS	Department for Homeland Security
DMZ	Demilitarised Zone
DoS	Denial of Service
DPA	Data Protection Act
DR	Disaster Recovery
EAL	Evaluation Assurance Level
EDGE	Enhanced Data Rates for GSM Evolution
EDI	Electronic Data Interchange
EDS	ETSI Documentation Service
EFTA	European Free Trade Association

ENISA	European Network and Information Security Agency
ERP	Enterprise Resource Planning
ETR	Evaluation Technical Report
ETSI	European Telecommunications Standards Institute
EU	European Union
FIPS PUBS	Federal Information Processing Standards Publications
FIRST	Forum for Incident Response and Security Teams
FoIA	Freedom of Information Act
FSA	Financial Services Agency
GATT TRIP	General Agreement on Tariffs and Trades, Trade Related Aspects of Intellectual Property Rights
GCHQ	Government Communications Headquarters
GFS	Grandfather-Father-Son
GIPSI	General Information Assurance Products and Services Initiative
GPRS	GSM Packet Radio Service
GSM	Global System for Mobile communications
HIDS	Host Intrusion Detection Systems
HIPAA	Health Insurance Portability and Accountability Act
HRA	Human Rights Act
HSDPA	High-Speed Downlink Packet Access
IA	Information Assurance
ICSA	Institute of Chartered Secretaries and Administrators
ICT	Information Communications and Technology
ID&A	Identification and Authentication
IDC	Inter-Domain Connector
IDS	Intrusion Detection System
IEC	International Electrotechnical Commission
IETF	Internet Engineering Task Force
IPR	Intellectual Property Rights
IPS	Intrusion Prevention System
IRC	Internet Relay Chat
IRT	Incident Response Team
IS	Information Security
IS	Information Systems
ISF	International Security Forum
ISMS	Information Security Management System
ISO	International Organization for Standardization
ITIL	IT Infrastructure Library
ITPC	Infosec Training Paths and Competencies
ITSEC	Information Technology Security Evaluation Criteria

ITU	International Telecommunication Union
LAN	Local Area Network
LOB	Line of Business
MIFID	Markets in Financial Instruments Directive
NDA	Non-Disclosure Agreement
NIDS	Network Intrusion Detection Systems
NIST	National Institute for Standards and Technology
OSA	Official Secrets Act
PACE	Police and Criminal Evidence Act
PAS	Publicly Available Specification
PCI	Payment Card Industry
PDCA	Plan–Do–Check–Act
PGP	Pretty Good Privacy
PIN	Personal Identification Number
PKI	Public Key Infrastructure
RFC	Request for Comments
RIPA	Regulation of Investigatory Powers Act
ROI	Return on Investment
SANS	Sysadmin, Audit, Network, Security
SEAP	Security Equipment Assessment Panel
SLA	Service Level Agreement
SOMA	Security Operations Maturity Architecture
SSL	Secure Sockets Layer
TOE	Target of Evaluation
UPS	Uninterruptible Power Supply
VOIP	Voice Over IP
VPN	Virtual Private Network
WA	Wassenaar Arrangement
WAN	Wide Area Network
WAP	Wireless Access Point
WiFi	Wireless Fidelity

Preface

Information has been important for a very wide variety of reasons for as many centuries as man has been able to pass valuable data to another person. The location of the nearest water hole, herd of wild animals or warm cave was a carefully guarded secret that was only passed on to those with a need to know and who could be trusted not to divulge the information to other, possibly hostile, tribes. The method of transfer and the storage of such information were perhaps rather more primitive than today but the basic principles of Information Security have not changed too much since those days.

Information Security, which is more accurately called Information Assurance, is now well founded in three major concepts – those of Confidentiality, Integrity and Availability. Managing these concepts is critical and, as information has increasingly become one of the modern currencies of society, it is the retention of assurance in an appropriate and cost-effective manner that has become of keen interest to businesses in all sectors, of all sizes and in all locations.

As an example, even within living memory, the quantity of numbers we are given and need to enable us to exist and participate in modern society has risen almost exponentially from virtually zero in the early part of the 20th century to several hundred (and still growing) now: PIN codes; licence numbers; credit card numbers; number plates; telephone numbers; employee number; health, tax and insurance numbers; access codes; customer numbers; train times; tram or bus numbers. We now know and need to remember them on a day-to-day basis and that is before we start work proper and have to deal with all those things that allow us to earn our salary where even more numbers and other elements of information will occur.

The mechanisms we use to manage information are the areas where we have seen very significant change, notably in the last few decades. The advent of computers in particular has altered the way we manage information extensively and has also meant that we have much more information to worry about than ever before. Information has become the key to success in almost any field of adventure and so the assurance of it has gained in significance and, perhaps more importantly, in value to a business or organisation. It may not necessarily be financial value that is the most important factor. Lack of knowledge of some issue, the way things are done, or knowing the currency of specific pieces of information may be more important than any financial valuation. Nevertheless looking after it properly is still very important.

One other factor that has significantly altered our need for assurance of information is that of mobility. When the only place we had business information, and where we were able to look after it properly, was the office, life was straightforward. To secure information we closed and locked the office door. Today we expect and need to have information in a wide variety of locations including wanting it on the move in cars and trains. With open plan offices and the increasing mobility of the office environment we now have a critical need for improved assurance if we are not to allow others to gain access to our information inappropriately.

The threats, vulnerabilities and countermeasures have also changed and grown in complexity in some areas, although it is still essential to consider the easiest and often cheapest countermeasures before getting into large or expensive solutions. The increase in capability of those intent on causing harm to companies, public bodies and other organisations means that the role of the Information Assurance manager and professional has increased in complexity to such a degree that it is now quite possible to have a full and very satisfying working life entirely within this field of expertise.

The legislation that is introduced by governments to address the increasing problems of Information Assurance in all its guises is also an area of concern and this book covers the most important principles and implementation of such laws. Once again though, it is important that readers understand that this book has been written in the UK and is based on English law. Other countries, even Devolved Administrations within the UK, may have further or different legislation with which you should become acquainted.

The technical aspects of Information Assurance including the technical details of Information Systems (IS), computer networks, communication systems, cryptography, and related areas are not part of the syllabus for this examination despite their importance. They appear in higher qualifications and so in this book reference is made to them in passing but they are not covered in any sort of detail. The syllabus and this book have remained technology neutral as far as possible.

This book accompanies the ISEB Certificate in Information Security Management Principles. This qualification, one of a series covering the whole area of Information Assurance management, is the first step towards a full understanding of the issues and the comprehensive management of the assurance of information wherever it may be. Whilst the British Computer Society (BCS) is clearly mainly concerned with the impact and effective use of computers, it is recognised that it is impossible to divorce the management of Information Security in computers from the management of information in any other media or from the security of the tools used to process information. Thus, in this book, the boundaries between different forms of information storage, processing, transmission and use are deliberately blurred or indeed removed entirely. It is not significant whether a particular piece of information exists in electronic form, paper form or indeed in someone's head. Its appropriate protection is the main factor and all aspects of its assurance must be considered from all angles.

The examination syllabus is the guide for the contents of this book. As a result of studying this book the reader should have a very clear understanding of the various elements of Information Assurance and should be able to consider taking the professional examination. It would naturally be useful to undertake a period of study with an approved training provider to enhance the understanding and those who deliver such training will inevitably add value to the reader's understanding, probably increasing the chance of success in the examination.

The sections of the book follow the numbering of the syllabus sections so that easy reference can be made both ways. A simple scenario has been introduced in order to help develop full understanding and to provide a close-to-life example of the real world. Activities based on the scenario are suggested throughout the book again to help bring reality into the concepts discussed and it is hoped that the reader will do these in an appropriate manner – formally or informally as suits them best.

Reference has been made to national and international standards applicable to Information Assurance but there is no requirement for detailed specific knowledge of any of those standards. They are naturally important but it is recognised that they will change over time and be more applicable in some parts of the world than in others. Readers should ensure they are familiar with the standards relevant to their country, their area of interest, their organisation and their business sector.

After studying this book and the related syllabus, the reader should be able to demonstrate a good knowledge and basic understanding of the wide range of subject areas that make up Information Assurance management. The examination tests the knowledge of principles rather than the knowledge of specific technologies, products or techniques. This means that where in the book specific technical examples are used to illustrate particular principles, it is the understanding of the principles that is of prime importance when considering the examples and not the examples themselves.

1 Information Security Principles

This chapter covers the basic principles of Information Security. It introduces some specific terminology together with its meaning and definitions and considers the use of such terminology across the field of Information Assurance management. It also discusses the way in which Information Assurance management relates to its environment. This chapter forms about 10 per cent of the CISMP examination syllabus.

CONCEPTS AND DEFINITIONS

As in any area of business, Information Assurance management has its own language although, being very closely related to the business need, it is limited in scope and complexity to enable the wider business population to appreciate the concepts with little difficulty. Each of the terms listed below will be further discussed and expanded upon later in the book in the appropriate section.

In the following sections the definitions in italics have been taken from the General Information Assurance Products and Services Initiative (GIPSI) Security Glossary and Terminology Definitions where available. GIPSI have taken the definitions from BS ISO/IEC 27001:2005 where the definition exists, from ISO/IEC FDIS 13335-1 or ISO/IEC 17799 when no 27001 definition is available, from other ISO standards where there was no 27001, 17799 or 13335 definition, and from SC27 or SD6 where ISO standards provide no definition. Where there is no extant definition this is provided by the Central Sponsor for Information Assurance (CSIA) or the authors with its source where applicable.

LEARNING OUTCOMES

Following study in this area, the reader should be able to define and explain each of the following terms and to describe their appropriate use as applicable.

Information Security

Confidentiality. The property that information is not made available or disclosed to unauthorised individuals, entities or processes (ISO 13335)

Information will often be applicable only to a limited number of individuals because of its nature, its content or because its wider distribution will result

1

in undesired effects including legal or financial penalties, or embarrassment to one party or another. Restricting access to information to those who have a 'need to know' is good practice and is based on the principle of confidentiality. Controls to ensure confidentiality form a major part of the wider aspects of Information Assurance management.

Integrity. The property of safeguarding the accuracy and completeness of assets (ISO 13335)

Information is only useful if it is complete and accurate, and remains so. Maintaining these aspects of information (its integrity) is often critical and ensuring that only certain people have the appropriate authority to alter, update or delete information is another basic principle of Information Assurance.

Availability. The property of being accessible and usable upon demand by an authorised entity (ISO 13335)

Information that is not available when and as required is not information at all but irrelevant data. Availability is one area where developments in technology have increased the difficulties for the Information Assurance professional very significantly. In the past, in an ideal world, all important information could be locked up in a very secure safe of some form and never allowed to be accessed – just about perfect assurance but naturally totally impractical. There will, therefore, always have to be a compromise between security in its purest sense and the availability of the information. This compromise has to be acknowledged throughout all aspects of Information Assurance and has a direct bearing on many of the principles covered in this book.

Assets and asset types

Asset. Anything that has value to the organisation, its business operations and its continuity (ISO 13335)

Assets come in as great an array of types as the mechanisms for using them. In Information Assurance, three main types of assets are considered although the sub-categories that fall within each of these main types can be numerous. The three main types are (i) pure information (in whatever format), (ii) physical assets such as buildings and computer systems and (iii) software used to process or otherwise manage information. When assets are considered in any aspect of Information Assurance, the impact on all three of these asset types should be reviewed. The value of an asset is usually estimated on the basis of the cost or value of its loss or unavailability to the business. There are, however, other aspects to consider including, but not limited to, the value to a competitor, the cost of recovery or reconstruction, the damage to other operations and even the impact on such intangibles as reputation, brand awareness and customer loyalty.

Threat, vulnerability, risk and impact

The understanding of these terms is critical to the whole of Information Assurance.

Threat. A potential cause of an incident that may result in harm to a system or organisation (ISO 13335)

A threat is something that may happen that may cause some unwanted consequence. As a simple example, if we see clouds in the sky that look large and dark we talk about the threat of rain. Naturally to some, farmers perhaps, this threat is not unwanted at all and so they would not have the same view of the clouds and its potential for rain and this is an important point to recognise. Threats to one organisation may well be opportunities to another – it is all very dependent on the viewpoint, the environment and the situation in which it is being considered.

Vulnerability. A weakness of an asset or group of assets that can be exploited by one or more threats (ISO 13335)

A vulnerability is a weakness, something that, if exploited, could cause some unwanted effect(s). To continue the example above, if someone was to venture out into the cloudy environment without an umbrella, this could be considered a vulnerability. If something else (the threat) happens (it rains) then the consequences could be detrimental.

Risk. The potential that a given threat will exploit vulnerabilities of an asset or group of assets and thereby cause harm to the organisation (ISO 13335)

Risk is then the combination of these two. If there is a threat (of rain) and a vulnerability (of not carrying an umbrella) then there is a risk that the individual concerned might get wet and ruin their expensive clothes. There may well be other risks associated with this same set of circumstances – damaged hair style, late attendance for an appointment, and so on. It is also important to recognise that sometimes there may be a combination of circumstances that lead to further more serious risks as well. The lateness of attendance at an appointment combined with a number of other similar occurrences could result in the termination of employment.

Impact. The result of an Information Security incident, caused by a threat, which affects assets (ISO 13335)

The impact of the risk actually occurring is perhaps the most important concept of all to grasp. It is the potential impact which has to be considered and managed in Information Assurance. If the impact is small and insignificant – a wet coat in the example above – then it may be entirely appropriate to accept the risk and to take no further action other than to monitor it. On the other hand, if the potential impact could be dismissal from a well-paid job then more appropriate countermeasures need to be considered – the purchase of an umbrella, hiring a taxi or similar. As far as businesses are concerned, the impact on the organisation and its daily activities is usually the crucial consideration and will often warrant further measures being taken.

Information Security policy concepts

Any organisation should have a policy for its management of Information Assurance. This would normally be a short punchy statement from the chief executive stating that they acknowledge the risks to the business resulting from poor Information Assurance and will take appropriate measures to deal with them. It should include statements that make it clear that the organisation regards risk as a serious issue with it being discussed at all appropriate meetings, with those with the correct authority and responsibility taking an active interest in it. It is common for organisations to form an Information Assurance working group to lead the activities necessary to ensure appropriate levels of assurance within the organisation.

The purpose of controls

Controls in the Information Assurance sense are those activities that are taken to manage the risks identified. There are four main types of control, although the actual implementation of each of these types can be very varied.

Eliminate. Risk avoidance – Decision not to be involved in, or action to withdraw from, a risk situation (ISO Guide 73)

This means taking a course of action(s) that removes the threat of a certain risk occurring at all. This could entail removing a particular item that is unsafe, choosing to do things a completely different way or any number of other options. This action is sometimes referred to as 'prevent', 'avoid' or 'terminate'.

Reduce. Risk Reduction – Action taken to lessen the probability, negative consequences, or both, associated with risk (ISO Guide 73)

This means to take one or more actions that will reduce the impact or the likelihood of a risk occurring. It is often necessary to use several of these measures in partnership to have the desired overall effect. This could include having contingency measures in place that mitigate the effect if the risk does occur – a backup plan or 'plan B'. This action is sometimes referred to as 'treat'.

Transfer. Risk Transfer – Sharing with another party the burden of loss, or benefit of gain, for a risk (ISO Guide 73)

This means to take steps to move the accountability for a risk to another organisation who will take on the responsibility for the future management of the risk. In practice this might mean taking out some form of indemnity or insurance against the risk occurring or perhaps writing contracts in such a way that the financial impact of a risk occurring is borne by a third party – liquidated damages. This action is sometimes referred to as 'share'.

Accept. Risk acceptance – Decision to accept a risk (ISO Guide 73)

This means senior management accepting that it is not considered practical or sensible to take any further action other than to monitor the risk. This could be for a number of reasons that further actions are considered inappropriate including but not limited to: the likely impact of a risk is too small; the likelihood of a risk occurring is too small; the cost of appropriate measures is too high in comparison with the financial impact of the risk occurring; the risk is outside the organisation's direct control. The decision would also be related to the organisation's risk appetite which determines the level of risk the organisation is prepared to accept. This is sometimes referred to as 'tolerate'.

Identity, authentication and authorisation

Identity. The properties of an individual or resource that can be used to identify uniquely one individual or resource (Authors)

Frequently there is a need to establish who is accessing information and the identity of individuals may well be required. This may enable, for example, audit trails to be produced to see who changed a specific item of data and hence to assign an appropriate level of confidence to the change. This concept is equally applicable to assets such as specific pieces of information which need to be identified uniquely.

Authentication. Ensuring that the identity of a subject or resource is the one claimed (Derived from Authenticity in ISO 13335)

This process ensures that the individual is who they say they are and confirms their identity to an appropriate level of confidence appropriate for the task in hand. This could be simply asking them, at the most basic, for their date of birth, through to completing a complex identity check using, for example, tokens, biometrics and detailed biographical-data checks.

Authorisation. The process of checking the authentication of an individual or resource to establish and confirm their authorised use of, or access to, information or other assets (Authors)

In order for anyone to use a system of information retrieval, management, etc. it is good practice to have a method of authorisation which makes clear the assets to which someone should have access and the type of access they should have. This authorisation will vary depending on the business requirement, the individual, the type of asset and a range of other aspects. Who has the authority to detail and approve such authorisations will vary according to the type of usage required.

Accountability, audit and compliance

Accountability. The responsibility for actions and processes (Authors)

When any action is carried out on an information system or as part of the Information Security management system, an individual needs to be accountable or responsible for that action. The person who has the accountability may delegate the actual work to someone else but they would still retain the accountability.

Audit. Formal review of actions, processes, policies and procedures (Authors)

This is the formal checking of the records of a system to ensure that the activities that were anticipated to have taken place have actually happened. The purposes of an audit could include identifying gaps in the system's functionality, noting trends over time to help with problem resolution or identification or a number of other requirements. It can also help to identify misuse of information or the inappropriate use of an authorisation, for example, and thus identify unauthorised activity.

Compliance. Working in accordance with the actions, processes, policies and procedures laid down without necessarily having independent reviews (Authors)

Ensuring that a system or process complies with the defined or expected operating procedures is compliance. This could cover a major operation, such as a whole organisation being compliant with a recognised national standard for Information Assurance, or could be much more limited with just certain aspects of the operation, or individual users, of a specific system being compliant. In general compliance should be independently audited to achieve certification against a standard, a legal or regulatory framework for example.

Information Security professionalism and ethics

The general awareness of the work done by Information Assurance professionals (as distinct from IT security professionals) is gradually growing as organisations become increasingly complex with more and more information being managed and processed. The adage that the staff are the most important asset of an organisation could now be seen to be outmoded since it is often the case that it is the information an organisation holds and uses effectively that has become its most important asset. Therefore looking after it has also gained in importance and the whole profession has grown to meet the need. New professional bodies, such as the Institute of Information Security Professionals which was set up in 2006 in the UK, have helped to raise the profile very significantly, as have the various qualifications ranging from this introductory level to master's degrees and beyond.

An Information Assurance professional will, inevitably, become party to some of the most important information an organisation might hold. This could be sensitive for a number of reasons but, in all cases, it is critical that the professional deals with it in the appropriate manner. Releasing information to a third party or other organisation, albeit with the best of intentions but without the approval of the owner, is probably one of the easiest ways to be dismissed. Non-disclosure agreements (NDAs) are now commonplace even in seemingly innocuous areas such as publishing and the retail marketplace as well as the more usual research and development, product innovation and financial areas.

The bottom line of all assurance is trust. Without it, it is impossible to operate in the world as it is today. The degree of trust is where there is room for manoeuvre and it is often the degree to which staff, customers, suppliers, shareholders and the like can be trusted that will determine the measures that have to be put in place. It is crucial though that the trust placed in Information Assurance professionals is not misplaced in any way. They must be above reproach and never be seen to compromise in this critical area.

The Information Security Management System (ISMS) concepts

Information Management Security System (ISMS). That part of the overall management system, based on a business risk approach, to establish, implement, operate, monitor, review, maintain and improve Information Security (ISO 17799)

The main principle behind the ISMS is that there should be a 'one-stop shop' for all information pertinent to the assurance of information within an organisation. As soon as there is a need to go looking for documentation, policies, practices or anything else to do with assurance, the chances are that someone will not bother and will do their own thing.

Whilst there may well be good reason for them not to do this in terms of rules, regulations, punishments and the like, human nature being what it is, they will find a reasonable excuse for going down a different route if only because 'I thought it was OK and couldn't be bothered to check if it was the right way to do it'. The result of this approach will inevitably be a reduction in the overall level of assurance. In addition, any system that is too complex or difficult to use will result in users finding ways to get around the security measures put in place perhaps again resulting in weakened assurance.

It is therefore critical that organisations make their information as freely and easily available as is possible, practical and necessary and this equally applies to the assurance rules controlling it. Naturally there will be elements of policy that have to be more secure, available only to those with a strict 'need to know', but in general everyone should be able to access easily and quickly the appropriate information and the assurance measures pertinent to it.

The national and international security standards

As a policy, the ISEB examination board have decided not to relate the syllabus for this examination to any national or international standards specifically, although there are several such standards that are applicable. The main reasons for this were two-fold – firstly to make the syllabus and the qualification as applicable internationally as possible, and secondly to reduce the need to update the syllabus at every change to the standards.

It is clear however that Information Assurance is the subject of several international and national standards and that these should be considered when studying for the examination. The questions set in the examination will never be specific to any one standard but will be generic to all best practice where applicable. The knowledge of the appropriate standards required for the examination is therefore limited to a general understanding of the principles involved as they reflect on best practice. In the UK, awareness of, for example, the ISO/IEC 27000 series and related British Standards would be helpful but not critical to the passing of the examinations. It is the broad principles that should be used as a basis for study as reflected in the examination syllabus.

There is though another aspect of this. When an Information Assurance professional is working in an organisation to deliver a secure and effective information management system, the relevant standards should always be viewed as the achievable goal for the system. Whether it is necessary to gain simple compliance or go the extra step to achieve certification is an arbitrary decision often based on other factors. Nevertheless it is considered good practice to base an effective Information Assurance management system on the principles of the relevant standards. The use of an internationally accepted standard such as the ISO/IEC 27000 series makes sense in the global nature of operations today.

The Group for the Appreciation of the Natterjack Toad (GANT) scenario

The Group for the Appreciation of the Natterjack Toad (GANT) is a conservation group which is keen to promote and preserve the well-being of the Natterjack toad. It has a significant number of members in a number of different countries around the world, all of whom are keen to promote the work of the Group which is a charity registered in the UK. All the Group's information is either on a web-based application available to members over the Internet or on old-fashioned, paper-based documents held by Dr Jane Peabody, the honorary secretary/treasurer.

The Natterjack toad is an endangered species which is gradually being destroyed by the development of areas where it prospers and through pollution affecting the brackish water and sand dunes in which it lives.

The membership of the organisation is growing and the system for managing the records of members is one area where there are some concerns about the information assurance. Details of the Group's activities, their meeting places, their website and other aspects of the Group's work have been compromised in the recent past owing to the server containing them having no significant security in place. The chairperson (Ms Rachel Jackson) believes it is the right time to take information assurance more seriously. She has heard a bit about Information Assurance but needs to be clear what it really means and, most importantly, what the benefits and costs would be to the organisation.

The GANT scenario is a fictitious scenario that will be used throughout the book to provide examples and to be the basis of some questions to aid your understanding of the theory. The main objective of the scenario is to implement an effective Information Assurance system but we will take you through various steps along the way to help with your understanding.

Activity 1.1

Assume that you have been invited to a committee meeting of GANT by the chairperson, who wants you to 'start the ball rolling' by explaining why it would be a good idea for GANT to think about Information Assurance.

To make your points most forcefully, she has asked you to define three threats to the organisation, three vulnerabilities and consequently three risks that any Information Assurance system would need to manage.

Solution pointers for the activities can be found at the end of the relevant chapters.

We have started above with developing an initial idea of the reasons for considering Information Assurance based on three possible problems. We will take that on to a more formal approach in due course – this is simply to get you thinking about some of the terms we have introduced in the first section of the book.

THE NEED FOR, AND BENEFITS OF, INFORMATION SECURITY

Any business will have information that is critical to its continued effective operation. Looking after this information in an appropriate way does not come free but has a price tag attached that can be, in some circumstances, very considerable. It is therefore essential that Information Assurance professionals are able to justify their recommendations for appropriate assurance measures in a sensible yet pragmatic manner which must take into account the specific environment in which the business is based.

LEARNING OUTCOMES

Following study in this area, the reader should be able to explain and justify each of the following concepts and to describe their appropriate use as applicable.

The importance of Information Security as part of a business model

Information Security – Preservation of confidentiality, integrity and availability of information; in addition, other properties such as authenticity, accountability, non-repudiation and reliability can also be involved (ISO 17799)

Neither information nor assurance operate in a vacuum. Both need to take into account the environment in which they are operating and to address the issues this environment brings with it. It is therefore critical that any Inform-ation Assurance system must be grounded firmly in the business world. This means that Information Assurance is not an issue only for the IT manager or the security officer but for the whole organisation. As soon as only one part of the organisation is given the task of running assurance, the rest of the organisation will bother less about it. All staff members of any organisation, regardless of its nature, its business, its location or any other factor, should be concerned about Information Assurance. It might be from a purely personal viewpoint (what happens to my personal data in this place?) or from a wider view of the effective continued operation of the organisation, but in either case all should be concerned and involved.

Assurance should not be viewed as an 'add-on' to be included only if there is the time and the money to do it. It has to be built in to business processes at all stages if it is to be truly effective. Whilst it might be possible in some areas to add in assurance measures at the last moment (an extra lock on a door or an additional staff security check) they will usually cost more and be less effective than if they had been added at the appropriate time earlier in the design process.

Different business models and their impact on security

In the last 20 years, the world of business has changed dramatically – perhaps more than in the previous 50 or 100 years. One of the principal reasons for this is the increased use of technology that has enabled business to be transacted remotely rather than in person. One of the consequences of this is that more people are able to make business transactions themselves rather than expecting others to act as intermediaries. No longer do we need to use travel agents to book our flights, local garages to obtain our cars for us or financial advisers to obtain investment packages for us. All these and many more transactions can be carried out directly with the supplier, often using the internet for communications, or with a trader in another part of the country or the world who can offer a better deal. Whilst the access to such facilities is a huge advantage and can provide very significant financial savings, it has brought with it major issues of assurance both for the individual and for the organisation wishing to trade in this way.

The other very significant change in business has been the shift in the UK away from manufacturing and related primary industries to service and financial industries where the use of technology has an even bigger impact.

It is clear that the use of technology in manufacturing has changed those industries too but, it might be argued, in a more controlled and manageable manner. In the service industry, the availability of information has increased many times over and has liberated the industry based on information in a manner that is similar to the impact of the steam engine or electricity in their day. This in its turn has increased the importance and difficulty of keeping the information securely.

Many organisations are now based in and operate in more than one country. With global organisations now moving very sensitive information or money around the world at a moment's notice, the need to ensure it is done securely and with proof of receipt, integrity and authority has grown too. Proving the authorised person sent the correct document at the appropriate time to only the intended recipients, not to mention ensuring that it arrives in the same state as when it left the originator, are all issues that the Information Assurance manager now has to deal with to the satisfaction of their management and any ambitious litigant. In addition, organisations that operate within different countries need to understand the differing restrictions that local legislation may place on how their information can be handled.

There are many further risks from this change in the business model. With an increasing amount of trade being conducted across the internet, organisations must be aware of the dangers of virus infection, denial-of-service attacks, unauthorised changes to their information in the public domain (e.g. internet websites) and the impact of any such issues on their reputation, financial status and other related areas. In addition organisations are having to deal with people about whom they know very little but with whom they still need to establish an appropriate level of trust. The ability of disillusioned employees, ex-employees or groups of activists to damage an organisation by taking, deleting, altering or otherwise misappropriating critical business information from the employer and either passing to a competitor, or simply using for their own ill-gotten gains, is now a very real issue. Whilst companies who have been the victims of such events are not inclined to increase the damage caused by making such acts public knowledge, there are so many apocryphal tales of the theft of client databases, deletion or alteration of critical financial data and other similar acts that it suggests that some at least are true.

There are also cautionary tales of laptop PCs containing highly sensitive or confidential information being lost or stolen from parked cars, to the embarrassment of the company or organisation.

The use of the internet for transactions, be it shopping for cars, food or financial services, as well as the storage of client, stock, financial and related information in a secure manner has further increased the problems to be managed. The ability of the consumer to deal directly with the manufacturer has increased the risks for industry as well as for the consumer where the problems of unreliable services or products still abound. With the rise of business-to-business transactions, just-in-time operations and other similar services that rely heavily on the timely and accurate movement, storage and retrieval of critical information, the loss of a computer system for a comparatively short while can and has created serious financial losses for the businesses concerned. In 2005 it was estimated by an independent research organisation that US$14.2 billion was lost by businesses worldwide through the business impact of malicious software (malware – viruses and the like) on their systems alone.

The effect of the rapidly changing business environment

'It is change, continuing change, inevitable change, that is the dominant factor in society today.' This quotation is from Isaac Asimov and it is now well understood that for a business to survive in the current climate of change, it must adapt and be able to adapt rapidly. This means that what was acceptable as a business practice last week may no longer be acceptable this week. Therefore any assurance system put in place must reflect this changing climate and be flexible enough to cope with it. However this does not mean that the assurance can be relaxed or reduced in any way. Indeed if anything, the flexibility should produce a higher level of security and assurance that risks are being managed effectively.

Balancing cost and impact of security with the reduction in risk

Life can never be risk free. Indeed it is often considered that life is all about risk and its effective management. The measures taken in an organisation to reduce risk to an acceptable level can, at times, become excessively expensive. A careful balance must be struck between the cost or business impact of a risk if it occurs and the cost of the measures taken to reduce its likelihood or impact.

A typical example is insurance. The insurance policy may help to offset the cost of a risk occurring by providing the necessary financial backing to be used to deal with the occurrence of a risk. However, if the cost of the insurance policy is too high, it may simply be cheaper to accept that the risk might occur and pay the smaller amount out to deal with its consequences. It must also be remembered that whilst it may be possible to transfer to a third party some of the impact of a risk occurring – that is the financial impact for example – it is frequently very difficult to transfer the other consequences of a risk, notably the impact on reputation, public opinion or other related results.

It is not uncommon for organisations to put in place extravagant measures to reduce the impact or likelihood of risk occurring when in reality the consequences of the risk occurring are limited, or the actual chance of it happening is so small that the expense is a waste of both money and effort in managing the risk unnecessarily. A second problem is that of maintaining the currency of risk countermeasures. Once defined and planned, it is critical that they are not simply put on the shelf to await the risk arising. The world around us changes and so the countermeasures may not be valid or may change in their effectiveness or cost as time moves on. Thus risk management, and the maintenance of the consequential actions taken, is a continual and iterative process that must not be allowed to whither through lack of action or misplaced belief that the situation will not change.

Information Security as part of company policy

Assurance is not an add-on. It is not possible to deal adequately with assurance by considering it as an additional expense to be avoided if at all possible. The most effective way to deal with it is to include it from the beginning in all areas of the organisation. To this end the inclusion of assurance as part of the operational policy of the organisation is the only cost-effective way of covering the issues adequately.

There are clear similarities between Information Assurance and health and safety issues. As soon as health and safety is seen as one person's problem (that of the health and safety officer) the battle for a safe working environment has been lost. Similarly, assurance is not the concern solely of the Information Security manager but of the whole organisation. It is essential also that this involvement is from the top of the organisation to the bottom. Just implementing Information Assurance at middle management or on the shop floor is meaningless and will inevitably lead to further assurance issues. Senior management have a critical role to play to ensure they engender a working environment where Information Assurance is the norm and accepted by all.

The need for comprehensive policy, standards, guidelines and procedures documentation

Just having an Information Assurance policy on its own is meaningless. It must be fully supported by a range of other documentation covering the standards expected, the guidelines of how to do things correctly and procedures for what must be done to preserve the assurance of the information in question. This documentation must be comprehensive in its coverage, must be written in a style that is understandable to the intended audience, which may well be the ordinary staff member with very limited experience or knowledge of assurance matters, and must be readily available in an appropriate format.

It is good practice to ensure that any procedures to be followed are detailed in an easily digestible format perhaps as desk cards or prompts for users, or as checklists for operators or support technicians. It must be remembered, however, that this is not only about computers. For example, procedures are also required for the management of physical assets such as filing cabinets including how they should be cleared before their disposal to avoid the inadvertent inclusion of a confidential file for the second-hand filing cabinet marketplace. Where information critical to the organisation's continued operation is held solely in the heads of its staff, it is almost inevitable that one day this will result in one of the key staff members being ill, having an accident or being otherwise indisposed when a crucial decision or operation is required. Considering the management of the information in staff members' heads is just as important as the effective management of technical systems – some might say more so.

Relationship with corporate governance and related areas of risk management

In recent years the advent of some very-high-profile commercial criminal investigations has resulted in much more stringent and invasive legislation regarding risk taking in companies. Sarbanes–Oxley from the USA, the effects on corporate governance of the Turnbull Report and the new Companies Act in the UK and related issues, have all had the effect of bringing risk management to the top of the agenda in many a boardroom. It is no longer effective or acceptable (even if it ever was) to delegate the responsibility for risk management down to the manager of the IT section.

The proper implementation of effective Information Assurance should lie at the heart of all organisations regardless of their sector, size or business. Properly implemented, the secure management of information can provide assurance that risk is being managed effectively in that area at least and can form the firm foundation for further risk management in related areas. If all information is covered by the measures implemented, then the financial, operational, Intellectual Property Rights and a whole range of other risk areas can be managed through the establishment of a single framework.

Security as an enabler delivering value rather than cost

In the information economy in which we all now live, the cost of the loss, corruption, non-availability or unauthorised release of information can be very high. The effective implementation of Information Assurance measures can have a very beneficial effect on the potential costs of such events. Thus it is easy to develop a convincing and compelling business case for the effective management of information through the use of an approved standard and related processes. Whilst it may not be possible to remove the risk entirely, it should be possible to ensure at least that the probability of the risk occurring is significantly reduced or that the effects of the risk materialising are significantly reduced in terms of the business impact.

The use of appropriate countermeasures and contingency plans can also have the very beneficial effect of making the work done by an organisation much more orderly by being based on best working practices. Piles of paper and computer disks left lying around on desks, floors and shelves can be the assurance disaster waiting to happen. With an Information Assurance standard in place such things should be a thing of the past and the need to spend many hours finding a specific piece of information should be long gone.

With the advent of photocopiers in almost every workplace, the ease with which a sheet of information could be reproduced became very much greater. This in turn meant that where originally there might be only the original and perhaps one handwritten copy to look after, there was now the possibility of many copies to worry about and to try and control. Many a leak from organisations, including governments, has been caused by the proliferation of photocopies, mislaid CDs or inappropriate, perhaps covert, use of USB memory sticks. With improved working practices instigated through effective Information Assurance, the need to reproduce information declines since those who need to see a piece of information can do so easily and in a controlled way through the appropriate use of technology perhaps without recourse to the production of ever more copies.

The role of Information Security in countering hi-tech and other crime

Crime is always advancing and developing, often a little quicker than the enforcement agencies who are established to combat it. The hi-tech industry (covering computers, the internet, digitisation, communications and related areas) over the last 30 years or so has provided criminals with ever-increasing opportunities for more advanced and profitable crime in a wide range of activities. Some crimes are the old ones which had effectively been removed from the criminals' handbook. One example is that of fraud which had been dealt a severe blow by the introduction of sophisticated security devices in bank notes, passports and the like, but, with the ever-increasing use of the internet, has now returned with increased 'effectiveness'. Emails with the 'too good to be true' heading, such as the lottery win notifications, have been estimated to have taken up to £110,000 from a single individual with the overall loss being well into the millions of pounds in the UK alone. All these are no more than old-fashioned fraud dressed up in new clothes. In addition, the ability to obtain personal information through phishing, key-loggers, screen-scraping or similar tactics has increased the opportunities for criminals to achieve their nefarious purposes.

Information Assurance can help to address all these issues, at least in the workplace. Good practices at work can also lead to better practices at home where the proliferation of computers in particular has led to increasing instances of criminal activity targeting the home user. The social duty of companies to help reduce the overall crime is well established and setting good work practices with the care of information is an excellent opportunity that should not be missed.

The growth of such crime has increased the importance of forensic investigation and notably the requirement to preserve evidence based on IT systems. Later in this book this subject will be discussed in more detail but in recent years it has been ever more evident that the skill of the IT practitioner in the preparation of evidence for trials has needed to develop very considerably from the early days of computing when IT evidence was rarely used except in the most complex of cases. Now, with internet crime on the increase and the use of IT becoming the norm for many areas of criminality, the use of investigative techniques based on the IT system has increased enormously. With effectively managed Information Assurance high on the priority list for all organisations, these techniques are now a vital piece of the jigsaw of helping to reduce criminality. The Information Assurance professional is now a crucial element in the fight against crime, both internal and external to the organisation itself.

Ms Jackson, the chairperson, has asked you to help to develop a sound business case for the implementation of an Information Security Management System (ISMS). She needs to be able to convince her fellow committee members to authorise the expenditure and so needs to be clear why this would be a good idea. The key aspect is the balance between the costs of implementing an ISMS against the costs of suffering a serious attack on their information.

Property developers are keen to know where the Natterjack toad currently can be found so they can either avoid buying the land or, if they already have ownership of the land, possibly 'remove' the toad in advance of the planning applications being submitted to 'avoid' any problems with the approvals required. This information is on the website which has no firewall protecting it.

It would cost GANT many thousands of pounds and several years of effort to re-introduce the toad to a habitat once it has been removed either by natural or man-made effects.

The funding for GANT is through members' fees, grants from other nature conservancy organisations and commercial companies who make donations.

Activity 1.2

Consider three main areas where the chairperson should gather more detailed information to allow the committee to make reasonable judgements on whether or not it is sensible to carry out the ISMS implementation.

Sample Questions

1. If the accuracy of information is a major concern, which of the following would be used to ensure this is covered effectively?
    a. Confidentiality.
    b. Integrity.
    c. Availability.
    d. None of these.

2. When a user logs onto a computer system and is asked for their mother's maiden name, which of the following aspects is the system ensuring?
    a. Accountability.
    b. Authorisation.
    c. Authentication.
    d. Applicability.

3. ISO 27001 is an international standard for Information Security. Which organisation is responsible for its maintenance?
    a. The British Standards Institute.
    b. The government of the country in which it has been implemented.
    c. The European Union Standards Committee.
    d. The International Standards Organisation.

4. How should the implementation of an Information Assurance system be seen within an organisation?
    a. As a problem for the IS department only to sort out.
    b. As a problem on which the senior managers should make a decision but then leave to others to deal with.
    c. As a whole organisation issue.
    d. As an issue where outside expertise is the best solution.

5. How should the use of an international standard for Information Security be viewed by senior managers within an organisation?
    a. As a good idea if there was the right business environment in which to implement it.
    b. As implementing best practice.
    c. As overkill unless there are very serious problems with assurance.
    d. As the pet idea of the IT director who thinks it will look good to shareholders in the next annual report of the organisation.

Pointers for activities in the chapter

Activity 1.1

There is a significant number of threats, vulnerabilities and risks to this organisation. You may have come up with others but here are three of the most serious ones. It is most important that you fully appreciate the differences between the three categories as well as being able to make some specific suggestions.

Three threats

These are areas where there is a potential for some adverse consequences if this threat should arise. In this scenario three threats might be as follows.

(1) Information about members might be accessed by unauthorised people.

(2) Information about the habitats of the Natterjack toad might be used by those who are not inclined to support its ongoing existence.

(3) The website might be compromised and unofficial messages added to it.

Three vulnerabilities

These are weaknesses in the system that might allow a threat to materialise. In this scenario and building on the threats given above, the vulnerabilities might be as follows.

(1) The records of the members are maintained in a variety of ways including paper and unreliable computer systems.

(2) The information about the toads' habitats is maintained on an old internet-based server with very limited assurance in place.

(3) There is no firewall between the website server and the Internet.

Three risks

There is a large number of risks resulting from the threats and vulnerabilities listed above. Three of them might be as follows.

(1) There is a risk that unscrupulous property developers might gain access to the personal details of members of GANT and take positive action against them or their property.

(2) There is a risk that a habitat of the Natterjack toad might be destroyed by someone who is not interested in the existence of the toad.

(3) There is a risk that someone might gain access to the code of the GANT website and change the messages to information that is offensive to those interested in nature conservancy.

Activity 1.2

The cost effectiveness or cost–benefit analysis for such an implementation would include a very large number of areas. Three of the most significant following on from the suggestions given above for Activity 1.1 might be the following.

(1) Members of GANT could be injured or their families and property adversely affected in some way. The cost of protecting the members and their families would be excessive and could not be found through the membership of GANT alone.

(2) The cost of re-introducing Natterjack toads into the wild after their habitat has been destroyed would be very considerable. This could be the consequence (impact) of allowing unauthorised access to the details of the toads' habitats.

(3) GANT relies very heavily on the goodwill of other nature conservancy groups and donations from interested commercial companies. If they were embarrassed by the content of the website, they might reduce or withdraw their support for an organisation they saw as unprofessional and poorly organised. This could be devastating for the existence of GANT.

Answers to sample questions

1. The correct answer is b.
2. The correct answer is c.
3. The correct answer is d.
4. The correct answer is c.
5. The correct answer is b.

2 Information Risk

Information Assurance is almost entirely about the management of risk. The concepts of Confidentiality, Integrity and Availability already covered in Chapter 1 are merely areas of risk which must be addressed in an Information Systems environment. In this section of the book, we will examine the component parts of risk – **threats**, **impact**, **vulnerabilities** and combining threats with the **likelihood** or **probability** that the threat will be carried out, the resulting **risk**. It introduces the basic terminology of risk and discusses the potential threats to, and vulnerabilities of, Information Systems, and the processes for understanding and managing risk relating to Information Systems. This chapter covers about 15 per cent of the CISMP syllabus.

THREATS TO, AND VULNERABILITIES OF, INFORMATION SYSTEMS

LEARNING OUTCOMES

Following study in this area candidates should be able to define and explain each of the key concepts of Information Risk Management and have a thorough understanding of the terminology used.

Threats

A threat is something that may happen that may cause some undesirable consequence. As a simple example, a feasible threat is that an unauthorised person might discover your username and password to a system or service. We won't dwell on the consequences of this just yet – that will be covered under impacts, but it is clear that someone else having knowledge of both your username and password is not a healthy state of affairs.

In order to have any validity, threats must be realistic. They may already have happened to someone else, so there may well be records of such incidents to support the validity of the threat. On the other hand, what might be a threat to one person may well be an opportunity to another. You may care to think about this the next time you try and find a free taxi when it is pouring with rain. To you, there is a very real threat that you will be soaked – to a taxi driver the combination of the rain and wet pedestrians represents an opportunity!

Threat categorisation

Threats can be categorised into two main areas – **accidental threats** and **deliberate threats**. Each of these areas may contain two further choices – **internal threats** and **external threats**.

In Information Assurance, accidental threats include a number of conditions, such as human error, system malfunctions, fire and floods. Some of these are referred to as **hazards**, especially when concerned with external events. The implication is that there has been no deliberate attempt to carry out the threat – it has simply happened. There may be no one to blame for an accidental threat occurring, but there may be a means of dealing with the threat as we shall see later.

Deliberate threats on the other hand occur when someone sets out with every intention of carrying out the threat. This type of threat includes hacking, malicious software, sabotage, cyber terrorism, hi-tech crime, and so on.

Internal threats arise – as the name suggests – from within the organisation itself, or from business partners and suppliers who have some degree of access to the organisation's Information Systems environment. Alternatively it might be that the partner's own Information Systems infrastructure is so closely linked with that of the organisation (perhaps for business-to-business trading reasons) that it is to all intents and purposes an integral part of it. Sources of internal threats include permanent and contract employees, trusted partners and managed-service organisations.

External threats arise from outside the organisation and its less closely linked business partners and suppliers. Typical external threats may arise from hackers of various kinds, competitors and protest groups.

Hazards, mentioned earlier, can be either internal or external in origin. For example a fire or flood may originate within the organisation's building, or may originate from outside – for example from a neighbouring building. Severe weather also frequently constitutes a major hazard to the operations of many organisations, especially in the winter months.

Vulnerabilities

A vulnerability is a weakness; something which, if exploited, could cause some unwanted consequence. To continue the example above, if you write your password on a Post-It® note stuck underneath your computer's keyboard, this would constitute a vulnerability, as a hacker could easily know or guess your username, and thereby have complete access to your information.

Many vulnerabilities are not of the user's making. For example, poor software design leaves systems vulnerable to attack – witness Microsoft's 'patch Tuesday', on which patches or fixes for problems, including security vulnerabilities, are released for system administrators to apply.

Whether or not a vulnerability might be exploited will depend on the likelihood or probability, which will be discussed later in this chapter, but often it is the most widely available or widely used software packages and operating systems which are most vulnerable to attack as they present a more easily available or inviting target for malicious software writers and hackers.

Vulnerability categorisation

Vulnerabilities fall into two distinct categories – **general vulnerabilities** and **information-specific vulnerabilities**.

General vulnerabilities include basic weaknesses in software (including poor design), hardware, buildings or facilities, people, processes and procedures.

Information-specific vulnerabilities include such areas as unsecured computers, including personal computers, hand-held devices and memory sticks, servers, un-patched operating systems and applications, unsecured network boundary devices, unsecured wireless systems, unsecured web servers, unsecured email systems, unlocked filing cabinets and the like.

The point here (for either general or information-specific vulnerabilities) is that the asset is vulnerable because something has not already been done to secure or protect it.

Threats are said to take advantage of, or exploit, vulnerabilities in order to succeed in achieving their goal.

Assets

An information asset can vary considerably in form. An asset does not even have to be tangible, although it could be a system, a database or a building. On the other hand, it could be intellectual property, a business service, an organisation's brand or the reputation of the organisation's chief executive. What is important about assets is that if they are lost, stolen or damaged in any way, the organisation will almost certainly suffer as a result, and if that damage is sufficiently serious, the organisation might never recover.

When we examine **impacts**, we will see that it is always an asset which is impacted by an incident, whether this is tangible or intangible.

Impact

The impact (or potential impact) of the risk actually occurring is perhaps the most important concept of all to grasp. It is this potential impact which has to be considered and managed in Information Assurance. If the impact is small and insignificant then it may be entirely appropriate to accept the risk and to take no further action other than to monitor it periodically. An example of this might be failure of 'hole-in-the-wall' cash dispensers – if just one machine in the bank's network fails, the impact would generally be very low.

On the other hand, if the potential impact could be the loss of vital company information, then more appropriate countermeasures need to be considered. As far as businesses are concerned, the impact on the organisation and its daily activities are usually the crucial considerations and will often warrant further measures being taken.

The business impacts of realised threats include the loss of confidentiality, integrity and availability, and frequently lead to financial loss, inability to trade, brand damage, loss of customer confidence, etc.

An example of this is when Gerald Ratner, the chief executive of Ratners, a high-street jewellery chain, made a comment to a journalist denigrating his own company's jewellery products. The result of this was that the comment was displayed in banner headlines across the next day's national newspapers and £500 million was wiped off the organisation's share price within a week. This was actually the **impact** as we shall see later, but the point here is that nothing tangible was damaged in the exercise, but the organisation was ruined, and eventually went bankrupt, just the same.

At the opposite end of the spectrum, immediately following the British Midland air crash at Kegworth, England, in 1989, Sir Michael Bishop, the airline's chairman, commented that he was not worried about the financial impact of the accident, but that he was more concerned about air safety. This reassured the media and the public and the airline is now one of the most successful in the industry.

Likelihood or probability

There are very few certainties in this world, and risk management is no exception. Some things are very likely to happen, while some will be very unlikely to happen. Most others lie somewhere in the grey area in between. It is generally accepted that the greater the vulnerability, the more likely an incident is to take place – i.e. the threat is carried out.

There are two basic ways in which likelihood can be assessed – quantitatively and qualitatively – and these will be discussed in greater detail later in the chapter. In quantitative assessment, there will be clear metrics to calculate the likelihood. These may be derived from previously recorded information including statistical data. In the case of qualitative assessment, the work is more subjective and relies on opinions rather than facts.

For example, companies who produce anti-virus software can point to the large number of viruses which their products can scan for and remove, from which one can conclude that without anti-virus software, the risk of infection is high.

On the other hand, one does not need to know the exact number of incidents to be aware that the likelihood of a breach of confidentiality or integrity is high without proper password protection.

Both methods of assessment have their place – the important thing is that likelihood assessments are carried out according to agreed criteria.

Risk

As mentioned earlier, the result of having a vulnerability and it being exploited by a threat results in a risk. The assessment of the risk for any particular threat is considered to be a combination of the impact and the likelihood that the threat can be carried out.

It is also important to recognise that sometimes there may be a combination of circumstances that lead to further more serious risks as well. For an unauthorised person to discover your username and password combination is one thing. If your files include a list of other usernames and their passwords, this would lead to further (and potentially more serious) security breaches.

Calculating the overall risk

When we wish to assess the degree of risk for an information asset, we must take all the above factors into account. We must identify as many threats or hazards as possible, and for each one try to estimate the potential impact of the threat or hazard occurring. Finally, we must identify any vulnerabilities associated with the asset which will lead us to an assessment of the likelihood or probability that the threat might be carried out.

The first stage of this is called a business impact analysis (BIA) in which we decide what the impact on one or more business assets would be for each threat. Once we have completed that, we assess the likelihood or probability that vulnerabilities might be exploited, allowing the threats to be realised.

From these two, we can draw a risk matrix which plots impact against likelihood, and gives us a formal risk assessment. This will be discussed in greater detail in the next section of this chapter.

Ms Jackson, the chairperson, has been reminded that all GANT's information is held on a single computer system which was recently compromised by a teenage hacker. GANT has no backup of the information and no suitable paper documentation from which to easily recreate their records.

She has realised that all GANT's information is highly vulnerable and has asked you to assess the consequences of loss or failure of this computer.

Activity 2.1

Looking at the records and information held by GANT, perform a business impact analysis based on the loss of their main computer system. Some possible threats to consider are loss of:

- membership details;
- Natterjack toad breeding ground details;
- financial records.

Solution pointers for the activities can be found at the end of the chapter.

RISK MANAGEMENT

LEARNING OUTCOMES

Following study in this area candidates should be able to understand the overall process of risk management, and the appropriate use of controls to enable them to manage risk in a cost effective and appropriate manner for their organisation.

Risk management process

Risk management consists of four distinct areas: identification of the threats; impact analysis and risk assessment; treatment of the risks; ongoing monitoring of the results. Risk assessments may take place at a number of levels, for example across a corporation, a business system or process or a physical location. While these are somewhat different types of risk assessment, the way in which they are conducted and the way in which the results will be used are essentially the same.

This process can be represented as shown in Figure 2.1.

Identify

**Risk
Management
Life Cycle**

Monitor

Analyse

Treat

FIGURE 2.1 *The risk management life cycle*

Identification

One way of beginning a risk management exercise is to identify the threats. This should be carried out in conjunction with the understanding of any known vulnerabilities. For example if the assessment is looking at the threat of possible hacking attacks on a web server, operating system and web server software vulnerabilities should be considered.

Sometimes this will result in the identification of more than one threat while, at other times, it will become clear that a number of different vulnerabilities will all be covered by a single threat.

Once each threat has been identified (often more will appear during the process of the work), each one should be considered in the light of its impact on the asset concerned. In the web server example, the threat of a hacker gaining control of the server could potentially result in loss of service – perhaps the failure of an e-commerce facility – loss of customer data, defacement of the web pages and so on, all of which would have a high impact on the company's profitability.

An alternative approach might be to start with a list of the assets that need to be protected and then to determine the threats to those assets. In either case the resultant list of assets, their threats and the potential impacts is taken on to the next step of analysis.

Analysis

Having identified the impact or impacts for each threat, the next task is to assess the likelihood of each occurring. It is tempting at this point to assume that because the system might be fully up to date with its security patches there is a low likelihood of a threat being realised. However, it must be remembered that this is ongoing work, and that if the patching falls behind, the likelihood of an attack being successful will increase.

Once this stage has been completed, the risk matrix can be drawn – an example is shown in Figure 2.2.

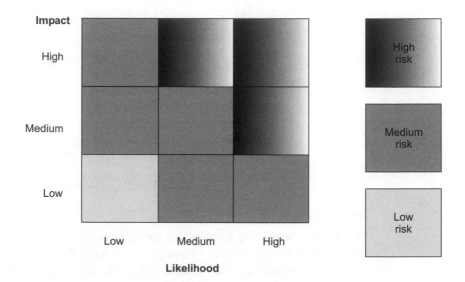

FIGURE 2.2   *A typical risk matrix*

The matrix itself can be drawn in many ways. It is generally accepted that the most simple form is a three-by-three matrix with High, Medium and Low ratings for both impact and likelihood as shown above. An organisation will use the size of matrix which is most appropriate to its risk programme. Five-by-five matrices are very common and provide a greater level of granularity in the results. However, there is no reason why the matrix cannot contain more ratings for either axis, and equally there is no reason to have the same number of ratings for each. It is entirely up to the organisation or the individual to decide what size and shape of matrix is appropriate. However, once a particular matrix has been chosen, it is recommended that this is used throughout the organisation, as it then means that all risk assessments are carried out on the same basis.

The output from the matrix will be a number of risk levels. Again, these are arbitrary, and can be agreed based upon the organisation's 'risk appetite'.

(This is the degree of risk an organisation is prepared to accept. Organisations which have a low risk appetite include pharmaceutical companies, where the introduction of new drugs sometimes requires years of rigorous testing before a product is considered safe enough to launch. Organisations which display a high risk appetite, on the other hand, include petrochemical companies who will spend tens of millions of pounds in searching for scarce oil reserves, and will often drill many 'dry' holes before finally finding a rich source.) The highest combination of impact and likelihood give the highest level of risk, and are risks which should be treated as soon as possible. Those lower down the matrix have a lesser degree of urgency, while those risks which carry low impact and likelihood may, if the organisation decides, be accepted without the need for treatment.

Whatever the risk, the assessment for each threat should be recorded on a risk register which will include details of the impact and likelihood for each threat, the level of risk calculated, possible treatment options, who would be responsible for carrying out the risk treatment, and a date by which the work should be completed. It is also considered good practice to note a review date for each risk as ongoing monitoring will show up whether either the impact or likelihood of any threat has changed since the last assessment. It may also be that other factors have had an effect to increase or reduce the threat, likelihood or impact of the risk.

Treatment

Having decided, from the output of the risk matrix, what options exist to treat the risks identified, a risk treatment plan must be produced. This will be dealt with in greater detail in the following section, and allows for four basic options:

- to avoid the risk completely (often by not doing something which might incur an unacceptable level of risk);
- to accept the risk – this is a common option where the level of risk assessed is low;
- to reduce either the likelihood or the impact of a risk – usually by some form of risk mitigation;
- to transfer some parts or all of the risk, for example by insuring against the eventuality.

Monitor

The final stage of the risk management cycle is to monitor the results of the risk treatment plan. The frequency of this process may vary according to the type of threat – some threats may change very quickly and will require monitoring at frequent intervals while others will change little over long periods of time and will only need occasional monitoring.

The cycle should also be repeated over time, as some threats might disappear completely and new threats might emerge. Again, the interval will depend largely upon the risk appetite of the organisation and may well be documented in a risk management strategy or policy document.

Options for treating risks

The output of the risk matrix will determine one of four courses of action in order to treat the risks. These will be:

Avoid the risk

Risk avoidance, sometimes called termination of the risk, is usually a fairly clear-cut option. Put simply, it means not doing something which incurs risk. For example, it might be to issue a security policy which states that users of personal computers must not install unauthorised software. This removes the risk of inappropriate software finding its way onto PCs within the organisation, and can be enforced by restricting the administrative capabilities of users. Another example would be not to do or to stop a business activity because it put the organisation at too much risk.

Accept the risk

When the level of risk assessed is very low, the organisation may decide that it is willing to live with or tolerate the risk and that it will be accepted. It is important that this is a conscious decision and that one or more individuals are held accountable for it by means of a formal sign-off process and by keeping a record in the risk register as to who has signed as accepting the risk. In some cases, the cost of treating the risk may equal or exceed the potential financial impact if the risk occurs. In this case, the business must decide whether to accept the risk or to implement the appropriate controls anyway, maybe as a means of maintaining customer confidence.

Acceptance of a risk is not the same as ignoring it – this must never be a course of action as risks which are ignored can cause problems at a later date. It is also important that risks which have been accepted are monitored at suitable intervals in case the impact or likelihood have changed since the initial assessment was carried out.

Reduce the risk

This is sometimes also referred to as risk mitigation or risk treatment. There are basically three possibilities – to reduce the threat, the vulnerability (and thereby the likelihood) or the impact. Actions which take place in reducing the risk are often referred to as controls.

Reducing the threat can be difficult. For example, although it would be nice to get rid of hackers completely, this would require significant social reform and is therefore an unlikely option.

Reducing the vulnerability or likelihood is a possibility. For example, by applying appropriate security patches to an operating system or tightening the security settings on a firewall the likelihood of hackers gaining access is reduced although not removed.

Finally, it is also possible to reduce the business impact if a risk does materialise. For example if the whole of an organisation's information assets reside on one main system, this would represent a potential single point of failure, and could be mitigated by introducing either a load-sharing system or a disaster recovery standby system.

Transfer the risk

Risk transfer can be achieved in a number of ways, but typically an insurance policy is an appropriate method when the impact of the risk can be measured as a purely financial one. Another means of transferring risk is to move it to a third party when the relevant expertise to manage the risk is not available within the organisation. An example of this might be when magnetic media containing sensitive information requires secure disposal, and the organisation outsources the work to a specialist company. In cases such as this, however, the organisation itself must still retain overall responsibility and ownership of the risk.

Like Information Assurance, insurance is also all about the management of risk – it is something in which insurance companies have specialised for many years. You pay the insurance company to do the worrying for you and in return, they expect you to take reasonable care to ensure that the worst does not happen. The insurance policy does not necessarily alter the threat or the likelihood of the risk occurring but, if it does happen, then the impact on you is reduced by the payout from the insurance company.

It must also be realised that it is highly unlikely that the full impact of a risk can be removed by transfer. It is more likely that the risk is ultimately shared between the two organisations with a formal acknowledgement of the responsibilities. For example, a travel insurance policy will reduce the financial impact on you if your flight is seriously delayed but it will have little effect on the consequences for your company of not making the critical business sales meeting where you lost a major contract. Indeed it is usual for these consequential impacts to be explicitly excluded from such policies.

Most aspects of risk treatment involve a cost element of some sort – this must be balanced against the potential losses which might be incurred if the threat should be realised. Where the level of the cost of the mitigation approaches or exceeds the potential losses, the decision to accept the risk is normally the correct decision.

Approaches to risk assessment

Qualitative

As has been mentioned earlier, one of the approaches to carrying out risk assessments is to use a qualitative method. While this is essentially subjective, it may be the best course of action when hard facts relating to impacts and frequency of events are hard to come by.

The fact that the method is largely subjective, however, should not prevent the assessment from being properly carried out. The main thing to agree is what constitutes 'high', 'medium' and 'low' for example, so that any assessment will have a good degree of rationality about it, making it easy to understand and straightforward to justify later on.

Alternatively, a 'standard' template can be used. For example, the UK Government has a standard method of risk assessment for use in civil contingency work:

Rating	Impact	Likelihood
1	Insignificant	Negligible
2	Minor	Rare
3	Moderate	Unlikely
4	Significant	Possible
5	Catastrophic	Probable

Quantitative

Quantitative risk assessments on the other hand take a much more factual approach, and can use statistical evidence to support both impact and likelihood assessments. For example, when assessing the risk of virus attacks, there will be plenty of numeric information available on the websites of anti-virus vendors to provide the basis for supporting a metric-based assessment. Whether their figures are to be wholly believed is of course another matter entirely.

Alternatively, you may be trying to assess the impact of failure of a system or service, and having no hard facts to support the assessment, you might decide that up to £100,000 constitutes a low impact; between £100,000 and £1,000,000 constitutes a medium impact, and above £1,000,000 constitutes a high impact. As long as all parties agree that this is a sensible method, then it is perfectly acceptable.

Statistical information to support likelihood assessments is also very likely to be widely available, but should also be treated with caution. The expression 'There are three kinds of lies: lies, damned lies, and statistics' has been attributed to many people including Benjamin Disraeli and Mark Twain, but remains true to this day. If you wish to explore the subject further, there are two books listed in the reference section of this book which may be of interest (Bernstein, 1996, 1998; Salkind, 2004).

Software tools

Unsurprisingly, there are a number of software tools available which will help in carrying out risk assessments. This book does not aim to offer any specific guidance on the good, bad or the ugly of these; merely to state that they exist, and that the reader should investigate these in greater detail to discover which (if any) are best suited to his or her needs.

Again, a word of caution here. It is very easy to become obsessed with choosing the right software tool and working through a complex set of analyses, only to find that the answers are not as you would hope. Very often a simple analysis tool can be created using a simple spreadsheet program, and is therefore very much easier to tailor to the needs of the organisation. Try to keep the work as simple as possible and reduce the impression of a 'black art' by making the results understandable to as wide an audience as possible.

Questionnaires

Ultimately, whenever you conduct a risk assessment you will need to visit various areas of the organisation seeking information from people who understand far more about their particular area of the business than you do. It is worthwhile therefore spending some time in preparing a questionnaire which will guide you and them through a series of questions designed specifically to discover exactly the information you require in order to carry out the risk assessment. Working with a questionnaire also helps to ensure that that there is a level of consistency across the answers provided.

It is usually best to begin with open questions – for example asking people to describe the processes and procedures by which things happen as this information will often point to the need for further questions. For example it may help to begin by asking for an explanation of what the person's department does. What are the inputs and outputs; what processes are involved; who carries out the work; where do they do this; what happens if one or more inputs ceases to work, and so on. This will very often highlight a 'single point of failure' in the process. Closed questions can then follow, drilling down into the detail and uncovering facts and figures which will help you to build up a more detailed picture, and which will allow you to provide a detailed analysis of what might happen and how likely this might be.

While some of this information might seem unimportant at first, it should be remembered that at some stage a business case will have to be presented in order to gain approval for funding to mitigate the most serious risks. This information will almost certainly play a key part in building the business case.

Identifying and accounting for the value of information assets

Before we can carry out any form of risk assessment on our organisation's information, it is obvious that we must first of all identify and document each of these 'information assets'. Much of the information to do this will come from the questionnaires referred to earlier, so it will be useful to list who is responsible for collecting and storing the information, where it is held, how and when it is used and backed up, and so on. On occasion the people themselves could be considered an information asset if, for example, they are the only source of business critical information or if they have unique skills within the organisation.

The value of each of these information assets will depend very much on its function, how long the business can manage without it, how long it would take or how difficult it would be to recover or restore it and how frequently the information changes. One of the key questions to ask when assessing the information value is 'how much will the organisation lose (or not make) if the asset is not available'.

Clearly if this is a Human Resources database, loss of access to it for a short period of time should not pose a serious threat – the impact would be low, but loss of a database holding on-line customer orders on an e-commerce website even for a few minutes would have a much higher impact.

Information classification policies

The value of information assets links us neatly into the subject of information classification. Some information held by an organisation (for example a product list) will be considered to be public domain information, and will be allocated a low classification – often referred to as 'unmarked' or 'unrestricted'. Other information will be more strictly controlled – for example a list of customer accounts and their annual spend must be kept within the organisation, and will therefore have a higher level of classification such as 'confidential'.

More critical information will have a higher level of classification again – for example documents relating to a merger or acquisition will not be available to many people within the organisation – perhaps only at Board level and a very few senior managers. These might be graded as 'highly confidential' or 'secret'. There is no limit to the number of classification levels which a company can use, although simplicity is again the key here. Three or four levels is considered to be about right.

Each information asset should be categorised according to the classification policy, and those assets which are not graded as 'unmarked' or 'unrestricted', must be protectively marked to indicate this. The classification policy should also identify the procedures for handling, storing and disposing of protectively marked information.

The need to assess the risks to the business in business terms

While it is very straightforward (after some practice) to carry out risk assessments, there will be a great temptation to describe and document these in risk management terminology. This is fine when discussing the assessments with like-minded or similarly experienced people, but when it comes to selling the concept back into the business, this terminology may not be well understood if people are unfamiliar with the jargon. Terminology which is alien to the recipient will diminish the effectiveness of the risk assessment and will make it more difficult to convince the reader that appropriate action must be taken.

It is always advisable for the risk assessor to be able to express the outcome in terms which are readily understood by managers within the business – talk their language in other words. This may mean that a number of risk assessments must be 'translated' for the benefit of different departments in the organisation. For example, different terminology is used in an organisation's Production and Marketing departments, so the output of the risk assessments must be adjusted so that the language used reflects their own specific terminology. This should not be seen as a patronising approach, but more as a pragmatic method of optimising the results to gain the maximum impact and buy-in. Likewise, the assessments themselves must focus on the areas which the individual departments recognise and to which they can relate, or the exercise will have been wasted time.

Balancing the cost of Information Security against the potential losses

Once the results of the risk assessments have been made available, there will be recommendations as to how the higher-level risks should be mitigated. While the organisation would not expect a detailed cost estimate to carry out the remedial work at this stage, it would be prudent to have a rough idea at least of the order of cost.

In this way, it is possible to present the results of the risk assessments in a more balanced way so that the decision-makers can take a more objective view.

For example, if the anticipated losses as the result of a threat being carried out are £50,000, the overall risk is deemed as medium. If the costs of reducing this to a lower level will amount to £25,000, the decision might well be to accept the risk rather than reducing it as the cost of the control is high in comparison to the possible impact.

On the other hand, if the anticipated losses are £1,000,000, the risk is high and it will cost £25,000 to reduce this to medium or low, then the decision to reduce the risk is much easier, as the balance is more in favour of risk reduction. Finding the balance is largely dependent upon the organisation's risk appetite, but in some cases (where the cost–benefit balance is not as clear cut) the decision will be more difficult to make and may require a more detailed cost breakdown. The experienced risk manager will recognise cases such as these and will be prepared for them. However, there may be circumstances in which the cost of treating the risk is not the main issue and other factors such as legal and regulatory requirements mean that the work has to be carried out regardless.

The role of management in accepting risk

The option to accept risk may sound an easy one to take, but it is not something which should be done lightly. Many organisations are unable to differentiate between accepting risk and ignoring risk (which is never an option).

If the recommendation is to accept a risk, then the decision to do this must be a conscious one, and should be fully documented. Although it is common practice for a single manager to 'sign off' a risk, where the impact is high, it is better practice to have a second manager sign off as well – preferably one who is more remote from the risk itself but nevertheless one who has a good understanding of the potential impact of the risk materialising.

For example, if a production manager signs off the risk of having only one machine of a particular type, a manager from an entirely different discipline (say finance) should counter-sign the risk in order to provide an objective confirmation that acceptance is in order. This reduces the possibility of individual departments covering up their own mistakes.

Once 'signed off', an accepted risk should still be monitored at regular intervals in order to verify that the threat, the impact or the likelihood have not changed, and that acceptance of the risk continues to sit well with the organisation's risk appetite.

Contribution to risk registers (e.g. Turnbull conformance)

Risk registers are a vital part of the overall risk management process. They achieve a number of objectives:

- they permit all risks identified in the risk assessment process to be documented in a formal manner;
- they allow an authorised observer (e.g. an auditor) to have visibility of the impact and likelihood of the risk and all the associated details and can assess the suitability of the responses selected;
- they allow ongoing monitoring of the status of the risk and can be used as management reports on the progress of risk mitigation and of any variation in the risks.

A risk register should contain as a minimum the details of the threat; its assessed impact and likelihood; the overall risk calculated from these; the recommended treatment (Accept, Avoid, Reduce, Transfer), and the actual action(s) to be taken; the person or department responsible for carrying out this work and the date by which it is expected to be completed. Other fields may also be included, but those listed above form the basic minimum information required of a risk register. It is common practice to review and update the risk register at intervals – typically monthly or quarterly.

> You have delivered your impact analysis to Ms Jackson and, although she now understands the consequences of loss or failure of the computer, she needs to understand the likelihood of your impact analyses actually occurring.
>
> She has asked you to carry out a risk assessment based on the threats you have already identified.

Activity 2.2

For each of the threats you identified in Activity 2.1, give an assessment of the likelihood of each taking place.

From the impact analysis carried out in Activity 2.1 and the likelihood assessment above, calculate the overall level of risk for each threat.

Draw a simple 3 × 3 risk matrix and illustrate the risks you have assessed.

Sample Questions

1. What are the four types of risk treatment that can be used?
   a. Accept, transfer, ignore, control.
   b. Avoid, ignore, transfer, mitigate.
   c. Accept, avoid, reduce, transfer.
   d. Reduce, transfer, mitigate, control.
2. A business impact analysis considers which of the following?
   a. The consequences of a threat being carried out.
   b. The likelihood of a threat occurring.
   c. The likelihood that a vulnerability will be exploited.
   d. The probability that losses might result from an incident.
3. A risk assessment is designed to achieve which of the following?
   a. To identify the likely impact if a vulnerability is exploited.
   b. To identify the degree of likelihood that a vulnerability will be exploited.
   c. To identify the likely impact if a threat occurs.
   d. To identify the degree of likelihood that a threat will occur and its likely impact.
4. Which of the following is **not** a threat?
   a. Failure of the local mains power supply.
   b. An easily guessed password.
   c. A transmission circuit cable break.
   d. Flooding of a data centre.
5. Once the key risks have been assessed, what action is unacceptable for very low risks?
   a. They can be ignored.
   b. They can be accepted.
   c. They can be treated.
   d. They can be terminated.

Pointers for activities in the chapter

Activity 2.1

Given several types of threat such as loss of membership records, details of the Natterjack toad's breeding grounds or the financial records of GANT, an impact analysis should look at the short-term, medium-term and long-term consequences.

You should try and look also at various types of impact – including financial loss, GANT's reputation and the possible effects on the toads themselves. You may find that the impacts may change over time – improving or worsening according to the type of impact, and this may (later) affect your recommendations as to how the risks might be mitigated.

Activity 2.2

Whereas impact analyses can be relatively straightforward to conduct, the likelihood assessments can be more complex as they can be very subjective if using a qualitative approach. To gain a less-subjective assessment it is necessary to carry out the risk assessment using a quantitative approach which may involve gathering statistical information such as frequency of previous events for example, which can sometimes be a time-consuming process.

For the purposes of this activity it is suggested that you take a qualitative approach and use your best judgement to come up with a Low/Medium/High likelihood rating.

You can number each threat and mark the numbers on the completed Risk Matrix diagram. You then need to decide what action(s) to take for each threat, and it might be useful to make a note of why you consider this to be the optimum approach – in the real world you would have to justify your recommendations, possibly with a cost-based business case, so it is worth getting into the habit early on.

Try to allow logic to influence your recommendations rather than emotions. You may feel strongly about a particular course of action, but others may hold a different view, and you might have to put up a convincing business-based argument to bring them round to your point of view.

Answers to sample questions

1. The correct answer is c.
2. The correct answer is a.
3. The correct answer is d.
4. The correct answer is b.
5. The correct answer is b.

REFERENCES AND FURTHER READING

Publications

Bernstein, P. L. (1996, 1998) *Against the Gods*. John Wiley & Sons, Inc. ISBN 0-471-29563-9.

Hiles, A. and Barnes, P. (1999) *The Definitive Handbook of Business Continuity Management*. John Wiley & Sons, Inc. ISBN 0-471-98622-4.

The Business Continuity Institute (2007) *Business Continuity Management – Good Practice Guide*, November.

The Institute of Chartered Accountants in England and Wales (1999) *Internal Control – Guidance for Directors on the Combined Code (Turnbull report)*, September. ISBN 1-84152-010-1.

The Institute of Directors (2000) *Business Continuity*. Director Publications Ltd. ISBN 0-749-43563-1.

Toigo, J. (1996) *Disaster Recovery Planning*. John Wiley & Sons, Inc. ISBN 0-471-12175-4.

Websites

American Society for Industrial Security (ASIS) Business Continuity Guidelines http://www.asisonline.org/guidelines/guidelines.htm

British Standards Institute http://www.bsi-global.com

Continuity Central http://www.continuitycentral.com

Continuity Forum http://www.continuityforum.org

Disaster Recovery Institute International http://www.drii.org

Global Continuity http://www.globalcontinuity.com

The Business Continuity Institute http://www.thebci.com

Virtual Corporation (BCMM) http://www.virtual-corp.net/

3 Information Security Framework

The purpose of establishing an Information Security framework is to ensure that appropriate control mechanisms are in place to effectively manage Information Assurance across the enterprise.

This chapter covers the basic principles for establishing such a framework within an organisation and will look at the general area of Information Security management. In particular we will consider the role and use of policy, standards and procedures, Information Assurance governance, security incident management and their appropriate implementation.

This chapter forms about 35 per cent of the CISMP examination syllabus.

INFORMATION SECURITY MANAGEMENT

LEARNING OUTCOMES

The aim of this section is to provide the reader with the basic knowledge needed to understand the principles for organising Information Assurance across the enterprise. Once completed, the reader should be able to define and explain not only the main concepts but also to draft documents to meet the general requirements in the following areas.

Organisation and responsibilities

Establishing an organisational structure to manage Information Assurance provides a framework to ensure that the assurance requirements of the enterprise are understood and that responsibilities are allocated appropriately across the enterprise to achieve this. Accountabilities need to be clearly defined, whether at an enterprise level or on a local basis, and assurance activities need to be co-ordinated appropriately across the organisation to ensure that they are being managed effectively. This section covers the necessary organisational arrangements that should be carried out to provide effective control of Information Assurance.

Information Security roles within the enterprise

There should be a nominated resource within the organisation that has responsibility for the day-to-day management of Information Assurance issues. This is to ensure that good Information Assurance practice is applied properly and effectively across the enterprise and for co-ordinating all assurance activities. In larger organisations, this function should be a full-time role and the manager of this function is often referred to as the Head of Information Assurance, the Information Security manager, the Chief Information Security Officer (CISO) or sometimes as the Chief Information Officer (CIO).

In smaller organisations, the role may be combined with other responsibilities.

In this section the role will be referred to as the Information Security manager. How this role is structured will depend largely on the size and culture of the organisation and is typically supported by other persons as part of a dedicated team.

The Information Security manager needs to understand the Information Assurance risks that the enterprise may face, what controls are in place and where the enterprise may be vulnerable. This information must be communicated effectively to senior management (who have ultimate responsibility for Information Assurance). This is to ensure that they understand the status of assurance within the enterprise so that the appropriate safeguards are put into place. The main activities of the Information Security Manager are:

- co-ordinating Information Assurance activities across the enterprise including those delegated outside of the team;
- co-ordinating the production of security policy;
- communicating with users so they understand their Information Assurance responsibilities and are aware of potential threats to the enterprise;
- understanding the enterprise's risk appetite and profile and how it may be evolving;
- monitoring the effectiveness of the enterprise's assurance arrangements;
- reporting on the effectiveness of the assurance arrangements to senior management and suggesting improvements;
- providing expert advice on Information Assurance matters to the enterprise;
- creating a culture of good information exchange and assurance practices.

There are a number of recognised standards that provide guidance on how to manage assurance arrangements and responsibilities within an enterprise such as the ISO/IEC 27000 series and the ISF (Information Security Forum) standard of Good Practice. These standards can be adapted to fit individual enterprise requirements.

Placement in the enterprise structure

Placement of the various assurance roles within an organisation will normally depend on the structure, the particular requirements and the culture of the enterprise. Therefore, there are no definite hard and fast rules as to where the roles should specifically sit, how they should be organised or what their scope should include.

In many enterprises, the Information Assurance function is located within the corporate compliance area. This is common in enterprises or industries that have a strong compliance culture such as banking or manufacturing.

In other enterprises the function is based in the Information Technology group because many (but rarely all) of the controls to protect the enterprise are reliant on computer technology. Sometimes, the function can be placed within a central facilities group since assurance responsibilities often span a number of management areas within an enterprise.

The scope of the Information Assurance function may vary. In some instances the assurance function may include responsibility for setting policy and direction but not for the actual implementation of the security control mechanisms, which then may be carried out by a separate area such as the IT department or local teams. Alternatively, the assurance function can also have responsibility for the implementation of technical security controls and solutions and for conducting investigations and monitoring compliance.

As a regulatory role, the Information Assurance function should be positioned as part of a formal structure so that it can facilitate the full management and co-ordination of assurance matters across the enterprise.

Board/Director responsibility

One senior person within the organisation should be given the overall responsibility for protecting the assurance of the enterprise's information assets and be formally held accountable. This role should be performed by a board member or equivalent to demonstrate the enterprise's management commitment to Information Assurance. Their main responsibility is to ensure that appropriate assurance controls are implemented across the enterprise and to:

- provide a single point of accountability for Information Assurance;
- ensure that assurance goals are identified and meet the enterprise's needs;
- ensure that adequate assurance resources are made available to protect the enterprise to an acceptable and agreed level of risk;
- assign specific assurance roles and responsibilities across the enterprise;
- provide clear direction, commitment and visible support for assurance initiatives, for example by approving and providing sign off for high-level security policies, strategies and requisite architectures.

The director has the necessary status to ensure that appropriate focus is placed on protecting the enterprise's information assets and to influence and sanction assurance activities. Implementing adequate assurance control mechanisms can in some cases be met with resistance from other parts of the business that are in competition for available resources, and therefore it is important to have a 'security champion' to ensure that priorities are met. Experience has shown that if senior support is not in place, assurance initiatives will probably fail.

There is an increasing amount of UK and worldwide legislation and regulation that demands this level of accountability and responsibility, for example Sarbanes–Oxley (USA) and the Companies Act (UK). The Turnbull Report in the UK states that a board member for a public limited company has to be responsible for ensuring adequate service continuity requirements are in place to prevent the enterprise going out of operation after experiencing a major problem. If these measures are not appropriately implemented, that person could perhaps face a custodial sentence. This potential outcome may be good for focusing the attention of senior management and for securing appropriate resources.

The director should establish and chair an ongoing high-level working group to co-ordinate assurance activities across the organisation to ensure adequate assurance measures are in place to protect the business to an acceptable and agreed level of risk.

This working group is often called a steering committee or a Security Forum. The working group should be made up of a cross section of individuals from the enterprise that are either stakeholders in requiring good assurance or have responsibilities for ensuring appropriate assurance arrangements are in place.

Membership should include one or more line of business (LOB) managers or departmental heads to ensure that assurance arrangements meet their business or organisational demands. It should also include the Information Security Manager and representatives from vested interest parties such as internal audit, personnel (HR), physical security and the head of Information Technology.

The group should meet regularly in order to ensure that the protection of the organisation's information is being managed effectively and that controls are in place to reduce risk to an acceptable level. This would include:

- ensuring that assurance is included in the enterprise's overall planning activities;
- approving and prioritising assurance improvement activities;
- reviewing assurance performance and changes in threats to assess whether the risk profile of the enterprise has altered;
- approving policies, standards and procedures that relate to Information Assurance;
- acting as evangelists for assurance within the organisation by emphasising its importance to colleagues.

The director will normally delegate authority for the development of Information Assurance initiatives and responsibilities either to individuals within the working party or to other members of the organisation. However, the director will be ultimately accountable for achievements or failures. The working party is the cornerstone of the Information Governance structure that will be covered later in this chapter.

Responsibilities across the organisation

Achieving good Information Assurance requires teamwork and a wide variety of skills ranging from managerial to technical and administrative. It is unlikely that any one person would have all the requisite skill sets or even the time to perform everything that is required; therefore roles need to be delegated to the appropriate teams or to specific individuals with the necessary skills. For instance the skill sets required to maintain an enterprise's anti-virus systems are different from those required for administering User IDs.

All those involved need to have a proper understanding of accountabilities and be given clear direction and support from senior management to achieve what is required of them. In many cases, individuals may be working together as a 'virtual team' that spans across separate management responsibility areas. For many individuals, their Information Assurance responsibilities will form just a part of their overall role. Therefore their activities require co-ordination and monitoring from a central Information Assurance function to ensure they are successful. It is therefore essential that all individuals have clearly defined responsibilities and that they understand their part in delivering the overall Information Assurance function within the enterprise. Their Job Descriptions or Terms of Reference should include:

- the scope of their responsibilities and their level of authority;
- the processes they should be following to carry out these responsibilities;
- the procedure they should carry out to report and deal with any security breaches that they discover;
- understanding confidentiality/non-disclosure constraints;
- requirements for regular reporting;
- what should take place if they leave the organisation;
- what will happen if they breach the agreed terms and conditions.

These responsibilities should reflect the enterprise Information Assurance policy and current legislation. They should be reviewed regularly to ensure that they remain current and are relevant and supplemented with additional guidance as necessary. Where the Information Assurance function does not constitute a full-time role, it is important that those engaged in carrying out assurance activities are given a clear mandate by senior management to do so and that the work is included as a formal part of their objectives. These individuals must have the sufficient skills and tools to be able to carry out these tasks and may need training and support to acquire the necessary knowledge and fully appreciate the critical nature of protecting information assets.

Many enterprises have local security co-ordinators that are the 'eyes and ears' at a local level to ensure that security policies are followed and for identifying any security vulnerabilities or breaches. They can offer feedback to the Information Security manager as to whether existing assurance processes and controls are effective, identify possible risks and help propose new assurance controls. The scope of the local co-ordinators will vary depending on the enterprise's requirements. In a large global operation it may be appropriate to have country or regional co-ordinators or it may be more relevant to have an individual responsible for a business unit or office location. In smaller businesses it may be better to nominate individuals who have responsibility for a specific department or business function.

Anyone who has access to the organisation's information assets will have a level of personal responsibility for its assurance and it is important that these are known and understood. User responsibilities need to be clearly set out in an acceptable information use policy and bolstered by education so that they can help protect against risk. Guidance on acceptable use policies is described in the next section and user awareness and training is described in more detail in Chapter 4. Individuals may have specific responsibilities for a particular application or system and in this case their responsibilities are best expressed in the system operating procedures. Third-party assurance responsibilities should be included in contractual terms and conditions.

Any information assets within an organisation should be associated with an owner of that information (i.e. head of department, business manager or process owner) who understands its importance to the enterprise and the resulting negative impact if its confidentiality, integrity or availability is compromised. This will help ensure that adequate controls and procedures are put into place.

Statutory, regulatory and advisory requirements

External factors can influence how an enterprise's Information Assurance should be managed and these requirements need to be understood so that the appropriate assurance controls can be adopted to enable the business to fulfil its responsibilities. These requirements can arise from a variety of organisations such as the police, utility companies, government, trade regulatory bodies or telecommunications suppliers. They may be statutory, regulatory or advisory.

Statutory requirements are legal requirements that must be fulfilled. For example, law enforcement agencies must be contacted should certain laws be broken or are suspected of being broken. The download of child pornography would be such a case. Compliance with these requirements may influence how an enterprise's incident reporting procedures are organised. For example, how, when and by whom should the authorities be contacted. Privacy legislation such as the Data Protection Act will influence how information is stored and managed within the enterprise and how resources are deployed to ensure that the enterprise complies with this legislation.

Regulatory requirements often are imposed by trade bodies and these specify how an enterprise should operate to conform to certain standards.

Although they are not legal obligations, regulatory bodies have extensive powers and failure to comply could lead to possible fines or in extreme cases exclusion from trading in a particular environment. The finance sector is a good example of this as it maintains strict controls to prevent financial malpractices such as fraud or money laundering. Official bodies such as the Financial Services Agency (FSA) within the UK have far-reaching powers. Another example of a regulatory authority is the government agency on health and safety in the workplace. Some of these regulatory requirements support or supplement statutory requirements in certain business operations.

Advisory requirements may arise from government agencies or utility companies and provide advice as to what arrangements should be put into place to help cope with instances such as fires, natural disasters and acts of terrorism. These requirements are not legally binding and are generally issued to help encourage best practice.

Maintaining relationships with relevant external bodies is beneficial to an organisation as it helps the enterprise to appreciate better the requirements placed on them and gain prior warning of any changes. By understanding the requirements of the emergency services, utility companies and government agencies, enterprises can more effectively design their contingency plans and incident management processes and procedures.

Provision of specialist Information Security advice and expertise

Those involved in the security function should provide specialist security information advice and expertise to the enterprise. A high degree of current knowledge on Information Assurance matters should be maintained on topics such as awareness of industry trends, changes to organisational threats, new control measures, analysis of risk, legislation and compliance requirements and the latest technological developments. It is not necessary to have all the answers but it is essential to be in a position know where to find this information or to have access to someone with this specialist knowledge as and when needed.

One way of achieving this aim is to keep in regular contact with special interest groups or by networking with Information Assurance peers in other enterprises via professional associations or security forums. Information about new technologies, products, threats and vulnerabilities or how to tackle particular assurance issues can be shared with one another and often a collaborative approach is useful in understanding and addressing these issues before applying them to relevant situations. Bulletin boards, websites and news groups also can provide early warnings of possible alerts, attacks and vulnerabilities and it is important to identify which ones may relate to the enterprise.

A certain amount of ongoing self education is needed to maintain this level of competency and to gain knowledge and understanding. Training courses are available to develop this knowledge with courses that range from specific topics on Information Assurance to training that covers a wider focus such as security management. There are also a number of professional accreditations that can be gained to develop your knowledge. It is also recommended to read the specialist Information Assurance publications and the wider IT industry ones in order to gain an understanding of the business issues that are of concern to our colleagues.

Creating a culture of good Information Security practice

Information assurance needs the co-operation and collaboration of everyone with access to the enterprise's information. Involving everyone in the assurance process will help to develop a culture of good Information Security practice.

As previously mentioned, it is important that Information Assurance is taken seriously by senior management within the enterprise and that they provide sponsorship and support for assurance initiatives. If so, then their support and commitment will cascade down through the organisation. Line managers will proactively take responsibility for adopting Information Assurance measures within their teams, and likewise end users will know that they must take their responsibilities seriously. Positive reinforcement of good assurance behaviour by the Information Assurance function and management helps to cement good behaviour and some organisations even include feedback on assurance behaviour in their performance reviews.

A key factor for success is ensuring that everyone that accesses the enterprise's information knows what is expected of them. Having in place clearly defined assurance roles and responsibilities, up-to-date security policies and standards and procedures will eliminate any ambiguities. They do need to be clearly communicated and be readily accessible. For example, assurance responsibilities should be included in employee job descriptions and for third parties they should form part of their contract conditions. All users need to clearly understand what will happen if they do not follow Information Assurance policies and that senior management will be involved should the rules be breached. Policy development is covered in the next section.

Education is also a vital component in creating a culture of good Information Assurance practice. If everyone understands the value of the enterprise's information assets and how they can be put at risk, then they are far more likely to appreciate why these processes and procedures are in place. Regular awareness campaigns initiated through the Information Security manager can help reinforce this message.

Activity 3.1
Miss Peacock has just returned from a conference and has realised that the enterprise does not have a formal Information Assurance function. She has asked you to put together a high-level proposal on what should be put in place.

POLICY, STANDARDS AND PROCEDURES

Organisations require both their staff and third parties to use, manipulate and interpret information and need their co-operation to ensure that their information assets are accessed in a safe and responsible manner. All users need to know what the enterprise expects of them with regard to this. Policies, standards, procedures and guidelines provide this guidance.

LEARNING OUTCOMES

The intention of this section is to provide the reader with the basic knowledge needed to develop, write and gain user commitment for assurance policies, standards, operating procedures and guidelines. Following study in this area, the reader should be able to explain and justify not only the main concepts but also to draft documents to meet the general requirements in the following areas.

Developing policies, standards, procedures and guidelines internally and with third parties

There is often confusion concerning the definition of policies, standards, procedures and guidelines so this should be clarified first of all. A policy is a high-level statement of an organisation's values, goals and objectives in a specific area, and the general approach to achieving them. Although they should be regularly reviewed, policies should hold good for some time as they are not intended to provide either detailed or specific guidance on how to achieve these goals. For example, a policy might say that each user is responsible for creating and maintaining their system passwords – although it doesn't say exactly how to do this. Policies are mandatory.

A standard is more prescriptive than a policy. It quantifies what needs to be done and provides consistency in controls that can be measured. For instance, passwords must contain a minimum of 8 characters, be a mix of numbers and letters and be changed every 30 days. Standards and policies are obligatory. They should support policy and state what 'must' be done and how it should be achieved. Standards can be either general (e.g. handling sensitive information) or technical (e.g. encryption of data) but they should always relate to a specific subject.

A procedure is a set of detailed working instructions and will describe what, when, how and by whom something should be done. Again, they are obligatory and should support enterprise policies and standards.

Guidelines are not mandatory but can provide advice, direction and best practice in instances where it is often difficult to regulate how something should be done (e.g. working practices when out of the office).

Whether it is producing policies, standards, procedures or guidelines, these documents should always be to the point and clearly written. Language should be concise, unambiguous and as free as possible of complex jargon and acronyms. Statements should contain positive rather than negative 'do not' rules as these tend to make users less responsive. A document should address a clear and well-defined subject area within its scope so that the target audience knows that it is relevant to them (e.g. this policy applies to all GANT employees in the UK).

Policies, and any attendant standards, procedures and guidelines, should be endorsed by senior management and have clear ownership (i.e. Head of Human Resources, Departmental Manager, etc.). In addition to senior management they should also be supported by the main stakeholders and especially those people tasked to enforce them. For example, if an individual is to be disciplined for a breach of policy, then Human Resources will need to support the policy to carry out any disciplinary action in relation to it. To have credibility, policies should be endorsed by all interested parties such as stakeholders and user communities.

Policies, standards and procedures need to be realistic and enforceable. It may be a great aspiration to expect people to keep their laptops with them at all times but it is far more realistic to state that they must not be left unattended in a public place. Similarly, if a technical control is stipulated (e.g. encryption of all data on laptops) it must be anticipated whether this is actually feasible. There may be instances where it is not possible to comply with policy and consideration also needs to be given to allowing exceptions to policy in the way of special dispensations.

To be enforceable policies must be consistent with other corporate policies and compliant with the law. All users need to know what will happen if they do not comply. They need to be regularly reviewed to ensure that they remain current, relevant and effective. This will be covered in more detail later under Information Assurance Governance.

The way in which policies, standards, procedures and guidelines are structured will largely depend on the organisation. Regardless, every organisation should have a (high-level) assurance policy which states the organisation's commitment to Information Assurance and what it expects to be done to protect its information assets. A security policy is a strategic statement of the organisation's approach to assurance and sets out the formal organisational stance on assurance matters for everyone to see. This security policy should contain statements on:

- how the enterprise will manage Information Assurance;
- the protection of information assets in accordance with their criticality;
- the compliance with legal and regulatory obligations;

- the means by which users will be made aware of Information Assurance issues and the process to deal with breaches to policy and suspected assurance weaknesses;
- the fact that this policy has the support of the Board and Chief Executive.

More detailed guidance on what to include in a security policy can be found in recognised standards such as the ISO/IEC 27000 series and the International Security Forum (ISF) standard of good practice. The high-level security policy should be signed off by the director responsible for Information Assurance. The policy should then be issued or made available to all individuals with access to the organisation's information and systems, both internal and external, in a format that is readily understandable and accessible by the user.

Third parties often require access to an enterprise's information assets in terms of processing information, offering support, providing services or processing facilities. It is important to ensure that there is no misunderstanding between the enterprise and the third party over what controls are to be put in place to protect the enterprise's information assets. Policies, standards and procedures should be extended to third parties where relevant, and specific policies may need to be written to cover third-party arrangements. These should be included within the terms of a contract. Access should not be given to an external entity until the enterprise can be assured that the appropriate controls have been put in place and that the third party has formally confirmed that they understand their obligations and accept their responsibility to comply.

As the relationships with third parties can be quite diverse, any terms associated with policies, standards and procedures may vary according to the type and nature of the relationship. Agreements with third parties should include the enterprise's assurance policy. Again ISO/IEC 27000 series and the ISF Standard of Good Practice contain guidance on the type of controls that should be considered for inclusion in third-party agreements but typically they should include the following arrangements:

- management of changes to the application/facility/service/resource;
- the right to audit and monitor assurance arrangements within the third party;
- notification and investigation of assurance incidents and security breaches;
- recruitment of personnel.

Care should be taken to ensure that sensitive information is not disclosed to or by third parties, and policies should reflect demands on the third party for confidentiality and non-disclosure of information. The third party may, in the process of delivering the service, use further sub-contractors or service providers (this can be controlled in the contract). Therefore it is important to ensure that any policies, standards, procedures and guidelines are applied to them too.

Balance between physical, procedural and technical controls

Physical, procedural and technical controls can provide very effective security mechanisms and do much to reduce the likelihood of incidents occurring. However, they each have their limitations and there are occasions where their use is not appropriate. Possibly their deployment would be far too complex or expensive given the perceived value of the information and the associated risk. For example a £1 million security application to protect a £10,000 information asset does not make much financial sense. In other cases a physical or technical control may be so intrusive that the users are prevented from efficiently carrying out their work. In many cases there may be no reasonable physical or technical controls that can be deployed to prevent a particular security breach from occurring or it may be that the security controls in place can be circumvented by the user in some way.

Users need to access Information Systems in order to carry out their tasks and this inevitably introduces a level of risk to the information. They may need to share this data with colleagues or external suppliers and make value judgements as to whether it should be released to them. Reducing this kind of risk is difficult to achieve through technical controls alone. Technical controls introduced by a documental security system for example may well provide a good level of security. There will, however, always be exceptions and these need to be handled in a consistent manner by having a policy and process in place. This might simply involve informing a senior colleague of the issue and the proposed course of action to deal with the issue in the short term.

Formal policies and procedures can be used to make users aware of their responsibilities and the risks relating to the data to which they have access. The policies can empower individuals to make decisions as to whether others should access this data. This can be an effective control measure but is obviously dependent upon users complying with these policies and associated standards and procedures.

Occasionally, due to time pressures, or perhaps because of expediency, policy rules may be circumvented or ignored. Ignorance or a failure to properly understand the policy will prevent compliance and in these instances users won't understand the risks to their information assets and are very unlikely to be fully aware of the threats to them. Policies and procedures rely on individuals knowing that the policy exists and understanding what the policy expects of them as well as gaining their agreement to comply with it. So policy controls have limitations.

There needs to be a sensible balance between using physical, procedural and technical controls to manage the risks associated with information assets. All three elements should be used to complement one another in a layered approach to manage risk to an acceptable level.

End-user code of practice

The development of a high-level security policy should be bolstered by an end-user code of practice or acceptable use policy which provides a readily accessible way of communicating requirements to end users. An acceptable use policy demonstrates the organisation's commitment to Information Assurance and must be approved by the director responsible for Information Assurance. It should be published to all users that need to access the organisation's information management systems and include all employees (permanent and temporary, full and part time), contractors and third parties. The acceptable use policy should detail what is expected from users to protect the organisation's information assets. Elements that may be included in this policy are:

- ensuring that user passwords and PINs are protected appropriately and not compromised and changed at defined intervals;
- ensuring that users only access information, facilities or equipment for which they have the requisite authorisation;
- logging-off from systems when leaving a workstation unattended;
- locking away sensitive documentation and media when not in use (as part of a clear desk policy);
- ensuring that all security incidents are reported.

An acceptable use policy can also include general statements regarding behaviour in the workplace such as making it unacceptable to make any sexual, racist, obscene, discriminatory, harassing or other offensive statements regardless of the method used to transmit such statements (email, telephone, text, paper or spoken word). All conditions of employment for permanent or contract employees should contain a statement that compliance with the enterprise Information Assurance policies is mandatory. To avoid against vicarious liability, the policy should also include statements that specify that users must comply with all appropriate legal and regulatory requirements placed on the organisation.

Consequences of policy violation

Anyone accessing the enterprise's information assets needs to know what are the consequences of a policy violation and this should be clearly stated in the policy, standard or procedure. Appropriate processes should be established for reporting and dealing with violations so that they are dealt with in a consistent manner. These processes should be documented and agreed with the relevant stakeholders when the documents are produced.

Violation of a policy may in severe cases lead to an employee disciplinary process being instigated, termination of supplier contract or the need to report the behaviour to the appropriate law enforcement agency. Therefore the rules and processes need to be understood, agreed and put into effect within the organisation before violations may need to be dealt with. Naturally it is essential to involve the HR and legal departments in the development of such policies to ensure the proposed course of action complies fully with all employment legislation as well as other relevant national laws.

However, it is a waste of time having a policy in place unless the organisation is prepared to enforce it. Senior management, and those that have to enforce the rules, need to support the processes to deal with any violations. If violations have not been dealt with appropriately, or have been ignored by line management, then this should also be considered as a violation of policy and treated seriously.

> ### Activity 3.2
> Miss Peacock has asked you to prepare an end-user code of practice for GANT. Identify the main areas that you would include in the policy.

INFORMATION SECURITY GOVERNANCE

There is an increasing amount of legislation and regulation that requires senior management to ensure that adequate controls are in place to protect the enterprise's information assets. To fulfil these obligations, senior management needs to understand the current status of existing assurance controls, where such controls are inadequate and how the risk profile of the organisation is changing. The necessary effort can then be made to improve security mechanisms and manage the risk effectively. This section covers the principles of the governance processes that should be implemented to enable this to happen and to provide senior management with sound and up-to-date information on the state of assurance within the enterprise.

LEARNING OUTCOMES

The intention of this section is to provide the reader with the basic knowledge needed to understand the principles of Information assurance governance. Once completed the reader should be able to explain and justify not only the main concepts but also to establish procedures and draft documents to meet the general requirements in the following areas.

Review, evaluation and revision of security policy

The production of policies, standards, procedures and guidelines has already been covered in the previous section but to ensure that they remain current, relevant and effective they should be reviewed regularly. Reviews should take place after any significant changes to either systems or resources or as part of a regular review schedule (e.g. annually).

A management review process should be established to ensure that policy reviews take place in an organised and timely manner. The review schedule should identify all the persons to be involved and a formal record kept of any revisions made – with an explanation as to why content has been incorporated or removed. Senior management should then approve the final version of any amended documentation.

The review should involve all the main stakeholders including external parties and, where applicable, regulatory authorities. The review should focus on factors that might influence or trigger possible amendments, such as:

- changes to technology, processes, organisation, resource availability or working practices;
- changes to contractual, regulatory or legal requirements;
- changes in threats and vulnerabilities;
- results, actions and recommendations from any assurance reviews or audits;
- findings and recommendations from either incidents or previous assurance breaches, or where there is evidence of non-compliance with the policy.

Once the review has been completed the revised policy should be communicated effectively to the relevant users, both internal and external to the organisation. This process should also be used for the maintenance of all other assurance documents such as security standards, procedures and guidelines.

Security audits and reviews

Audits and reviews provide a good opportunity to understand how well things are working within the enterprise and provide senior management with valuable information on the assurance of their environment. Regular independent assurance audits and reviews should be carried out across the business to ensure that its Information Systems are compliant with existing security policies, standards and controls. Possible vulnerabilities to these systems can be checked and the effectiveness of existing controls can be tested. Audits and reviews should be carried out periodically or when a significant change (e.g. a system upgrade) has occurred.

To introduce a measure of impartiality into the review, it should be carried out by an independent party, which will also bring to it a fresh set of eyes. Ideally, a member of an audit team or a manager that has no conflict of interest in its outcome could do this. Alternatively, reviews can be carried out by a third party such as an external auditor or a consulting company. In the case of technical reviews it is often beneficial to engage a company with specialist knowledge in areas such as penetration testing. They can bring with them their experience of having audited similar assurance-based scenarios in other organisations. Reviewers must have sufficient expertise so it is prudent to verify their abilities before commencing. Technical testing should only be carried out by recognised and approved technicians and engineers. Any organisation providing testers should also be able to verify that the individuals' CVs and background have been checked to ensure that they have a suitable level of personal integrity. Information on technical testing and assessment is covered in more detail in Chapter 4.

A programme of Information Assurance audits and reviews should be introduced by senior management. The scope of each individual review and their deliverables should be agreed by senior management and the area owner (i.e. head of department, line manager, etc.). A scoping exercise should be completed before the audit or review is started and a checklist should be developed to measure the efficacy of the assurance controls. The outputs should show whether the defined controls (e.g. policy, standard, procedural or technical) have been implemented correctly and are effective enough to reduce risk to an acceptable level.

Access rights to systems or information assets for those performing the audit or review should be restricted to only what is necessary on a need-to-know basis. These should be monitored and logged to create a reference trail of their activities. Wherever possible, auditors and reviewers should be given read-only access to isolated copies of the system. Audit tools should be restricted to prevent any possible misuse or compromise to data. The legal implications of providing third parties with access to sensitive information should be considered as should the disposal of any information, reports and scripts that result from the audits or tests. Non-disclosure agreements (NDAs) should be put in place if the information being reviewed is sensitive.

Audits and reviews should be planned well in advance to minimise the risk of disruption to the normal operation of the enterprise. Some audits such as penetration testing may produce some unexpected activity on a computer system or network. Change management processes should be followed to ensure that all parties that could be affected are aware of the planned activities and potential change in activity levels.

The results of the audit or review should be recorded within a formal report and presented by the reviewer to senior management and the manager whose area has been reviewed. A plan of corrective action should be agreed with them, including time scales for implementation. The plan should be regularly monitored to ensure that actions are being progressed. Any risks identified during an audit or review should always be added to an information risk register – maintained centrally by the organisation. All documentation produced should be filed securely so that it can be referred to when planning the following cycle of audits and reviews.

Checks for compliance with security policy

Regular checks should be carried out to measure compliance with security policics, standards and procedures. Carrying out compliance checks helps to identify whether controls are still adequate and relevant. Compliance checks also help to gauge the level of user understanding and awareness of their assurance responsibilities and whether or not these are being taken seriously. If regular checks are not carried out, then over time there can be a tendency for users to show less regard for them. Assurance is weakened as users become aware that monitoring does not take place and that they are not likely to be challenged.

If an instance of non-compliance has been identified then it is necessary to discover why this has happened. This could be due to lack of training, misunderstandings or perhaps simple disregard of procedures. It may have resulted from a change in business processes which has not been recognised in the assurance documentation. The compliance checker should then decide what action should be taken and whether measures need to be put in place to prevent further occurrences. Action taken should reflect the scale of the non-conformity; minor incidents such as an isolated instance where a procedure has not been followed could be dealt with in an informal manner but any major non-conformance such as widespread password sharing should be addressed more formally. If corrective action is recommended, subsequent reviews should identify that it has been implemented.

The results of compliance checks should be recorded and serious instances of non compliance reported to senior management. The findings from the checks can be fed into subsequent policy reviews. Compliance reviews should also be carried out to ensure that the enterprise is using licences, for example for software, in accordance with terms stated in the purchase agreement.

Reporting on compliance status

The finance industry has a long history of regulation and most stock exchanges have their own regulatory controls to prevent financial malpractice but governance controls have gradually extended to other operating spheres. Many countries have produced their own codes of ethics often in response to large corporate failures or in response to public pressure. The Sarbanes–Oxley Act in 2002 was introduced following a number of high-profile financial accounting scandals in the USA. The European Union's governance legislation was revised in 2004 via the Companies (Audit, Investigations and Community Enterprise) Act, which at the time of writing is being implemented across the member states and will replace most of their local company legislation.

The type of strategy deployed by the enterprise to meet their Information Assurance compliance obligations will depend on the risk appetite of the organisation and the external requirements placed on them. The enterprise needs to understand what their specific obligations are so they can implement the necessary controls and reporting mechanisms. In some situations highly specific governance requirements do apply but mostly they ask the enterprise to demonstrate that good Information Assurance controls have been implemented. Generally regulators will want assurance that senior management are committed to protecting the enterprise's information assets, understand the enterprise's risk profile and have implemented controls to manage risk to an acceptable level. Regulators will also want assurance that the controls in place are working effectively and that any gaps identified are being addressed.

Senior management and any regulatory or compliance bodies need to have access to sufficient information to be able to demonstrate compliance. To do this the following types of information need to be made available:

- high-level risk assessments for the enterprise and for critical systems and services;
- a risk register showing how identified risks will be managed;
- an up-to-date set of security policies with a review process;
- a register of any dispensations from security polices;
- the results from assurance reviews and security testing and compliance reviews;
- reports from any assurance breaches or incidents;
- plans to address any compliance weaknesses.

The relevant information has to be gathered, reviewed and presented in a format that is acceptable to the regulator. This activity can be very time consuming so it helps to develop a repeatable and efficient process for reporting on compliance issues and to reuse controls for each of the regulatory groups. This process may form part of an enterprise Information Assurance policy.

There are various models (comprising a methodology, structure and processes) that can be adopted by an enterprise to provide this level of information. All the models tend to be based upon the principles of implementing a formal control process for:

- understanding risk;
- identifying control requirements to reduce risk to an acceptable level;
- implementing effective security controls;
- monitoring how effective the controls are;
- periodic re-evaluation of risk levels;
- the efficacy of controls to enable continual improvement and to ensure that the risk level is maintained.

Current models include ISO 27001, Security Operations Maturity Architecture (SOMA) and the Committee of Sponsoring Organizations of the Treadway Commission (COSO) and they all offer levels of accreditation to enable the enterprise to demonstrate their competency to other organisations and regulatory bodies. The ISO 27001 model provides an approach for establishing, implementing, operating, monitoring, reviewing, maintaining and improving assurance within an organisation. The standard uses a 'Plan–Do–Check–Act' (PDCA) approach to provide a cycle of continuous assurance review and improvement.

SOMA, produced by the Institute for Security and Open Methodologies, provides a framework for measuring the operational security and management process and is structured in maturity levels that can be adapted to work at different levels of assurance maturity within the enterprise as well as being used with other standards. COSO, produced by the Treadway Commission, provides a framework for evaluating effectiveness of assurance by establishing a set of objectives for assurance control and measuring against them. This is often used for testing the effectiveness of accounting controls.

Importance of effective Information Security governance from the highest levels of organisational management

As discussed at the beginning of this chapter, one senior person within the organisation should be given the overall responsibility for protecting the assurance of the organisation's information assets and be formally held accountable to ensure that appropriate security controls are implemented across the business. This director should be supported by a working group to ensure that adequate assurance measures have been put in place to protect the organisation to an acceptable level of risk. Involving senior management will help to endorse the governance process, ensure that adequate resources are made available, ensure that controls are implemented efffectively and that any identified security gaps are addressed.

> ### Activity 3.3
> After the recent loss of information, Miss Peacock is concerned that she needs to demonstrate to the regulators and external auditors that good assurance controls are in place within GANT. How would you provide her with evidence to demonstrate that assurance is being managed effectively?

SECURITY INCIDENT MANAGEMENT

No matter how careful you are in conducting the day-to-day business of the organisation, and regardless of the extent of the assurance controls in place, security incidents happen. These don't just affect the confidentiality of assets, the impact can equally relate to their integrity or availability. It is important to have plans in place to deal with these eventualities before they occur, because trying to implement solutions afterwards is seldom likely to be effective.

LEARNING OUTCOMES

The intention of this section is to provide the reader with the basic knowledge needed to manage assurance incidents and plan and conduct a forensic investigation. Once completed, the reader should have an understanding of the following.

Incident reporting, recording and management

Having an incident response plan that has been worked out in advance and tested is like having a good insurance policy. Trying to get one afterwards is too late. Do not think that you can quickly improvise something after the event, because this is a complex subject and in the ensuing chaos you will not have the luxury of time to come up with a good plan.

The first priority is to ensure that all the people within the organisation know how to recognise an incident and to whom they should report it. This can be done in a number of ways including awareness training, a section on a company intranet or portal and by carrying out exercises.

There are normally five phases in the management of an incident:

(i) reporting;

(ii) investigation;

(iii) assessment;

(iv) corrective action;

(v) review.

In order to ensure that enough information is captured it is good practice to have a standard form to hand on which to record the information given by the person making the initial report. This form should capture:

- who they are;
- where they are – geographic location and department;
- contact details – address, telephone (desk and mobile), email;
- brief description of incident;
- whether there any danger to life, health or company assets;
- other potential impact to business operations;
- description of anything they have done to date in response;
- time first noticed.

From the moment of the first report and until the incident is closed, a log should be kept of information, decisions made and the consequences of any actions. These records will be invaluable later – both for internal use and also for possible use by external agencies including those for law enforcement.

Incident Response Teams and procedures

An Incident Response Team (IRT) must be appointed in advance and all members of that team should be properly briefed and prepared. The members need to come from a cross section of the business to ensure that there is sufficient breadth of knowledge to deal effectively with the situation. They need to be senior and experienced enough to have the authority to make decisions on the spot. They must also be empowered to call upon additional resources, internal and external, as they see fit to use in resolving the incident.

There needs to be a documented escalation process for the team to reach the most senior members of the organisation as and when necessary. It is advisable to give each of the team a set of the incident response plan documentation and make sure they have a pager or mobile phone so they can be contacted immediately it is decided to activate the plan.

Ideally, one or more persons should be designated as note-takers. Their job is not to be involved directly, but to observe and record all details of the incident in a logbook for reference later. It is a good job for someone who is learning about information assurance in general, because they get to see first-hand what does (and does not) work.

The procedures must be quite broad in their contents, because it is difficult to predict what the nature of the next incident will be. Some idea of likely events can be gained from looking at the Risk register and the output of the Risk Treatment planning process to identify high probability and high impact events. There are some events though, such as terrorist activity or freak storm damage, that are not part of the normal threat profile but can happen. One of the authors of this book has lost three IT systems to terrorist action and participated in an incident response after a law enforcement organisation had one of their buildings destroyed by fire bombs – all since 1997.

Links to corporate incident response management systems

Large organisations will probably have in place an infrastructure to support Incident Response Teams (IRTs). There is often a centralised function with access to resources and expertise to help deal with the incident. The latest procedures and contact lists may well be publicised on the intranet or information portal. It is possible that other offices will start to make preparations to send in specialist staff to help with managing and recovering from the incident, or to cover for the affected location, or to prepare to receive staff re-located from affected premises. Even if your organisation is not in the 'big league' it is worth approaching a large organisation located near yours. In return for the offer of help (perhaps an office with phones and internet access) in the event of a major incident their IRT may well be prepared to help you with advice and guidance based on their experience and training. It is worthwhile getting to know these people because the better prepared you are the better you will be able to handle the incident – whatever it may be.

Working with law enforcement organisations

There are times when it will be necessary to involve law enforcement or other similar organisations in the response to an incident. If there is any likelihood of criminal activity or other deliberate action, the appropriate authorities should be notified. It is important that senior management has a good understanding of the legal requirements for reporting certain events. It is, for instance, mandatory in the UK to inform the police if there is a suspicion of terrorist activity or that child pornography has been viewed or processed through the IT systems of an organisation. Recent UK legislation also requires the reporting of suspicious financial activities.

Another possibility is that of attempted extortion and blackmail by use of a denial of service attack. In this case the Serious Organised Crime Agency is the appropriate body in the UK to contact. Activity of this sort or malware (malicious software) discovered in UK government departments should lead to a report being passed to the Centre for the Protection of the Critical National Infrastructure (CPNI). In other countries there will be similar organisations and law enforcement agencies who will be the key point of contact for such incidents.

One last possibility is that an organisation may be visited by law enforcement officers conducting an enquiry into activities of which management has no knowledge. They may have a warrant to search the premises and remove items, or they may simply be conducting enquiries. The modern UK police force is aware of commercial sensitivities and the nature of intellectual property. While the organisation is best advised to take appropriate legal advice from internal or external sources, an open and co-operative response is almost always the best policy. One example of this is that the organisation must ensure it is abiding by the requirements of the country's Data Protection Act before providing any information to a third party, even if they are a law enforcement body. It may be necessary for the law enforcement body to obtain a warrant to enable the organisation to provide information without fear of later repercussions from the Information Commissioner or other regulatory body.

Processes, tools and techniques for the conduct of investigations

If it does become necessary to work with an external law enforcement organisation, they are going to want to collect evidence for use in further investigations and possible prosecutions. The UK's Police and Criminal Evidence Act (PACE) defines very strict standards of conduct in order to allow the police to demonstrate that the evidence is valid and admissible in court. The required course of action where IT assets are concerned can be very complex and it is very easy to render evidence inadmissible. It is strongly recommended that the Incident Response Team is properly trained in how to deal with these requirements and work with law enforcement representatives to achieve the desired outcomes.

Whether or not there is the possibility of involving a law enforcement organisation, it is good practice to observe the same high standards of rigour when investigating an incident. The findings could be used for a prosecution or an internal disciplinary hearing. A hearing that leads to the dismissal of an employee could then go to an employment tribunal and having evidence that is legally admissible through following good practice will be a great help in winning the case.

It is advisable to have someone designated as the Evidence Custody Officer. This person is responsible for collecting and securely storing evidence while maintaining a good documentary record to preserve what is often referred to as the 'chain of evidence'.

There are forensic tools available to collect and examine evidence from IT systems. They should only be used by skilled and properly trained investigators because of the ease with which evidence becomes contaminated and inadmissible. Many organisations will not have this kind of resource in-house but if a list of forensic specialists has been prepared in advance, they can then be quickly and easily located and contracted in when required. In some cases a 'retainer' or framework agreement may have been set up in advance to ensure a rapid response.

Security issues when procuring forensic services and support from third parties

If the organisation needs to go outside its own resources in order to complete the investigation or response, there are some important considerations to take into account.

One of the main ones is that of non-disclosure. In the previous section we mentioned a framework agreement. This sets out in advance all the contractual issues. Such an agreement can take time to negotiate and agree so it is preferable to put it in place before an incident occurs. In addition to the normal contractual terms about payment, provision of service levels and dispute resolution there also needs to be a section that defines a non-disclosure agreement (NDA) between the signatories. This document provides legally binding confidentiality, so that the third party is required under obligation to provide the same level of confidentiality to the information seen or facts discovered as a permanent employee of the company.

It should be noted that these agreements are still subject to the over-riding requirements of the law. The third party is legally required to notify law enforcement of any suspected child pornography or terrorist activity, even if they have signed an NDA.

The document should also define the requirements for the following:

- standards required in preserving evidence and accompanying documentation to those defined in PACE or equivalent for legal admissibility;
- the handover, assured destruction or secure erasure of all materials obtained by the third party at the end of the incident;
- participation in any review at the end of the incident to improve the response process.

Activity 3.4
The last external audit identified that there was no process in place to deal with any assurance breaches. Miss Peacock has asked you to produce a simple process for managing assurance incidents. How would you approach this and who would you involve?

INFORMATION SECURITY IMPLEMENTATION

An Information Assurance programme provides a high-level view of how the organisation will address its assurance needs. It can help to develop a common understanding of information risk and enable the organisation to prioritise and focus on implementing controls that address the risks that matter most. This section looks at various aspects of assurance planning and how to implement an assurance programme within an enterprise. It is not intended to offer guidance on either project or programme management. There are many publications that address this subject including the BCS publication Project Management for IT-related Projects, which provides the textbook material for the ISEB Foundation in IS Project Management.

LEARNING OUTCOMES

The intention of this section is to provide the reader with the basic knowledge needed to understand the principles of how to implement Information Assurance measures within an enterprise. Once completed the reader should be able to define and explain not only the main concepts but also to draft documents to meet the general requirements in the following areas.

Planning and ensuring effective programme implementation

Good planning is the foundation of any successful Information Assurance programme implementation. It can be used as a powerful tool for gaining support from both senior management and key stakeholders and to demonstrate how the assurance programme is helping to reduce risk within the enterprise. This builds support for further initiatives.

To have credibility, an Information Assurance implementation programme has to be realistic, be achievable and address accurately the needs of the enterprise. A programme will need to fulfil agreed objectives within the time scales set and to demonstrate quality and value for money and overall benefit to the organisation. A programme usually consists of a number of projects with each addressing either a function, application or information asset.

When planning a programme implementation it is necessary to understand the current status of assurance within the enterprise and what the programme needs to achieve. Ideally, a prior risk assessment should have been carried out. The outputs will help to define and shape the implementation programme and provide justification as to why it should be delivered. Guidance on carrying out a risk assessment is covered in Chapter 2.

Work should be prioritised to deal with the most pressing issues. A mix of tactical and strategic approaches may be used to address the issues involved. If possible, try to identify where there are some quick wins to be had. Those which have a high probability of success using only minimal resources will do much to raise the overall credibility of the implementation plan within the organisation.

When planning an implementation, consideration should be given to how long it will take to implement controls, how easy the implementation will be, what the associated costs are and what is the appetite of the organisation in wanting to resolve these issues. The main steps to developing an implementation programme and plan are to identify:

- how the implementation programme will address risks within the enterprise and reduce them to an acceptable level;
- the controls or work streams that need to be set up to achieve this;
- the level of effort that will be required and from whom;
- who will be accountable for the each part of the programme;
- the costs and time scales associated with implementation;
- how progress will be tracked.

High-level support is essential to the success of the programme and it should always have a senior responsible owner (sponsor). The programme and approach should be agreed with the main stakeholders and signed off by the sponsor. A steering committee should be set up to track the success of the programme and deal with any issues that arise. Resource and budget will need to be secured before the programme starts.

Depending on the scale and size of the programme it may be necessary to split the programme into a series of separate projects each with their own planning and tracking mechanisms. During the course of the programme there may be a need for planning revisions due to changes in enterprise priorities, budget cuts, unavailability of key human resources or similar. Such factors can affect what can be achieved. Therefore, the overall plan should be kept at a high level with its key deliverables and main milestones clearly expressed allowing the progress of the programme to be readily monitored. Detailed planning should be carried out near to the time of implementation where there is greater certainty of a settled environment and an appropriate understanding of what needs to be done at that point.

The plan should focus on the key deliverables and work should be divided into manageable amounts that can be measured (a milestone). Unless human resource is fully dedicated to the project, it may be necessary to calculate how much of a person's time has been committed to it. Project work can be allocated accordingly and enable resources to meet both project activities as well as other commitments they have.

The project plan should be regularly reviewed. The frequency of the reviews will vary depending on the type of implementation (daily, weekly, monthly). The purpose of these reviews is to maintain a vision of its actual progress by understanding what has been achieved thus far, comparing progress against the schedule, handling variations and making revisions to the plan, identifying problems and applying corrective action. Progress should be reported regularly to both the programme sponsor and any stakeholders and review meetings should be set up to enable them to agree and support programme alterations to meet changing requirements.

How to present Information Security programmes as a positive benefit

An Information Assurance programme should be seen as delivering positive benefits to the enterprise. Managing down information risk can bring about tangible benefits in terms of greater stability of Information Systems and improved protection to sensitive information. They can show the rest of the organisation that assurance priorities are aligned with the priorities of the enterprise.

Communicating with senior management, line managers and users in general, in a manner that relates to their own particular interests, can do much to change the view that the assurance function is an inhibitor to one that is an enabler, by demonstrating how it can add value to the organisation.

Similarly, establishing good interpersonal relationships with stakeholders and colleagues in general will always help to present assurance programmes as a worthwhile activity. It is essential to be sensitive to their needs and ensure that they understand what the programme means specifically to them and how it will affect their role. Initially colleagues may be cautious and wary of an implementation programme. Including them within the planning process will help gain their confidence and appreciation. By aligning assurance objectives with the overall enterprise culture and values it can be seen that you are working together to achieve the same shared goals.

As with all initiatives it is essential to have the support and commitment of senior management. Usually, they are not assurance specialists and do not have a full understanding of the Information Assurance risks and issues facing the organisation. It is important to present the positive benefits of the assurance programme in a manner that is concise and free of jargon. To support the programme senior management needs to understand:

- the risks facing the organisation;
- the cause and potential impacts of these risks;
- the benefits they will see from their investment;
- where there may need to be changes to ways of working;
- how they can support or sponsor the programme.

The programme should be formally presented to them by way of a sound business case and be accompanied by all the necessary facts to enable an informed decision to be made. Senior management is generally more favourable to persuasion if they can realise a return on their investment. By quantifying impacts and explaining where the enterprise may be vulnerable, it is possible to demonstrate that a reduction in impacts can lead to a reduction in operating costs. Return on Investment (ROI) is a mechanism that can be used to justify assurance expenditure and gain budget approval.

By calculating a positive financial return on an assurance investment it is possible to put forward a persuasive case for its implementation by balancing potential financial rewards against the costs of implementing the controls. This is achieved by calculating how much it would cost to purchase and implement a particular security control and then estimating, in cost terms, what expense the organisation could incur as a result of assurance incidents.

Demonstrating that good assurance controls can be used by the enterprise for competitive advantage can also help to present assurance programmes as a positive activity. For example, many organisations insist that an enterprise has certification to particular security standards such as ISO 27001 as a prerequisite before they engage with them. This provides them with an assurance that the enterprise has implemented effective assurance controls. Enterprises that have had assurance breaches can often suffer financially through fines and lost business as their trading partners and customers lose confidence in their abilities to protect their information. For some organisations a security breach can have an enormous negative impact on their brand value. A low instance of security breaches and good assurance controls in place can provide commercial advantage over competitors.

Information Security strategy and architecture

Information security strategy and architecture are two relatively new concepts in Information Assurance implementation. This section will look at some of the high-level principles regarding these concepts.

An Information Security strategy is a plan to take the assurance function within an organisation from the reality of where it is now with all its problems and issues, to an improved state in the future. It provides a road map or vision as to how this can be achieved. A strategy should normally cover a period of time where it is possible to implement a significant level of change but short enough to be able to predict changes in technology and organisational objectives. Typically, this is over a three to five year period.

An Information Security strategy has the elements of an implementation programme but covers a longer period of time and is pitched at a much higher, less detailed level. It should demonstrate how it will enable the enterprise to achieve its objectives and how it will protect it against current and future threats. It should consider:

- the current state of assurance and the strengths and weaknesses of existing controls;
- how the risk profile of the enterprise is likely to change in response to changing business objectives and working practices;
- trends in threats and vulnerabilities to potential types of incidents;
- expected developments in software and hardware;
- legal, compliance and audit requirements and any anticipated changes;
- areas where cost savings can be made.

As it is a vision, this high-level document should be written in concise non-technical language so that the target business audience can clearly comprehend the bigger picture and the vision being presented. The strategy should remain a living document by being regularly reviewed and updated to reflect changes in technology and organisational priorities as they are likely to change over the period of its existence.

Having a strategy in place shows a degree of maturity of the Information Assurance function within the organisation. It provides an assurance that the organisation is committed to good Information Assurance Governance. Increasingly, there are pressures exerted from external bodies (via legislation and regulation) for organisations to have a security strategy in place.

The second concept is an Information Security architecture which can be used in conjunction with the Information Security strategy. The architecture translates organisational requirements for assurance into a set of controls that can be used to protect the enterprise's information assets. The Information Security architecture should aim to provide a common and consistent framework of global assurance controls and arrangements to be used across the enterprise rather than in a piecemeal fashion. Traditionally, IT-based architectures focused purely on technology but, as Information Assurance behaviour extends beyond technology to include policies, processes, procedures and user behaviour, so it follows that an Information Security architecture should also encompass these aspects.

An enterprise Information Security architecture should provide system developers and administrators with a consistent framework of assurance controls that can be used across multiple systems and environments within the enterprise. It can be adapted to fulfil different circumstances which means that effort is not duplicated every time a new set of controls is implemented. Efficiency and productivity can be increased whilst costs can be reduced by providing leverage and economies of scale. This should enable the assurance function to react more quickly to commercial, organisational and technological changes and be able to implement assurance solutions more quickly, efficiently and at lower costs.

An Information Security architecture works on a set of 'Principles' that express the type of controls to be implemented. They act as positioning statements that will be adopted within the architecture. An example of this is 'auditing and monitoring controls will ensure that the organisation complies with security policies and legal obligations'. Having identified a set of principles the architecture can then be modelled through increasing layers of complexity and detail starting at a high-level conception view of controls though to a detailed specification and design.

Components within the enterprise with similar security requirements can be grouped together into 'Domains' so that common sets of security controls can be developed to protect them. For example, all enterprise systems with web-enabled interfaces can use the same Domain controls. The term 'Services' is used to describe the type of controls that will be used to protect these components.

The need to link with business planning and risk management and audit processes

The aim of an Information Assurance programme should be to reduce information risk within the enterprise. As we have seen throughout this section, Information Assurance planning and implementation processes should not work in isolation. To be effective an implementation programme needs to understand the enterprise's business objectives and goals so that it can identify the appropriate assurance control measures to ensure that the enterprise is sufficiently protected to meet these goals.

Information Assurance implementation programmes need to work closely with other organisational and assurance processes to manage risk to an acceptable level. The risk management process should provide awareness and understanding of the risks faced by the enterprise and identify where risks are not being managed effectively. The outputs from risk assessments should determine what controls should be implemented and assess how urgently they need to be addressed.

Similarly, assurance governance processes will identify where existing controls are inadequate and where improvements need to be made. This may be through the reporting of assurance breaches or via auditing or testing of security controls. Governance processes will also determine changes in regulatory or legal requirements that may require additional controls to be put in place.

All implementation programmes should support the enterprise's Information Assurance policies, security strategy and security architecture. All security controls should support its long-term vision for Information Assurance and should be seen to add value or business benefit to the organisation.

Activity 3.5
Miss Peacock is very pleased with the work that you have done so far on Information Assurance and has given you a budget to implement some additional access controls within GANT. How would you approach this?

LEGAL FRAMEWORK

This section covers the general principles of the law in relation to Information Assurance management. This will cover a broad spectrum from the assurance implications on compliance with legal requirements affecting business (e.g. international electronic commerce) to laws that directly affect the way information can be monitored and copied. It will also make reference to certain pieces of legislation to explain concepts and highlight the legislative variances between separate countries.

LEARNING OUTCOMES

The intention of this section is to provide the reader with the basic knowledge of some of the general principles of law, legal jurisdiction and associated topics and how they affect Information Security management. Following study in this area, the reader should be able to explain and justify each of the following concepts.

Background

Our legal system has evolved over a long period of time. Within Britain, it can be traced back as far back as Roman and Anglo-Saxon times, and laws that were in place years ago can still exert an effect on the legislation of today. Legislation is continually evolving to adapt to the changing needs of modern day life and reflects the cultural development and values of our society. Understanding this can help to explain why there is variance in the legislation between different countries.

Countries which have some form of Federal Government will have multiple levels of law such as the USA, Canada or Switzerland – where there are local state laws which are ultimately subject to national or Federal laws. Within the European Union (EU), there are European directives (agreements between the member states), which have been produced to harmonise pieces of legislation across member states. Each country has to incorporate the legislation into their own legal system and this can result in subtle yet significant differences as each country interprets the directives in their own way.

The legal systems across the world do share many similarities and common legal concepts. However, as enterprises increasingly operate or perform transactions in more than one country it is necessary to have an understanding of their particular legislation and how it can impact on the enterprise's information as it crosses international boundaries. Organisations should always consult with a qualified lawyer to be sure what legislation is applicable to them.

The requirements from one legislative system may be inconsistent with another making compliance with all of the relevant laws of multiple jurisdictions difficult. Understanding legislation can be complex and pieces of legislation can sometimes conflict with one another. ISO/IEC 27000 series provides organisations with guidance regarding compliance legal requirements and covers the following areas:

- intellectual property rights;
- protection of organisational records;
- data protection and privacy of personal information;
- prevention of misuse of information processing facilities;
- regulation of cryptographic controls.

Non-compliance with legislation could prove costly for an enterprise through incurring financial penalties, operating restrictions or, in extreme instances, custodial sentences for senior executives. Therefore, it is essential that advice is taken from a trained legal specialist before making any important decisions that could put the organisation at risk.

Protection of personal data and restrictions on monitoring, surveillance, communications interception and trans-border data flows

Privacy laws exist to protect the rights of the individual. Most organisations hold and process information about people such as employee or customer information. Organisations need to be aware of the legal restrictions placed on them to protect this information and how it may be used and monitored.

The last few years have seen an increase in privacy legislation and this should be considered when processing personal information. Many countries have legislation to protect the individual and restrict and control the amount of information held and how it should be used and monitored. Although they do share common principles there are significant differences in the legislative approaches and this can cause difficulties when working across different legal jurisdictions. The European Union has a legal framework via the Data Protection Act to protect all types of personal information, whereas the USA protects personal information via a number of federal statutes. These tend to target specific areas such as protection of customer information by financial institutions (via Gramm Leach Bliley) or preserving privacy of medical information (HIPAA – Health Insurance Portability and Accountability Act).

The scope of legislation can also vary from country to country. For example, the Canadian Personal Information Protection and Electronic Documentation Act applies to the records of people for up to 20 years after their death, whereas in the EU any protection ceases at the time of death.

The Data Protection Act within the European Union protects the individual by ensuring that information is collected and processed lawfully, is accurate and is appropriate. Individuals have the right to have access to information held about them, know who can access it and have any inaccuracies amended. The Act also has provision to ensure that information is handled and processed in a secure manner and places controls on transferring it out of the EU to countries that have less stringent privacy controls. It also covers both electronic and paper-based records. The main points to remember when handling personal information are as follows.

- Personal information must be surrounded by proper robust assurance controls and working practices to protect the data from unlawful processing, accidental loss, corruption or destruction and unauthorised disclosure.
- Processes should be implemented to ensure that information is entered into computer systems correctly and that staff understand that no per-

sonal information should be disclosed to any third party without the appropriate written authority being in place.

- Paper records should be kept locked away and computer screens should not be left displaying personal information or able to be over-looked. Information no longer required should be destroyed by shred-ding or other secure forms of destruction.

Privacy laws often place restrictions on transferring information between countries. For example, the EU Data Protection Act states that personal information must not be transferred to countries that do not have such sim-ilarly strict rules. Certain countries such as Argentina, Canada, Hungary and Switzerland operate a data protection model which is comparable to the EU model and there are no restrictions with these countries. For other countries safeguards need to be considered to enable trans-border data flows to take place legally. The European Commission and the United States Department of Commerce developed the **Safe Harbor** framework to enable American organisations to be compliant with European Union (EU) privacy legislation. American companies that are likely to exchange personal information with EU-based organisations can amend their assurance arrangements so they are compliant with the Safe Harbor framework. For other countries, such as for transfers to the Indian sub-continent, it may be possible to make the data transfer if a number of prior safeguards are put into place. These guards would be undertaken via approved contractual terms that are acceptable to the legal body responsible for protecting personal information.

In the UK, the individual has a right to a level of privacy which is protected by legislation that restricts how their personal information can be monitored or intercepted. This legislation may often pre-date the computerisation of data storage such as the Public Records Acts of 1957 and 1967 within the UK. Any monitoring and collection techniques employed by an enterprise must comply with these laws. If the monitoring controls are to be used across more than one legal jurisdiction then there may be differences in the rights of the individuals being monitored. Within the European Union, the Regulation of Investigatory Powers Act 2000 (RIPA) was introduced to restrict covert monitoring of an individual's information. It was introduced to take account of new developments in communications technology, the Human Rights Act and the Telecommunications Directive.

Employment issues and employee rights

Depending on the legal jurisdiction, employees have certain rights when using the enterprise's Information Systems – such as the right to privacy and the right to know what information is held about them by the enterprise. In the UK, for example, under the Data Protection Act, individuals can request a copy of any information that an organisation may hold on them. This is called a subject access request.

Rights may also extend to monitoring controls. Within the European Union employees have the right to know the type and scale of monitoring that is being carried out by the enterprise and why it is being done; for instance an employer might consider it necessary to protect the enterprise from offensive or pornographic material, or perhaps they need to understand the volume of email traffic being propagated for performance purposes. The enterprise must communicate this information to employees. The easiest way to do this is to include a statement about the extent of monitoring in the enterprise's Information Assurance policies or employment contracts. If this is not done it may be necessary to gain specific consent from individuals to allow their information to be monitored. An assessment of the monitoring strategy should be carried out to demonstrate that the monitoring techniques that are being used are justified, not excessive and meet legal requirements.

If monitoring tools detect information that is clearly personal then care must be taken not to violate the individual's right to privacy. For example, a clearly personal email should not be opened by the employer or an individual's email account should not be accessed unless agreed with them beforehand. These can cause operating issues. For instance, a colleague may need to quickly obtain important company information previously sent to an individual – whilst that person is away on holiday. Employees should be asked to remove any of their personal information from IT resources when they leave the enterprise to avoid it being viewed by others.

Monitoring tools should not be used to target any particular individual and covert monitoring is rarely justified – exceptions might include situations where there are clear grounds that criminal activity or malpractice is taking or has taken place. Internal investigations may lead to an employment tribunal or a court case. It is important that any information that is collected meets the legal requirements that might include, for example, the UK's Freedom of Information Act or the equivalent in other countries.

Common concepts of computer misuse

Much of the legislation that currently applies to the misuse of computers has not been written specifically to address computer crime. It can be said that crime is crime and criminals simply use whatever means are available to carry it out. Blackmail, fraud, deception, theft and so on have always existed, but developments in technology have enabled criminals to now exploit computing devices in their activities. Similarly, privacy rights can be abused via electronic eavesdropping, hacking or cyber stalking, rather than by an actual physical presence. Therefore, existing laws that pre-date computers are often used to prosecute computer misuse.

Legislation has been produced to target specifically crimes committed using computers. The USA introduced the Computer Fraud and Abuse Act in 1984 and this legislation has since undergone several amendments. The UK was the first European country to enact a law that specifically addressed computer crime and this legislation formed the basis of the EU directive on Computer Misuse. The Computer Misuse Act 1990 introduced three new offences: unauthorised access to a computer, unauthorised access with the intent to commit or facilitate further offences and the unauthorised modification of computer material. The misuse of computers can include:

- illegal access (hacking) to computer systems;
- illegal interception of information;
- interference with information and systems;
- computer-related fraud and forgery;
- commercial infringement of copyrights;
- download of illegal material such as child pornography;
- trafficking in passwords, digital signatures and encryption keys.

The motives for the misuse of computers can vary. Fraudsters may misuse a computer for financial gain; hackers may try to gain access to a system for the intellectual challenge; a disgruntled employee may sabotage a computer system as an act of revenge.

Computer fraud is the term used to describe stealing money or goods by using or involving a computer. There are various ways that this can be achieved, either by entering incorrect information or by altering the information already held on a computer. It can also be carried out by creating or altering computer code. Misuse of computers in this manner is becoming an increasing problem as organised criminals find ever new opportunities to use computers to commit fraud. The increasing use of the internet to trade and shop enables criminals to commit fraud and steal the identities of others to commit fraud. Phishing is the term used where criminals entice individuals to disclose their financial details, for example by sending an email to an individual that purports to have been sent by their bank. This constitutes obtaining information by deception.

Hacking (despite its benign origins as a term for a general interest in discovering how computers work) is the term given to accessing a computer system without the express or implied permission of the owner of that system. A hacker is the name given to the person that carries out this activity. Hackers often modify information or software programs – which can subsequently cause considerable havoc. Website defacement is an example of where a hacker changes the information displayed on a web page. Sometimes, hackers will change information held within a database. Hackers often gain unauthorised access to a computer system simply for the thrill of being able to circumvent assurance controls and then sharing their conquests with other like-minded individuals. However, hacking is now increasingly being used as a tactic by criminals to carry out crimes such as fraud or blackmail.

Malicious code (or malware) is the term used to describe programs that have been written to cause security breaches or damage to computer systems by installing unwanted and unauthorised code onto them. Malicious code can cause a number of undesirable impacts including the deletion or corruption of information, the capture of information or the hijacking of computer resources to launch further attacks onto other computers. Malicious code comes in a variety of forms such as viruses, Trojan horses and backdoors. Malicious code is being increasingly used by criminals especially to capture financial information held on a computer that can be used for fraudulent purposes. Ransomware is an example of malware that infects the target computer by encrypting the owner's personal files. The victim is then contacted and offered a decryption key to decrypt the files in exchange for cash or information.

The download of illegal material onto a computer is another form of computer misuse. Many countries have in place legislation that prohibits the download of paedophile pornography and of the 'sexual grooming' of children using the Internet. In many countries there is a legal obligation for enterprises (and individuals) to report the discovery of this type of activity to the law enforcement agencies. It is very likely that legislation such as the Obscene Publications Act would be used to prosecute cases of child pornography, as the penalties are more severe than in computer misuse legislation.

Computers can be misused by a person to harass and stalk another individual (cyberstalking), for instance by sending threatening emails that cause distress. You should ensure that policies are in place to provide clear guidance to all computer users as to what constitutes computer misuse.

The illegal or unauthorised use of software such as programs, computer games or electronically stored music is known as piracy and is another example of computer misuse. You should ensure that only legitimate software and material are used in line with licence agreements and provide guidance to computer users that the use of unlicensed material is not allowed.

Requirements for records retention

Certain documents or records need to be retained by an organisation for legal or regulatory purposes for a period of time. These can include company board minutes, financial reports and accounts or technical specifications. The duration for which documents need to be retained varies by the document type and the legislation of the country in which it is being used. In multi-national organisations, records may be passed over to other countries within the same enterprise; meaning that the same data is then subject to different legislation requirements – which might even conflict with one another.

Although most retention requirements state a minimum length of time for keeping data, some legislation conversely states when a record must be destroyed. These usually relate to personal privacy, such as the Data Protection Act 1998 (EU) or the Fair and Accurate Credit Transaction Act 2003 (US).

An organisation may be asked to produce these records (or proof of destruction) either by a government agency or by an opposing party in a legal dispute. Failure to comply with this could result in a legal judgment against the organisation, heavy fines, closure of business or adverse publicity.

To help in compliance with legislation, you should have in place within your organisation a record retention policy and schedule. This should be communicated to staff so that they are aware of their responsibilities. In the case of international organisations, more than one schedule will need to be kept to deal with variances in requirements. A document that needs to be retained should be stored in a format that can ensure its protection (for example on a secure central repository rather than in a personal file so that it is not deleted or lost inadvertently). For larger enterprises there are document management solutions on the market to do this.

There are a number of externally produced standards that are available to help enterprises understand how best to cope with legal requirements such as ISO 15489 : – Record Management Standards produced by the International Standards Organisation – or standards produced by the American National Standards Institute (ANSI).

Intellectual property rights, for example copyright, including its general application to software and databases

Individuals and enterprises invest a lot of time, money and effort in creating original works, products, methodologies and ideas. They can be significantly out of pocket if they are unable to realise the benefit of their investment because other parties have used their ideas without compensating them. 'Intellectual property rights' (IPR) is the term given to the legal rights which protect creative works and most countries have legislation in place to protect such intellectual property.

Copyright law was originally designed to protect original artistic works such as pieces of music, but its use can also be applied to software programs, computer games or other types of work made using a computer or generated by a computer. Copyright is automatically associated with the piece of work upon its publication and has to be deemed as original. It usually remains in place for a fixed duration such as 50 years in the case of music. Copyright gives the creator exclusive rights over certain aspects of the work such as copying, issuing, performing or adapting it. Abuse of these rights by someone else is called infringement. Piracy is the term commonly used to describe the unauthorised use of computer software and is a breach of copyright law. Where software has been developed by an enterprise, the copyright is normally owned by the enterprise rather than the individual(s) involved unless a special provision has been agreed beforehand.

Copyright legislation is prevalent in most developed countries but there are some countries that take copyright less seriously such as in Asia and the East. There have been a number of initiatives to harmonise copyright protection internationally such as the GATT TRIP agreement 1993 (the General Agreement on Tariffs and Trades; Trade Related Aspects of Intellectual Property Rights). Within the European Union there is a directive to harmonise certain aspects of copyright and associated rights in relation to Information Systems.

In addition to copyright there are other pieces of legislation that aim to protect intellectual property and it is useful to have an awareness of some of them. The Common Law of Breach of Confidence (often described as a tort) aims to protect secrets – personal, commercial or governmental. These can only be applied for as long as the data is not in the public domain and covers breaches of confidence made between two or more parties. Trademarks such as Microsoft® or Apple® are there to protect brand strength by demonstrating their uniqueness in terms of quality, reputation, reliability, ubiquity, originality, value for money or whatever the brand strives to promote.

Passing off is the term used when an object is trying to seem the same as something else in order to cash in on the originator's reputation or ideas. This legislation is to protect the public from deception and to stop misrepresentation. An example of infringement that could apply to Information Assurance is where someone has set up an internet domain name which uses a very similar name to another better known site. The 'impostor' site is branded in much the same way as the original so that people who have mistyped the address believe they have gone to the intended site.

Patents are used to protect the intellectual property invested in the development of new products or in the creation of inventions and, like copyright, they are in place to prevent other people from copying or manufacturing the product or invention so that the creator is able to realise their investment (in both time and money) in creating their original work. Within information technology, patents tend to be used to protect physical devices such as a new type of computing device. Patents are of a fixed duration but can often be renewed by the owner. Patents tend to apply only to the particular country in which it has been applied for. Extending patents to cover many countries can be expensive as multiple applications may have to be submitted, and expert advice should be sought.

Contractual safeguards common of security requirements in outsourcing contracts, third party connections, information exchange, etc.

When developing contracts with third parties it is important to ensure that you put in place controls to protect the information assets of the enterprise to an acceptable level. In effect you need to ensure that they would take the same level of care in protecting your information as you would internally. The types of safeguards required will vary depending on the type of service being provided and the sensitivity of the enterprise data.

Contract conditions should include clauses to ensure that proper assurance controls are in place. Security conditions are often handled via a security schedule within the contract. The type of clauses needed to provide adequate protection might include clauses to:

- carry out regular assurance reviews and health checks;
- apply security patches in a timely manner;
- protect information against malicious code;

- provide business continuity arrangements that meet agreed service levels;
- vet new staff to an appropriate level;
- discipline against any security breaches;
- manage security incidents (including reporting any incidents to you);
- protect against disclosure of sensitive information;
- allow the enterprise the right to audit and monitor the services being provided;
- prevent further sub-contracting without written authorisation.

Collection of admissible evidence

There are a number of rules and processes that need to be followed when collecting evidence so that it can meet certain criteria when used in a court of law (described as admissible evidence). If legal guidelines are not followed, the evidence may be excluded as being inadmissible. This could result in a court case being lost, adverse publicity, loss of face and financial penalties to the prosecuting party.

This generally means being able to demonstrate that it is authentic, has not been tampered with, and has been gathered in an acceptable manner that meets legislative requirements. This includes being able to retain and document the state and integrity of items at the crime scene. Most countries have produced legal requirements that specify how evidence should be handled. Examples are the Federal Rules of Evidence (US), the Police and Criminal Evidence Act (PACE) and the Civil Evidence Act (UK). The appropriate guidelines should be followed when collecting evidence.

Developing a procedure for dealing with investigations and gathering evidence will help to avoid mistakes when working under pressure. Only trained personnel should carry out securing of evidence. Some organisations, such as banks, may have an in-house facility for carrying out investigations as they may need to do this regularly. In other organisations, where investigations are rare, it may be better to call in an external specialist organisation to manage the investigation and collect the evidence.

Each person that has handled any evidence may need to testify in court that the evidence is in the same state as when it was processed during the investigation. Therefore, keeping the number of people involved in the investigation to a minimum helps to simplify the presentation of evidence and preserve confidentiality. Evidence needs to be presented in a form that is understandable to the judge, jury or adjudicator.

Evidence can be excluded because it has been gathered without the correct authorisation or in a manner that contravenes guidelines. Sometimes, a warrant may be required to seize evidence although this is not necessary, for example, if the evidence is in plain view or consent has been given by the individual.

Collection of digital evidence can be complex. It can come in a variety of forms such as audit trails, application logs, firewall logs and CCTV footage. Some of the information may be deleted, incomplete or partially overwritten. It is more difficult to isolate and preserve evidence from a communications network as it is in a state of constant change and the sources of evidence may reside in different locations. *The Good Practice Guide for Computer Based Electronic Evidence*, published by the British Police Force, provides detailed advice on recovery of computer-based evidence. The guide states four principles when handling digital evidence.

- No action taken by the police or their agents should change data held on a computer or other media that may subsequently be relied on in court.
- In exceptional circumstances where a person finds it necessary to access original data held on a target computer, that person must be competent to do so and to give evidence explaining the relevance and the implications of their actions.
- An audit trail or other record of all processes applied to the computer-based evidence should be created and preserved. An independent third party should be able to examine those procedures and achieve the same results.
- The officer in charge of the case is responsible for ensuring that the law and these principles are adhered to. This applies to the possession of and access to information contained in a computer. They must be satisfied that anyone accessing the computer, or any use of a copying device, complies with these principles.

Use is often made of organisations that specialise in recovering and securing lost data from computer disk drives.

Securing digital signatures

Traditionally, a handwritten signature on an original document proves who signed it and any alterations can be detected. In the electronic world the original is indistinguishable from a copy and therefore there is potential for fraud. Digital signatures are a form of electronic signature that addresses this problem. A digital signature electronically binds the sender of a message to the contents of the actual message to prove that it is genuine. It also proves when it was sent, who it was sent to, that it has not been tampered with, that it has been kept confidential and that neither party can deny its transmission.

Enterprises are increasingly using digital signatures to conduct their business and legislation has been developed to facilitate and control their use. However what is acceptable varies across legal jurisdictions so it is important that you should obtain legal advice before adopting the use of digital signatures.

Within the EU, the legal directive states that electronic signatures will not be denied legal effect or admissibility simply on the grounds that they are in electronic form. Electronic signatures will be treated as handwritten signatures if they are backed by qualified certificates, which are provided by a certification service provider and created by a secure signature creation device. Electronic signatures are admissible as evidence in legal proceedings both in relation to the authenticity of the transmission and as to the integrity of the contents of that communication. In the UK, this directive was incorporated into local legislation as the UK Electronic Communications Act 2000.

There is much emphasis on the certification authority to be deemed trustworthy. Certification authorities generally have their signatures verified by other certification authorities to build a greater degree of trust. Certificate authorities may be liable for any compromise to the integrity of digitally signed documents authorised by them so to limit their liability many certification authorities stipulate a financial cap on transactions.

Some legal jurisdictions control the extent to which foreign certificate authorities can issue certificates that meet local laws. In the EU, there has to be a recognised arrangement between the EU and the country that has issued the certificate.

Restrictions on purchase, use and movement of cryptography technology

Cryptography is a powerful tool for protecting privacy that can be used by businesses, governments, criminals and individuals to protect confidential information. Governments argue that it is in the national interest for them to control cryptographic activity in order to protect the individual and to prevent and track criminal or terrorist activity. As such, there are numerous controls in place over its use. Cryptography legislation varies greatly from country to country. In some countries the controls are quite draconian, especially where repressive political regimes are in government. It is important that organisations which operate internationally understand the local operating restrictions as penalties can be extremely harsh (i.e. for treason) and the death penalty is included in some statutes.

In China, foreign organisations and individuals have to gain permission to use cryptography under the China State Council directive 273 of the Regulation of Commercial Encryption Code. In Pakistan, all encryption hardware and software has to be inspected and approved by the Pakistan Telecom Authority. Even within the European Union, there is variance on acceptable use of cryptography. France has a number of very specific requirements as to how cryptography can be used that are in addition to the EU directives.

The export of cryptographic controls is controlled in many countries by the Wassenaar Arrangement (WA) 1996. The purpose of this agreement was to ensure that transfers of conventional firearms and dual-use goods and technologies between countries was carried out responsibly and did not further the development of hostile regimes. There are 40 participating countries and, although export controls are implemented by each individual WA Participating State, the scope of export controls is determined by Wassenaar directives.

Cryptographic controls should be used in compliance with all relevant agreements, laws and regulations. Local legislation may disallow or restrict the use of strong cryptography. It may restrict its sale and movement to another country or put regulatory controls and registration requirements for its use. You should seek legal advice to ensure compliance with any national laws and regulations, and when transferring encrypted information or tools from one legal jurisdiction to another.

ISO/IEC 27000 series advises that the following factors should be considered:

- restrictions on import and export of computer hardware and software for performing cryptographic functions;
- restrictions on import and export of computer hardware and software which is designed to have cryptographic functions added to it;
- restrictions on the usage of encryption;
- mandatory or discretionary methods of access by the countries' authorities to information encrypted by computer hardware and software to provide confidentiality of content.

For organisations that are subject to regulatory control, the associated regulatory body may define additional constraints on how cryptography should be used. For example, the finance industry may specify use of particular security standards. These factors also need to be taken into account when applying cryptographic controls.

Activity 3.6

Miss Peacock is worried that after the information leak GANT's controls for protecting personal information may be weak. She has asked you to carry out a review of the privacy legislation affecting GANT to ensure that the organisation is compliant. What would be the main areas that you would look at?

SECURITY STANDARDS AND PROCEDURES

Standards impact on many aspects of our daily lives and they have been developed to ensure that products and services are safe, reliable, and efficient. They also provide for interchange ability (interoperability between products and systems). Today, there are recognised standards in place for almost all aspects of commerce, industry or government, and Information Assurance is no exception to this. Standards are produced by recognised standards bodies and they enable organisations to demonstrate a requisite level of technical, operational or administrative competency. There are many standards and technical regulations in existence and many organisations worldwide producing them. This chapter will look at how externally produced standards impact on Information Assurance management within the enterprise.

LEARNING OUTCOMES

The intention of this section is to provide the reader with the basic knowledge of some of the main externally produced standards that apply to Information Assurance management. Following study in this area, the reader should be able to explain and justify each of the following concepts.

National and international standards

In the area of Information Assurance there are many standards that apply. These typically define a set of requirements for products, processes or procedures and they are produced by organisations known as standards bodies. They collaborate with industry experts in different areas whether representing vendors, scientific research agencies or government departments, to produce best practices that can be applied by others. The jurisdiction of a standards body may extend to a specific industry sector, a particular country or internationally. The standards that will apply to an enterprise will vary depending on a number of factors; these may include the actual country in which the enterprise is based, whether it works internationally, the industry sector in which it operates, or perhaps engagement in government contracts. Most standards are produced by non-profit making organisations and are funded by the various parties that have a vested interest in their existence. Typically, they do not actually regulate the adoption of their standards, although some do provide certification or accreditation to organisations to allow them to demonstrate compliance to the set standards.

Although not mandatory, failure to implement or comply with accepted standards may have a significant adverse impact on an organisation. For instance, if their product or service is not certified as being compatible with other vendors' offerings then this may dissuade potential customers from placing orders. Alternatively, the organisation may not be able to demonstrate a sufficient level of competency in managing particular processes. Therefore it is important to have an understanding of the standards that can or need to be applied within the enterprise. The remainder of this section will look at some of the common standards related to Information Assurance as well as the standards producing organisations themselves.

The International Organization for Standardization (ISO) is the world's largest developer of standards and has published over 1600 international standards since it was established in 1947. The organisation was founded to facilitate the international co-ordination and unification of industrial standards. ISO standards are mainly technical and cover a wide number of sectors including agriculture, construction, engineering and information technology. ISO standards are developed collaboratively by committees from over 150 participating countries. Each standard is reviewed at least every five years to ensure that it remains current and those that are no longer relevant can be withdrawn. Editions of these standards are formally published by the ISO and can be purchased.

The ISO works in collaboration with two other international standards organisations, the International Electrotechnical Commission (IEC) and the International Telecommunication Union (ITU), to form the World Standards Cooperation. These organisations have been extremely influential in producing standards that affect the information technology industry. The naming convention for standards approved jointly by IEC and ISO is ISO/IEC and there are a number of joint standards that directly affect Information Assurance management. The two most significant are the ISO/IEC 27000 series and ISO/IEC standard 13335 – Guidelines for the management of IT security.

The ISO/IEC 27000 series are the current standards for Information Security management. The numbering of the standards within this series can sometimes be confusing for UK organisations. This is because some were previously known as a British Standard or other earlier standards and may be referred to using their old names and numbers. The two main standards in this series that are currently in use are ISO 27001 and ISO 27002. More standards are being developed within the series to cover Information Assurance topics such as risk management. ISO 27001 (originally as BS7799 part 2) specifies the Information Security Management System requirements standard. Organisations can be formally certified against it and this will be covered in more detail later in this chapter. ISO 27002 (originally BS7799 part 1, then ISO 17799 in 2000) provides a code of practice for Information Security management. It is probably the most influential standard for Information Assurance management. It describes a high-level set of controls to protect the confidentiality, integrity and availability of an organisation's information assets, and looks at the various aspects of assurance such as security policy, Information Assurance organisation, asset management, human resources assurance and compliance. ISO/IEC 27002 is not a formal specification like ISO/IEC 27001 but is a generic advisory document. In order to use the standard, the organisation will need to assess the risks of their enterprise and apply the recommended control measures from the standard – as are applicable to mitigate these risks.

The ISO/IEC standard 13335 – Guidelines for the management of IT security focuses primarily on technical security control measures. It originally started life as a technical report before evolving to become the internationally recognised standard for Management of Information and Communications Technology Security. This consisted of a set of guidelines which is divided into five parts covering:

(1) concepts and models for information communications and techno-logy security (ICT) management;

(2) techniques for information and communications security risk man-agement;

(3) techniques for the management of information technology security;

(4) selection of safeguards (technical controls);

(5) management guidance on network security.

Parts 1 and 2 were revised in 2004 into ISO 13335-1 which provides con-cepts and models for the management of Information Communications and Technology (ICT) security and addresses the general assurance manage-ment issues of planning, implementing and operating security. The remain-ing parts are currently in the process of being incorporated into other ISO standards as they evolve.

Other international organisations produce standards on security manage-ment. For example, the International Security Forum (ISF) has produced a Standard of Good Practice for Information Assurance which is reviewed by them every two years. The standard focuses on how Information Assurance can support an organisation's business processes and provides guidance on implementing appropriate protection. Controls are grouped under several categories such as implementing security management controls, controls to protect critical business systems, computer installations, network imple-mentation, system development and end-user environments. The ISF mem-bers (who are in the main corporate organisations) fund the forum via an annual subscription, and then collaborate with them in developments for best practices in IT security and information risk management.

There are many other standards that have been produced (not exclusively for Information Assurance) that do impact on Information Assurance man-agement. These cover other related business functions or processes such as retention of records (ISO 15489), the implementation of business continuity (PAS 56 and 77), project development (COBIT), the management of inform-ation technology services (ISO 2000 ITIL) and quality assurance (ISO 9000). If these standards have been implemented within your enterprise it is neces-sary to ensure that Information Assurance management controls are com-patible with them and support their requirements. For example, ISO 2000 ITIL includes requirements for operational security.

It is necessary to be familiar with the standards that apply to the country and industry sector in which the enterprise operates. The financial and man-ufacturing industries are subject to a wide range of standards that need to be adhered to, and an inability to meet these requirements could, for instance, prevent an organisation from actively trading in the financial services market.

Certification of Information Security Management systems to appropriate standards

Gaining Information Assurance certification is a means of demonstrating that you take Information Assurance seriously and that good assurance processes and controls have been implemented. An increasing number of organisations now look for certification in their trading partners and, for some, certification can be a prerequisite for doing business. Certifications can apply enterprise wide or to a specific set of processes within the organisation. Certification usually involves the enterprise undergoing an external audit by an accredited third party.

The ISO runs a number of certification schemes against its standards, including ISO 27001 which enables an organisation to have its Information Assurance governance and management processes certified against ISO 27001. To gain accreditation, the organisation's ISMS (Information Security Management System) has to undergo an external audit carried out by an accredited third-party organisation. The auditors use standard processes to check the organisation's ISMS policies, standards and procedures against ISO 27001 requirement and then look for evidence that they are being used within the organisation. The findings from the audit are reported back to the organisation and certification will be granted if successful. After the initial certification periodic follow-ups (reassessments) will take place to ensure that the standards are still being met. There is also an ISO standard (ISO 27006) which is used to guide the accredited certification bodies on the formal processes for certifying or registering other organisations' Information Assurance management systems.

In the UK, industries such as financial services require that certification to certain standards are in place, and serious instances of non-compliance can lead to sanctions from the Financial Services Authority (FSA) – such as heavy fines or withdrawal of their registration. An example of an applicable standard is the Payment Card Industry (PCI) Data Security Standard. It was originally implemented in the USA but has now been extended to include other countries. It was introduced to reduce credit card compromise and deal with increasing cases of fraud. It specifies the protection measures that organisations processing payment information must put into place. Failure to comply may result in an organisation receiving substantial fines or steps being taken to prohibit the organisation using cards as a payment method. This could seriously jeopardise the organisation. PCI merchants, retailers and service providers must store credit card account data securely as specified by the standard and to demonstrate compliance to their Acquiring (merchant) Bank. All Acquiring Banks need to have certified proof of PCI compliance from their merchants or they will be liable to fines themselves from the FSA.

Product certification to recognised standards

Many products require independent testing and certification before they can be launched onto the market, to ensure that they conform to safety requirements, technical specifications or other compliance regulations. It is useful to have an independent third party to verify that a new product does meet expectations and that it can be trusted. This particularly applies to security products as it is often difficult for the consumer to be able to test the security of the product for themselves. Certificates provide customers with the assurance that the security features do offer the level of protection that is claimed by the vendor. It is helpful to know that a standards-based approach has been used to do this evaluation as this will aid understanding as to how rigorous it has been. Test results produced in a standardised format will enable straightforward comparison with other competing products.

Security testing, evaluation and certification have mainly been carried out by either government agencies or organisations serving the defence market. Different countries have developed their own evaluation and certification systems using a variety of classification models and approaches. This has often made life complex when dealing with other internationally recognised certification schemes. It has meant that products have had to be re-certified each time for use in different countries or industry sectors – which has exacerbated an already time-consuming and expensive process.

Over recent years there has been rationalisation of the various certification schemes. In the 1990s the European Union harmonised the various schemes of its member states into the Information Technology Security Evaluation Criteria (ITSEC). More recently this scheme was itself harmonised with other models such as the Canadian Trusted Computer Product Evaluation Criteria (CTCPEC) and the American US Federal Criteria (TCSEC – often referred to as the Orange book) to form the Common Criteria for Information Technology Security Evaluation (CC). This evaluation system is increasingly becoming the internationally accepted approach for security certification replacing national and regional systems. In 1999 the ISO incorporated its evaluation criteria into a standard with ISO 15408: the Common Criteria for Information Technology Security Evaluation. This is now the most widely used certification model.

The ISO 15408 standard specifies a number of functionality and assurance classes that can be tested. The standard has seven levels of assurance to describe the level of rigour used to carry out the testing, from the entry level of EAL 1, which tests claimed functionality to the highest classification, to EAL 7, which provides a formally verified design which has been subjected to rigorous testing. The higher the classification, the more complex and rigorous the testing is. Gaining classifications EAL 5–7 is generally less common for commercial organisations as testing requires very specialist security engineering techniques and is complex. These higher classifications tend to be used by the military and government organisations.

The developer of the product or system has to define what is being submitted for evaluation (known as the target of evaluation (TOE)) and specify the assurance level for which they are aiming. Certification is carried out by an approved testing agency. Within the UK, security certification is managed by the Communications-Electronics Security Group (CESG) (part of the Government Communications Headquarters (GCHQ) at Cheltenham). This is the UK Government's national technical authority for information assurance.

The evaluation is carried out within Commercial Evaluation Facilities (CLEFs), which are commercial organisations appointed by the CESG. Any vulnerabilities that are found during testing have to be resolved before the tester can submit the evaluation technical report (ETR) to the Certification Board for approval. The Board will then issue a certificate when satisfied with these results. Upon certification, the product has to enter a maintenance scheme to ensure that it can still provide the agreed level of protection as vulnerabilities and threats change over time.

To enable the international use of existing certificates, agreements have been put into place to enable security certificates to be recognised by other countries. For example, the Common Criteria Recognition Arrangement (CCRA) enables Common Criteria (CC) certificates up to EAL 4 to be recognised within all participating countries.

Awareness of key technical standards

There are a numberof technical standards that are applicable to Information Assurance management. This section will examine some of the more well-known technical standard producing bodies.

The Internet Engineering Task Force (IETF) is a large open international community that develops and promotes standards for the Internet. Its governing body meets two or three times a year. Standards are developed by working groups of interested parties such as network designers, operators, vendors and researchers that each focus on a particular topic. The standards generated are known as RFCs (Request for Comments); and upon production are subsequently issued to the IETF community as draft RFCs for comment and review. Once an RFC has been issued it is not withdrawn – although it may in time be superseded by further RFCs. This in many ways can show the development of standards. The published RFC documents have a status of either a proposed standard or an informational statement.

Federal Information Processing Standards Publications (FIPS PUBS) are standards and guidelines developed and issued by the National Institute of Standards and Technology (NIST) for Federal Government computer systems within the USA. Where possible, the US Federal Government uses existing (internationally recognised) published industry standards but, should none be suitable, it will ask NIST to help develop them. NIST collaborates with national and international standards committees such as IETF and other interested parties (such as vendors and industry bodies) to produce FIPS PUBS.

Within Europe, the European Telecommunications Standards Institute (ETSI), based in France, has official responsibility for standardisation of Information and Communication Technologies (ICT). It is recognised by the European Commission and the European Free Trade Association (EFTA) secretariat. Its main purpose is to provide technical specifications (or standards) that may be used in European Directives and Regulations or by manufacturers to show that their products are compliant with these Directives and Regulations. Products demonstrate conformance by attaching the 'CE' mark on their goods. ETSI members represent areas that have a vested interest in the process and include manufacturers, network operators, administrations, service providers, research bodies and users. They come from a wide selection of countries both inside and outside of Europe. The members determine the Institute's work programme, allocate resources and approve its deliverables. Documents can be downloaded from the ETSI website via their documentation service (EDS).

Sample Questions

1. Which of the following activities should **not** be handled by the Information Assurance function?
   a. Monitoring the effectiveness of the enterprise's assurance arrangements.
   b. Providing advice on Information Assurance.
   c. Effectively delivering a secure environment across the enterprise.
   d. Reporting on the effectiveness of the enterprise's assurance arrangements to senior management.
2. Where should the Information Assurance function be placed within the enterprise so that it can facilitate full management co-ordination of assurance across the enterprise?
   a. Within the compliance function.
   b. At board level.
   c. It will depend on the structure of the enterprise.
   d. Within the IT group.
3. What is the main role of the board director with responsibility for Information Assurance?
   a. Ensure that appropriate security controls are implemented across the enterprise.
   b. Have a detailed understanding of the threats facing the enterprise.
   c. Implement Information Assurance solutions across the enterprise.
   d. Provide day-to-day management of the Information Assurance function.
4. Clearly defined responsibilities for Information Assurance should include which of the following?
   a. Operating procedures and reporting requirements.
   b. The scope of the responsibilities and level of authority granted.

    c. Disciplinary procedure.

    d. None of these three.

5. Which would be the best way to hear about and plan for any regulatory changes to your industry that may affect Information Assurance?

    a. Permanently employing consultants.

    b. Scanning bulletin boards and websites for snippets of information.

    c. Waiting until the changes were announced the press.

    d. Maintaining a relationship with regulatory bodies for the industry.

6. Which of the following groups of people should have access to the high-level security policy for the enterprise?

    a. Senior management and all line management.

    b. All staff within the enterprise.

    c. Third parties that have access to the enterprise's Information Systems.

    d. All of the above.

7. Which of these security documents is **not** mandatory?

    a. A policy.

    b. A standard.

    c. A guideline.

    d. A procedure.

8. Which of the following statements best describes an Information Security architecture?

    a. A technical overview of assurance controls applied within the enterprise.

    b. A framework of assurance controls that can be applied across the enterprise to protect its information assets.

    c. The physical security controls applied within security locations.

    d. A blueprint for future security controls.

9. Which of the following is the security standard that applies to the accreditation of security controls within products?

    a. ISO 27001.

    b. ISO 15408.

    c. ISO 9000.

    d. ISO 13335.

10. Privacy legislation is in place to protect the rights of:

    a. Criminals.

    b. Companies.

    c. The individual.

    d. Data Protection Officers.

11. Which of the following is **not** a phase in incident management?

    a. Assessment.

    b. Investigation.

    c. Reporting.

    d. Elimination.

Pointers for activities in the chapter

Activity 3.1

The plan should include the following components.

- A senior member of staff, for example Miss Peacock, should be given board member responsibility for Information Assurance and provide high-level sponsorship for assurance.

- Someone should be given the role of day-to-day co-ordination of Information Assurance across GANT – full time responsibility – suggest yourself.

- Detail what you will be able to deliver within the assurance function, for example

  - co-ordinating assurance activities across GANT;

  - providing advice and guidance on assurance;

  - producing a security policy;

  - monitoring the effectiveness of assurance controls;

  - reporting on the effectiveness of controls;

  - raising awareness about assurance with GANT and ensuring that people understand their responsibilities.

- Identify people who can help support you within GANT, decide what they need to do and request that assurance responsibilities are built into the roles.

Activity 3.2

An end-user code of practice for GANT could include statements on:

- access to systems;
- protection of passwords;
- leaving information unattended;
- measures required to protect information about GANT members;
- protection of information and equipment if taken out of the office;
- acceptable behaviour when using GANT systems;
- use of the internet;
- use of GANT systems for personal use.

Activity 3.3

The following types of activities will help Miss Peacock to demonstrate to auditors and regulators that assurance is being managed effectively:

- establishing a governance process with regular governance reviews that can be chaired by Miss Peacock;

- setting up a risk register to record GANT's information risks and documenting how the risks are being treated;

- defining a schedule to show that assurance is regularly reviewed, for example compliance and policy reviews;

- setting up a documentation library to demonstrate that assurance review work and planning has been completed and formally recorded. The library could contain current security polices, outputs from risk assessment, results of audits and compliance reviews, minutes from governance reviews, GANT's risk register, risk assessments, incident reports, dispensations to policy, etc.

Activity 3.4

As GANT is a small organisation a simple process for managing assurance breaches will be adequate. The main elements should include:

- staff (with deputies) should be nominated to manage assurance breaches;

- a procedure for reporting, recording and managing incidents should be developed so that they can be dealt with in a consistent way;

- all staff and members should be told who they should contact and what they should do if they suspect a breach;

- personnel responsible for managing incidents should be trained to understand how they should deal with potential incidents and when they should engage with either specialist third parties or law enforcement agencies.

Activity 3.5

A sensible approach would be firstly to carry out a high-level risk assessment to identify where the main risks are and which areas cause the most concern and why. This should involve major stakeholders such as Dr Peabody and Miss Peacock. A high-level plan, including time scales and effort, should then be developed to address the most pressing issues quickly with tactical improvements and longer-term strategy to improve control overall. This should be supported by a business case that communicates the benefits, including outline costs. A simple presentation in business terms should be put together to communicate this information to Miss Peacock so that she can make a decision on what work should take place. Once agreed, a more detailed plan can be put in place to carry out the work and be regularly reviewed to check progress.

Activity 3.6

To ensure that GANT complies with appropriate personal information legislation, the following types of activities should be carried out:

- review local legislation and how that applies to GANT;
- review whether personal information is passed to any other legal jurisdiction and if so what are their requirements;
- understand if local laws require that the holding of personal information is registered and if so is the registration up to date and accurate;
- identify if there a policy in place to specify how personal information should be held and is it up to date;
- identify which systems are holding personal information;
- identify what controls are in place to protect personal information being held;
- identify who has access to the information and do they understand their responsibilities;
- identify if any information is shared with third parties and if so what controls are in place;
- understand what monitoring takes place and does this comply with local legislation;
- identify whether the enterprise has communicated to individuals what monitoring takes place;
- document finding where there are compliance issues and make recommendations to resolve;
- discuss findings and recommendations with a legal expert.

Answers to sample questions

1. The correct answer is c.
2. The correct answer is c.
3. The correct answer is a.
4. The correct answer is b.
5. The correct answer is d.
6. The correct answer is d.
7. The correct answer is c.
8. The correct answer is b.
9. The correct answer is b.
10. The correct answer is c.
11. The correct answer is d.

4 Information Security Controls

In this chapter we discuss in more detail the controls that are implemented to provide protection against security incidents. This includes the detection, prevention and mitigation of such incidents.

There are three main types of control:

- physical, for example locks on doors and secure cabinets;
- procedural, for example checking references for job applicants;
- product and technical controls, for example passwords or encryption.

The latest version of the ISO 27001 standard contains 133 controls within 39 functional groups, and this does not cover everything. Hopefully this gives you an idea that the subject of controls is an almost bottomless pit. All we can do here is explain the principles of the generic use of the major controls within Information Assurance. More detailed information about specific controls is outside the scope of this publication.

This chapter forms about 40 per cent of the CISMP examination syllabus.

PROTECTION FROM MALICIOUS SOFTWARE

LEARNING OUTCOMES

The Intention of this section is to provide the reader with the basic knowledge needed to put in place effective controls to manage the risks from malicious software. Once completed, the reader should have an understanding of each of the following concepts.

Types of malicious software

The topic of malicious software is very large and could easily fill a book of its own. In this section the barest basics are described and enough information is given to allow the reader to continue their studies elsewhere if they so wish. Malware (from MALicious softWARE), as it is often known, is one of the largest threats to the users and managers of Information Systems. An understanding of the capabilities of malware and those who write it, along with the controls that are needed to counter that threat, are essential for most Information Assurance practitioners.

A simple definition of malware would be something like: 'An unauthorised piece of code that installs and runs itself on a computer without the knowledge or permission of the owner. It then conducts data processing and other operations that benefit the originator, usually at the expense of the system users or the recipient of the output from the malware.'

The traditional idea of malware is the virus that infects your computer, attempts to spread itself to others, then trashes the contents of your hard disk or displays a message to show that it was successful in infecting your machine. A lot of the early malware did just this. Things have moved on, however, and the main emphasis now is not on 'spreading chaos while gaining kudos', it is about money. The FBI announced that, in 2006, organised crime gangs in America made more money from cybercrime than they did from dealing in drugs for the first time ever. It is big business in many parts of eastern Europe too. The chances of being caught are much lower than for drugs operations and the sentences, if convicted, are also much shorter.

The old malware writers wanted you to know that they had succeeded in infecting your machine; now it is changed round completely. The vast majority of modern writers know that if you realise you have an infected system they have failed, because you will disinfect it.

Modern malware can be split into the following major categories of payload.

Viruses. These cannot spread on their own. They need to be attached to another piece of data or program to reach and infect another computer. They are often triggered by opening an email attachment or executable received by email or on removable media such as CD or USB stick.

Worms. The difference between a worm and a virus is that worms contain the code needed to spread themselves without any user action. They will seek out other computers on any networks they can find. These can spread very quickly. It is estimated that the Slammer worm infected 90 per cent of the world's vulnerable computers within 10 minutes of being released.

Rootkits. These are complex software packages that hijack the operating system and attempt to make themselves invisible both to the user and to the software designed to find and remove malware. They are insidious in that they still perform all tasks that the user requests but they often make copies of sensitive data such as passwords, account details and logins and then send them to another computer, often to enable financial fraud such as identity theft.

Backdoors. The idea of the backdoor is to do just as it says. It provides a means for a third party to access the computer and use it for their own purposes without having to carry out the normal authentication checks. These can be used to turn the computer into a 'bot' (short for robot) that is effectively under the remote control (usually via IRC – Internet Relay Chat – channels) of the attacker. It can then be used to distribute spam or act as part of a distributed denial of service attack on a third party that cannot easily or quickly be traced back to the attacker.

Spyware. A common example of this is the use of cookies by websites. Some are designed to be permanent and to track and report the web usage back to a third party without the knowledge of the user. They can also log keystrokes and look for specific information such as bank account or auction site login credentials. They have been known to install diallers that call premium rate numbers (on modem-connected computers) to generate revenue for the perpetrators. These can also be installed by software that performs a legitimate service, and freeware is often offered as a means of getting a user to install spyware.

Trojans. The Trojan is the hackers' 'weapon of choice' today. Far more successful attacks use Trojans than any other attack vector. These are often disguised as another piece of software or are hidden inside compromised copies or other programs that users are lured into downloading and running. They often successfully avoid security countermeasures because users tend to have accounts with administrator privileges that allow the Trojan to run.

Another very successful infection root is through compromised websites. It is estimated that one in three websites contains malware of some sort. Trojans can download themselves without the user having to click on any buttons or links on the page. Simply going to an infected web page can be enough. More and more groups, criminal and otherwise, are writing increasingly sophisticated Trojans to attack computers in order to extract data, particularly via web protocols, where the malware scanning technology is often much weaker than the email countermeasures.

Active Content. This is the means by which a Trojan is often downloaded to a computer running the viewing browser. Modern web applications use active code such as Flash, Java, Active-X and even mime headers to perform complex tasks within the web page to 'enhance the user experience'. There is no question that they are good at this, but they are also good at installing malware on the target computer. If the right level of security is not set in the browser policies, the compromised code will install and run itself on the target without the user having any knowledge of it happening. A typical attack is where a banner advert runs on a well-respected and heavily used website, with the code for the banner being supplied by a third-party advertiser. The attacker subverts the third party and adds the Trojan into the banner code. People view the website, thinking it trustworthy because of the reputation of the organisation, little realising that the advertising hosted there is busy trying to infect their computer. The payload of an Active Content/Trojan can be any of the forms of malware described in this section.

Whatever the type, detecting a piece of malware on a computer is a cause for concern and should be investigated without delay. It should also be noted that malware is actively and very widely spread; it is not a case of if you receive some malware, but when and how often. It is almost inevitable.

Zero day exploits

No matter how good and comprehensive the defences that are in place, there is always a possibility that a new form of attack can get through them.

Hackers talk about 'zero day exploits'. These are ones that have yet to come to the attention of the companies selling anti-virus and firewall products, so they have not issued an update to detect and remove them. In theory these exploits can get past the scanning engines because they are not on the 'stop' list that the updates contain. Some products are better than others in spotting types of behaviour and their analytical tools can identify many new versions of malware because they exhibit behaviour that is known to be unacceptable or has similar code to that found in other known malware. There is even a trade in zero day exploits, with hackers selling the knowledge to others. Some zero day exploits for the latest version of a very well-known PC operating system were on sale for US$400 not long after the beta version was released.

Routes of infection

Most of the routes have already been mentioned in passing but a more comprehensive description is provided here.

Infected media. Any piece of media that has been out of your control or supervision should be considered suspect – CD, DVD, floppy disk, USB stick, etc. It should be scanned for malware, ideally on a stand-alone 'sheep-dip' computer before being allowed into an operational computer. It may have been infected by any system with which it has interacted before it reaches your system. Even CDs that come with a magazine or as part of a special promotion should not be trusted. Do not assume they have been properly checked before mass-production. These have been issued containing malware on more than one occasion in the past, causing much embarrassment for the organisation giving them away. USB sticks are another source of infection. Malware can use them to travel from one system to another.

The most common routes today are via email, as an attachment or a macro in a document or even disguised as another file type, and through websites, as described above. Worms can propagate across networks, wide or local area, and may spread through unprotected systems.

It is also possible for malware to infect your system through a wireless networking connection, Bluetooth or infrared port. Do not have these enabled unless you require them at the time and have a malware scanning application that protects those ports as well as the standard ones. If these functions are never used, don't even install the device drivers for them if you can avoid it.

Malware countermeasures

The countermeasures required to detect and defeat malware depend upon the configuration of the systems and networks to be defended and continually need to be updated to deal with the latest threats. A single computer, connected to a broadband connection at home, is very different from a global corporate network or a small organisation.

Even for the single user, because of the different possible routes of infection, a basic anti-virus package is not enough. The user requires a personal firewall package too. This will provide a defence against worms and web Trojans. Good-quality products also contain a profiling and access control tool. When installed they scan for existing malware and remove it, then build a profile of all the existing executables, putting them on a 'whitelist' of allowed products. Any new, unknown, executable or active content can be blocked from running unless manually approved by the user as the result of a prompt on the screen.

In an ideal world, large organisations that have separate systems to receive email and perform web browsing will need products or services for each system, for example:

- content scanning for web traffic and some means of controlling web access to stop prohibited sites from being accessed;
- email content and source checking software;
- firewalls that block ports and check content;
- network intrusion detection or prevention systems;
- 'Sheepdip' malware scanners for untrusted media;
- personal firewall or application control software on individual systems including checking files when they are accessed;
- use of managed services providers to scan mail and web traffic – inbound and outbound.

It is not the place of this textbook to recommend specific manufacturers' products, but it can list functionality that users should check for when acquiring such countermeasures:

- high degree of effectiveness in detecting and removing malware – read independent reviews;
- frequent and easy to deploy updates to signatures and scanning engines;
- ability to create and maintain a whitelist of accepted executables, active code and open network ports;
- support from a reputable company that can provide prompt updates to major threats and support;
- minimal impact upon operation of the systems.

Taking regular, secure, backups is also a good way of countering malware. If something does get in and compromises the integrity or availability of data, it is possible to restore from the last good backup to minimise the impact upon the organisation. Use of the Grandfather-Father-Son system is highly recommended to provide defence in depth and allow rollback to dates further back in time if necessary.

It is important to remember that there is a never-ending 'arms race' between malware writers and the developers of the countermeasures. The hackers are continually developing new ways to infect systems – new types of code and new routes of infection. Some malware is quite sophisticated and can even defend itself to some degree against countermeasures and other malware.

Methods of control

There are several approaches to controlling malware that need to be implemented at the same time if an organisation is to manage successfully the associated risks. The first one is not always obvious and doesn't relate to any form of specialist malware application. This approach is patching. The operating system or application that does not contain any bugs or vulnerabilities has not yet been written. Patches and upgrades are released quite frequently and every organisation should test and install patches at the earliest opportunity. Hackers keep a close eye on patch releases and the more capable ones will reverse-engineer the patch to identify the weakness it resolves. They then write or modify malware to take advantage of that weakness. The Slammer worm took advantage of a weakness for which a patch had been issued over 8 months previously. The worm was so successful because a lot of organisations had not applied the patch. The time from a patch being released or a vulnerability being described to an exploit appearing 'in the wild' is now down to as little as three days. Organisations must not only apply patches, but also do it promptly to provide adequate protection from new malware. User awareness is important too. Users that have been educated about the threats are less likely to click on a suspect link or fall for a social engineering attack that tries to trick them into loading malware.

Another approach is to 'harden' the operating system by not installing unnecessary features or applications and to ensure that default passwords and open configurations are not used. This is not the place to discuss the detail of how to perform these tasks, which is best left to experts. Suffice to say that an operating system installed using all the default settings recommended by the manufacturer is often very easy to compromise either manually or by malware.

The further approach has already been mentioned – use of anti-virus and personal firewall software. Some operating systems come with versions of firewall and malware-removal bundled in as part of the product. Experience and much independent testing have shown that these are often not the best products to use, certainly at the date of publication of this book. Larger organisations need to investigate and select specialist products to protect high-bandwidth routes in and out of the organisation, such as email and web interfaces. Good firewall products also contain malware checking applications, and specialist appliances are available to monitor activity on internal networks.

The last, but equally important, approach is to harden the settings in the web browser in use. By default these often have much too low a level of security, allowing active code to run by default and accepting cookies from any source. Change the settings to only accept cookies from the original source and either disable active code completely or at the very least prompt the user to authorise a pierce of code to run each time it tries to do so in the browser.

None of these products are of much use unless they are kept up to date. Many new items of malware are identified every day. The application and product providers issue regular updates to the signature files and sometimes to the scanning engines themselves. The same approach as for patching is required: download the updates and install them promptly to benefit from the protection they offer against new threats. Good products are capable of automatically distributing updates across the network to all clients, saving time and resources.

The officers of GANT have decided that they need to establish a better means of communicating among themselves and with the members of the society. Some members report that they have been the targeted by persons sending them malware in emails or attempting to extract data about toad populations. The officers have no knowledge of this area of computing and need advice on how to protect their systems, at home and in the GANT office, against malware.

The loss or unauthorised disclosure of sensitive membership or toad population data would be embarrassing and potentially harmful to human and amphibian alike.

Activity 4.1
What advice would you give to the society with regard to the countermeasures they need in order to provide an adequate level of protection from malware?

PEOPLE

LEARNING OUTCOMES

Information Assurance is a lot more than just a series of technical countermeasures. It is as much about the people as it is anything else. They have to be educated, motivated and appropriately regulated. The intention of this section is to provide the reader with the basic knowledge to understand how people and organisations should be managed within a culture of assurance.

Security culture within organisations

The most sophisticated Information Assurance system on the planet is worthless if the people, whose data it is designed to protect, are not security conscious. They need to be made aware of the dangers, how relevant they are to them and their data, and how to use the systems to make sure that the information assets are protected. This is very, very important and the lead must come from the top of the organisation. As mentioned earlier in this book, there should be an Information Security policy document, signed by the Chief Executive or equivalent, which says words to the effect of:

> 'We take information security and assurance very seriously and it is a high priority to us. It is the responsibility of everyone within the organisation to be security conscious and to abide by our Information Security policy and procedures when dealing with colleagues, suppliers and customers. If you are uncertain as to the correct course of action or are suspicious about a set of circumstances, your duty is to consult the Information Security Manager for advice.'

Rather than just pinning this to notice boards, it needs to become part of the culture of the organisation, and this will only happen if those in senior management lead by example. Do not expect people to do as you say if you do not stick to your own rules. Be proactive in promulgating this culture throughout the organisation and keeping the topic fresh in people's minds. Over 50 per cent of assurance incidents are caused by the inappropriate actions of an organisation's staff. Far more problems are caused by accident than maliciously. A security-conscious culture will reduce the number of incidents. Without it people will either not use the countermeasures or find ways round them. That increases risks or undoes the work done to manage them.

Security awareness

A large part of creating and maintaining the culture is the security awareness programme. It is no use telling people that 'there is a risk to our organisation and its assets'. That means nothing to the majority of the staff; it has to be made interesting and something to which they can relate. There should be a program of training for all employees and it should be included as part of their induction training programme too. Make sure that everyone is aware of the particular risks to your organisation – and why they are risks. This may include training in specific laws and industry regulations that apply to your organisation. Give them examples of organisations that have suffered as a result of security incidents. If you can show them that the organisation will lose money or be prosecuted, that means something to them – it could affect their job security.

It is also important to make people aware that this isn't just about confidentiality. Introduce them to integrity and availability too. In today's fast moving business world it is often these two aspects where greater problems can occur and have a much more significant effect.

If possible, keep a record of assurance awareness training – who, when and what. It has several uses. First, it allows you to identify when refresher training is required, for example, the passage of time or changes to risks or the law. Second, it could prove very useful in the event of legal action by helping to prove due diligence.

Contracts of employment

A contract of employment is a very important document because it has legal standing. It will define the terms and conditions of employment, including the responsibilities of the employee towards the organisation, and anyone else with whom they interact on behalf of the organisation. The document also defines the obligations that the organisation has towards the employee. It will include all the standard information about pay, leave, illness, training, health cover, etc.

In many cases the document, once signed, will not see the light of day again, but in some unfortunate circumstances, such as disciplinary cases, it will need to be referred to and quoted. The contents may end up being cited at a tribunal or produced as evidence in a court of law. This is why it is important to get the contract right, including the parts that define:

- acceptable standards of behaviour and conduct;
- ownership of intellectual property;
- acceptable use of company assets;
- grounds for disciplinary proceedings and the disciplinary process;
- adherence to all applicable laws and regulations;
- duty of care to the organisation and other staff;
- non-disclosure/confidentiality of information.

Service contracts and security undertakings

The nature of the modern world means that almost every organisation now has a service contract of some sort with a supplier and customer defined within it. Both parties give undertakings about the meanings of certain standards and naming conventions, such as protective markings, and the identification of policies and procedures to be observed. This document can be amended by mutual consent without having to resort to contract re-negotiation.

The security details for such contracts are normally contained in a Security Aspects Letter, which is often included as an appendix to the contract, issued by the client to the service provider. This forms a binding part of the contract and is to be observed by all parties to the contract. It will also often contain the possible consequences of not complying with the assurance requirements set out with any consequential damages specified.

Codes of conduct

The most obvious elements of a code of conduct in the context of this book are the obligations placed upon employees regarding Information Assurance – confidentiality, integrity and availability, which are described elsewhere. A code of conduct can cover a lot more than that. It is also a means of expressing the ethics and standards of the organisation. It will contain examples of the kind of behaviour expected of employees in their dealings with each other and other people, be they customers, suppliers or anyone else.

This can include rules on accepting (or not) hospitality, guidance on accepting and declaring the receipt of gifts and inducements from third parties. It is not unusual for the rules to say something along the lines of 'Gifts should be accepted when it would cause offence to refuse, but they must be declared to the organisation at the first opportunity'. Sometimes staff are given the option to buy the gift at a fair price, it might be used by the company or it may become a prize in an annual raffle or prize-giving.

Conversely the code may state that staff must not offer gifts, inducements or unreasonable levels of hospitality to others, or that alcohol is not allowed on company premises without approval of senior management, and usually only for entertainment of clients.

The ethos of customer relations can also be included in this heading, for example, 'always be helpful, polite and approachable to everyone, employees or otherwise'. Many supermarket chains have a program along the lines of 'Every Customer Offered Help', which is why they will ask if one needs help with packing nothing more than two packets of chewing gum and a new toothbrush.

Whilst some of these areas may seem a distance from Information Assurance, it must be remembered that one of the most important areas of assurance is that of social engineering. Members of staff may be provided with extravagant gifts or put into embarrassing situations by others who want some information or access to other assets of the organisation; this is a type of social engineering. There are many other situations where those intending to damage an organisation or its assets use the social behaviour of staff to achieve their aims.

The passing of jokes or amusing emails is another type of social engineering. Providing an email with an attachment of an amusing photograph that is readily passed around the staff may seem innocuous enough. If that email's attachment contains a worm or other malware infection, this is also a very efficient way of compromising the whole IT system.

This sort of attack is not limited simply to IT systems though. In the more complex, perhaps higher-value world, gaining access to keys to buildings, access codes or passwords for security systems is also often achieved by variations of social engineering. It is in this light therefore that, for example, banning gifts helps to reduce the threat to some degree although it would be very naive to think this would stop social engineering in its entirety.

Acceptable use policies

The acceptable use policy also known as an end-user code of practice is the document that defines the standards for the use of organisational information and communications systems by employees. This serves as an adjunct to the contract of employment to protect both the organisation and the individual from the actions of others. In law, an organisation can be held accountable for the actions of employees under what is known as 'vicarious liability'. The only defence an organisation has is to show due diligence in telling its staff that they are not to break the law or any relevant regulations. This document can also help to protect staff from harassment or malpractice by employers and other employees.

In this document the management must make clear the level of infringement (e.g. misconduct, gross misconduct, etc.) for each offence and the disciplinary steps that will be taken against those who are considered to have broken the rules. It is advisable to consult staff before introducing a document of this kind, to ensure that they understand the reasons why it has to exist and support it as being fair and reasonable. It is common practice to include a brief on the implications of this document in an induction training course and this is an effective way of dealing with a lot of related issues whilst also ensuring full understanding by the staff members. This topic is also discussed within policy in Chapter 3.

Segregation of duties and avoiding dependence

The segregation of duties is the concept that one person may not perform the duties for more than one role where there could be a conflict of interests. The requirement for segregation of duties has two functions:

(i)   To limit the scope that any one individual has to attack and compromise the Information Assurance of the organisation. A commonly used term for this kind of activity is system misuse.

   If one individual has all the passwords, access rights and privileges for the entire organisation they have the ability to systematically alter, extract or destroy any or all data within the control of the organisation with little or no risk of discovery. Many risk management systems consider one person having full access to be a serious risk. There should be separation between the roles of system administrator, system user and system auditor in order to manage the risk of collusion and fraud. Some legal and regulatory bodies require high levels of segregation and mandatory third party audits. Examples of this include the (UK) Financial Services Authority and the (US) Sarbanes–Oxley legislation.

(ii) To limit the dependence that an organisation has upon any one individual.

   This is about the obvious fact that if the organisation relies on the knowledge or skills of one person it is vulnerable. If that person falls under the proverbial bus or resigns, taking their knowledge with them, the organisation has a real problem. This is very a difficult problem if staff numbers are low, especially in IT. Good documentation can help, providing that it is kept up to date, as can cross-training and succession planning which are discussed elsewhere in this book.

Obligations on third-party suppliers of goods and services

It is sometimes overlooked that the obligations upon an organisation need to be taken into account when dealing with other businesses. There may be times when contracts for goods, services or both are outsourced. The contracts to cover this will need to include legally binding clauses that cover the Information Assurance aspects of the data and services concerned. The information owner has a legally binding duty of care to ensure that the external body is competent to process the data securely and will observe the same high standards as the organisation on behalf of which it is performing the work.

This stipulation (and the enforcement) of obligations has two benefits for the data owner:

(i)   it manages the risk of loss of goodwill, and punitive or corrective action as a result of an Information Security breach;

(ii) it manages the risk of leaving the organisation exposed to the impact of a business continuity risk event happening at a supplier. Setting obligations upon suppliers to use good practice to manage their own risks improves the level of confidence in ones' own business processes not being affected or at least being minimised.

It is important to note that the obligation should include the right of the organisation to audit suppliers (either directly or via a specialist third-party auditor) to ensure that they are complying with the requirements. This may be in the form of planned or no-notice inspections.

The profile that GANT has among the public has started to rise, thanks to an inspired publicity campaign. The workload is such that volunteers and one or two full-time specialists are now working for the organisation from an office. There are the beginnings of what may well become a full-blown IT infrastructure as time passes. Owing to the limited resources, some work is to be outsourced to service providers who will be much cheaper than staff doing the work in-house for the time being.

Activity 4.2
Now that the number of officers and volunteers working for GANT has started to rise, what do you think needs to be done in order to promote the need for assurance awareness among staff and service providers to the organisation?

Activity 4.3
How would you advise GANT to manage the risks that the use of third-party suppliers can bring?

USER ACCESS CONTROLS

LEARNING OUTCOMES

The measures taken to provide Information Assurance within an organisation are often referred to as controls. This section describes the basic building blocks upon which many other controls are predicated – the access controls. Without these, most of the other possible strategies would count for nothing. This section provides an overview that is essential knowledge for every Information Assurance practitioner.

The intention of this section is to provide the reader with the basic knowledge to understand how people and organisations should be managed within a culture of assurance.

Authentication and authorisation mechanisms

The process of authentication and authorisation is generally referred to by the acronym 'ID&A', which stands for 'identification and authentication'. Firstly, the user has to tell the system who they claim to be (identification) by entering a unique username. The system will then challenge them to prove that identity by providing some form of knowledge that can only be known, or possessed, by the individual that they have claimed to be. The system compares the data it receives against a known value it holds and, if they agree, it provides access to the system.

Traditionally, the second value has been a password, which the user is supposed to remember and not tell anyone else. The reality is that some people do write them down on a Post-it note that they keep near their machine, or they choose something that is easy to guess, like a date of birth, name of spouse/child/pet, car registration, sports team, etc. Many Information Assurance professionals believe that too much faith is placed in the ability of passwords to control effectively the access to systems.

 The traditional defence against password guessing has been to allow the user three tries and to lock them out if they fail three times to enter the correct password. Unfortunately this provides a form of Denial of Service (DoS) attack – allowing an attacker to disrupt the availability of a system by deliberately locking out users. In addition there are well-known techniques to capture passwords travelling across a network or to grab copies of the file on the authentication server that holds all the values for comparison. Copies of programs that will attack and 'crack' these are easy to find on the internet, meaning that this form of attack is relatively easy to conduct. People are also very easily fooled into giving out their passwords through social engineering attacks, mentioned earlier, for example where they believe they are talking on the telephone to someone in IT support. A survey a few years ago discovered that 40 per cent

of people asked would reveal their password to a total stranger in exchange for a bar of chocolate. Passwords are not strong security, they are actually fairly weak. Do not put your faith in them to protect you.

In order to provide a more effective level of assurance, many organisations are now starting to use two-factor authentication. This is where the user has to enter a password and something else as well before the system accepts their claimed identity. Quite often this involves use of a token, such as the RSA™ SecurID™ device. The traditional type is the size of a keyfob and has an LCD. This displays a 6-digit number that changes every 60 seconds. The values displayed are based on an algorithm and secret key value that is known only to the organisation that owns the system. The sequence of numbers displayed is not predictable and has resisted attempts to break it for many years. The sequence for each user is different, so they cannot be interchanged with other users. The user is asked to enter a 4-digit secret PIN supposedly known only to them and then the value showing on the token. This is compared to the value calculated by the authentication server. If the values match, access is granted.

The PIN provides protection against the token being stolen, providing time for the loss of the token to be detected and that particular unit to be disabled. Some banks and online trading organisations are starting to issue their customers with tokens. There is no doubt that they provide a greater degree of security. The downside is the cost of buying the system and tokens, which normally have to be replaced every three years (battery life limitation). Other kinds of token system do exist but this is the most popular and widely accepted one at the time of writing this book.

Another approach that is starting to gain acceptance is the use of biometrics. This is the use of a characteristic of an individual that is unique to that person, either anatomical (e.g. fingerprints), behavioural (e.g. signature) or a combination of both aspects (e.g. voice). Although the concept has been known for a long time, their introduction has been delayed partly due to the technical challenges in producing a system that is appropriately reliable and partly due to issues of public perception and acceptability. Work needs to be done by the Security Manager to overcome concerns about safety of the devices and the perception of 'Big Brother' that they can cause.

Many of the early systems were regarded as being too intrusive and required a high degree of training to make the interaction with the device work properly. In addition, there are still some issues to do with the false reject (often called the 'embarrassment factor') and acceptance rates that need resolving before the technology achieves wide-scale introduction.

Biometrics have distinct advantages over many other forms of identification and authentication methods:

- they are free with every user and very difficult to steal or lose, they even self-repair, although in certain trades and professions (for example the manual trades), fingerprints can wear away for considerable lengths of time;

- the person to be identified can be required to be physically present at the point of identification;

- identification based on biometric techniques reduces the need to remember a password;

- you can't write down a biometric on a piece of paper for someone else to find.

They do, however, require the use of sensors that can reliably read a biometric and detect attempts to defeat the system. These require capital outlay and integration into the security management system.

Effective use of controls

Now that we have described how to control access through the perimeter of Information Systems, we need to look at how to limit the access a user has once they are granted entry. Users should only be granted the minimum level of privilege to perform the role assigned to them. For example, a person working in a warehouse may need access to the stock records but they should not have access to the detailed financial or personnel records of an organisation. They simply do not need to know. The concept of 'need to know' is very important. We have already described how over 50 per cent of attacks originate from within the organisation; this is another line of defence to help in securing information. There is also the issue of privacy of data and legislation such as the Data Protection Act to be taken into consideration.

In order to make this limitation possible we need to assign attributes to users and to data, describing their profile to the remainder of the systems. This information can then be used to control access to data and systems, providing another level of protection for data and the users.

The first concept is that of User Groups to grant role-based access. Those users who perform a similar function are grouped together (e.g. 'Accounts', 'Sales', 'IT', etc.). This can be used to control access to applications, or functionality within large integrated applications such as Enterprise Resource Planning (ERP) systems. An example of this could be that access to the payroll system is only permitted for finance and human resources group users. A user can be denoted as being a member of more than one group if their role requires it. This type of designation may be based on some other attribute such as geographical location. All users in country A will have access to the data relevant to their own country but no access to the data of country B, and vice versa.

One other kind of user account we must mention is that of the System or Application Administrator. This role has access not just to the data (quite often all of it), but also to the software and operating system itself. The 'sysadmins' can add and delete users, groups or levels of privilege, rebuild the system, erase data, grant or deny access to applications, change passwords and even alter or destroy event logging or auditing data. These accounts have great power and wide-ranging capabilities and their use must be tightly controlled and safeguarded. Their potential to disrupt operations, accidental or otherwise, is enormous.

This degree of protection can be extended to the data as well. The standard approach is that there are three levels of privilege:

- each file has a designated owner, who has full control of the file;
- other members of the same user group as the owner who may have some degree of access (as described below);
- there is the 'rest of the world', i.e. other users in other groups, who may also have some limited access as described below.

There is another level of granularity that can be provided, which is to say whether the user can do the following:

- Read – the user can see the contents of the file or database, but not change them.
- Write – the user can change the contents of the file or database. This includes deletion privilege, since the user could overwrite the data to destroy it.
- Execute –the user can run this if it is an executable or a command script file. This implies full ownership, including Write privilege.
- A final option is not to grant any level of permission to one or more users, so that they cannot even open the file.

The actual names for these functions vary from one operating system to another, but the concept is the same.

The attributes on a file may then be as follows:

- User/Owner – Execute permission, allowing the file owner to Read, Write and Run the script or application, if that is what it is.
- Group – Write permission, allowing other members of the same user group to update the file.
- Other – No permission, so that the data or application cannot be read, amended or run by anyone who is not a member of the same group as the owner.

Administration of controls

The administration of access controls is another of the important jigsaw pieces that makes up the whole picture. Their use at the appropriate time is essential. The levels of privilege that each user or administrator has should be reviewed and updated regularly. This takes into account the fact that people change role (e.g. get promoted or transfer to another team). New privileges needed should be granted, but ones no longer required (i.e. old group memberships) should be removed.

The role of the administrator should include the following.

- Enrolling new users in the system after appropriate validation of identity. Without access they cannot do any work.
- Removing user access rights when they leave the organisation to prevent any further access.
- Modifying user access rights if they change role within the organisation. They may not be able to perform their new role without a change in rights and they may no longer need access to data they previously accessed.

People who leave the organisation should have their accounts deleted and all rights removed on the day they leave. Ownership of any data assets should be transferred to another user.

Role-based access is an issue that often gets overlooked. The roles of system or database administrator (very high system privilege required) and those of standard user (lack of high-level privileges is a good security countermeasure) must not be combined into a single account. The separation of these roles provides protection against accidental and deliberate abuse of the system. It also ensures a higher quality audit trail. It is a legal requirement in some industry sectors to separate out not just the 'sysadmin' functions, but whole departments, especially in finance and banking.

If the size of the organisation is such that the same individual is required to perform more than one duty often within the IT department, then the segregation of duties must still be enforced. This can be achieved through the requirement to log in using a different account with the appropriate privileges when performing the different duties. Whilst this may seem bureaucratic, it provides an effective audit trail and also helps to reinforce the serious nature of Information Assurance. There must always be someone else (another individual either internal or, as a last result, external) who is used to audit the work of the main 'sysadmin' function.

There can be occasions when access is needed to other areas of the system in order to meet an unusual or temporary operational requirement (e.g. to cover for a colleague on leave). There should be a process for users to apply for additional privileges to be granted temporarily so they can do the work. The approval should specify a start and end date for these, and those dates should be rigidly enforced.

These procedures must also be applied to any temporary staff who work for the organisation. A regular check should be made for obsolete roles, user accounts and privileges to guard against any lapses in the process.

Access points

An access point is any location from which the internal systems of the organisation can be accessed. This can be via one of three main types:

- direct connection from a hard-wired terminal;
- wireless network access within the perimeter;

- remote access over a third-party network, such as for example via a web client, broadband from home or dial up from a hotel.

There are two main security concerns with giving access:

(i) to ensure that the user completes the ID&A process successfully;

(ii) to protect the data being used to complete the authentication process and then the session itself.

If a user is connecting from a hard-wired terminal, then they are probably located within the premises of the organisation. This provides a degree of physical security to manage the risk that the person sat at the terminal is not an authorised user. The main risk is that someone is watching the user either visually or electronically with a 'network sniffer' or key-logger to capture the ID&A data. It is best to make sure that the login session is encrypted as it passes across the network in order to stop the data from being re-used to impersonate the user later.

Remote access presents additional challenges of physical and network security. It is quite likely that the network connection used is not controlled by the same organisation. This means it is even more important to protect not just the ID&A traffic, but all the data. This is usually achieved by setting higher requirements for ID&A, such 2-factor authentication using the tokens described earlier, and protecting the data connection using encryption, such as a Virtual Private Network (VPN) tunnel or Secure Sockets Layer (SSL) via the secure 'https' protocol.

The latest challenge is created by the rise in popularity of wireless networks. These have a lot of advantages, primarily large savings in cabling costs, but they also have disadvantages, mainly to do with security. The radio waves do not stop at the physical perimeter of the organisation or house. They travel outside and allow unauthorised access to attackers if not properly configured and located in the network architecture. Readily available aerials mean that a determined attacker can connect from a range of several miles rather than being sat outside in a car and therefore fairly easy to spot. If they are in a nearby building (e.g. your neighbour) they can be almost impossible to spot. Wireless access points must be strictly controlled in terms of installation, configuration and their physical links to the network. Many organisations connect them into their 'DMZ' (demilitarised zone) on the network, so that users have to authenticate to a higher standard and their traffic is screened by a firewall before having access to the internal network.

Another significant risk is that wireless users in your organisation may accidentally connect to an unsecured wireless network belonging to someone else in a nearby location, exposing your data to them or possibly even leading to accusations of hacking.

Protection of data

The protection of data by means of an information classification system (also referred to by some organisations as Protective Marking) is one of the oldest, yet most effective, security countermeasures yet invented. The point to remember is that the definition of the word data has changed, and continues to change. Originally the data was only in the form of paper files and knowledge inside the heads of the employees. Now it includes all forms of media, whether in storage or in transit from one place to another, including:

- magnetic – hard and floppy disks, USB sticks, magnetic tape, PDAs, mobile phones, digital cameras;
- optical media – CD, DVD, microfiche;
- paper – printed files, punched tape, blueprints and plans;
- data on physical and radio frequency networks;
- physical – some devices may have a protective marking because of their design or content;
- email.

All of these are considered to be information assets and thought must be given to their value to the organisation. This is not limited to their immediate commercial value, for example the design for a new product, but also the impact they could have on the organisation or other people if their contents were to become known to a competitor, foreign country or the public. The impacts can range from 'negligible' through to a 'grave impact on national security' for a government or 'major loss of goodwill with the public' for a commercial organisation.

All such assets need to be identified and valued against an agreed impact system; it is another form of risk assessment. Governments may well have a system that is along the lines of:

- Top Secret;
- Secret;
- Confidential;
- Restricted;
- Protect;
- Unclassified.

Whereas a commercial organisation may have a system such as:

- Highly Confidential;
- Confidential;
- Internal only;
- Public.

Once values have been assigned, a set of rules for handling and distribution must be drawn up to define their use. The most fundamental guideline is universally referred to as the 'need-to-know' principle – information should not be made available to people who do not need to know it. The fewer people that are aware of the knowledge, the easier it is to protect, yet that also presents a challenge in that enough people need to know to make best use of the information. There are even regulations in place to control the distribution of knowledge in some organisations. For example, in finance the concept of the 'Chinese wall' is used to guard against conflicts of commercial interest and insider dealing of shares. The trick is understanding where the ideal balance point lies for each piece or type of data.

Each level of classification requires protection appropriate to the value it has or, more accurately, the impact its inappropriate release or knowledge would have on the organisation or individual. The controls will not be just physical, but procedural and people-related too. Data of the 'Internal only' variety is probably sufficiently well protected by the normal ID&A mechanism for the system, the standard business rules and the locks on the doors of the building. Data that is Top Secret is often required to be kept in very strong safes inside heavily guarded buildings and handled in strictly defined ways, and can only be accessed by people who have been through an extensive security screening process.

In addition to these protective markings, data can also be given 'caveats'. These are additional markings that define a finer layer of protection and discretion. Some examples are:

- 'Human resources only' – personnel files containing sensitive personal data;
- 'Board member eyes only' – not to be shown to anyone who is not a Board member;
- 'Commercial in Confidence' – not to be shown to any competitor organisations;
- 'Intellectual Property' – subject to non-disclosure rules and possibly pending a patent application.

The key point overall with using any system of this type is that once a piece of information has been given a security classification, it automatically imposes certain constraints on the methods that can be used to process, store, transmit, dispose of or otherwise deal with it. These conditions are imposed on anyone who may come into contact with that information.

The growing numbers of members and their records mean that it is high time for GANT to register with the Information Commissioner. This means complying with the requirements of the Data Protection Act 1998 for the proper protection and processing of personal data. In order to achieve this, it has been recognised that GANT must have some policies to control user access to the IT systems and the data.

This requires a survey of the IT equipment in use and the methods used to access it, together with the places from which the internal systems can be accessed.

Activity 4.4
What do you think needs to be included in the policy documents for access control?

> ### Activity 4.5
> You have been asked to conduct a survey of the IT systems in use and the means used to access them. How would you set about conducting a survey and what would you look for?

> ### Activity 4.6
> The unwelcome interest in the activities of GANT by some groups and the data it holds requires special measures to protect some of it. How would you identify that data and label it to indicate the handling and processing requirements?

NETWORKS AND COMMUNICATIONS

LEARNING OUTCOMES

The intention of this section is to provide the reader with the basic knowledge to understand the issues that organisations should take into consideration when identifying and managing the security risks to their networks and communications links.

Entry points in networks and principles of authentication techniques

There is an old joke that 'if it wasn't for the users we wouldn't need security'. That can equally apply to the network and any connections to it. Not having a network would reduce the security requirement by a factor of ten. The network and communications links exist to make the systems connected to them available to authorised users. Unfortunately it also makes them available to all the unauthorised ones. If there is an internet connection somewhere then there are more than two hundred million potential unauthorised users. Experience shows us that some of them are up to no good and will try to compromise your network in some way. Even if it's only a tiny fraction of one percent, that is still a very big number when it is part of two hundred million.

Any location, logical or physical, from which a user or device can gain access to a network is considered an entry point. Where the whole system is hard wired these are fairly easy to define. These include but are not limited to:

- a terminal or PC in an office;
- a console on a server;
- a dial-up modem(s) or broadband connection(s);

- a router for a connection from another network – internal or external;
- a firewall protecting a connection from another network – internal or external.

If any aspect of wireless networking is involved the perimeters become much harder to define because of the ability of an attacker to use advanced radio devices to greatly increase the effective range from which they can access the network. The existence of a Wireless Access Point (WAP) within a network will add enormously to the challenges of securing the network against unauthorised access. The fact that the hardware is relatively cheap and installing a WAP has been made so easy presents two more challenges:

- users can buy and install their own hardware without the knowledge of the IT department;
- the default configurations are almost always insecure, with open settings and standard passwords known to all.

The other insidious threat is that other organisations in close proximity may also be using wireless networking and users may accidentally or intentionally connect to the wrong network. There is a real risk of sensitive data being compromised by this kind of activity. It is also possible for an attacker to use a wireless connection while sitting in their car or a neighbouring building to view, download or upload unacceptable content. This could lead to a visit from the police with a search warrant for activities that were not conducted by an employee and of which the organisation has no knowledge. It is usually too late to try and explain to the MD after the event has been reported in the papers.

The principle of authenticating to a network is very similar to that described in the section on user access controls for identifying and connecting to a computer. It may even be that a Single Sign-on system is in use that authenticates the identity of the user to the network and then grants appropriate privileges and access rights for all the systems for which that user has authority.

There are protocols designed specifically for centralised access control (e.g. Radius, TACACS, Kerberos and Diameter) which work well for networks. These provide authentication of the user and software on a dedicated server. This may be just username and password or it may involve some kind of token and code input or possibly a challenge-response mechanism.

Partitioning networks

Partitioning a network is another way of protecting essential systems. It is the same principle as physical access control to limit access to sensitive areas of the office or the 'need-to-know' principle where only certain people are allowed to have knowledge of some information to manage the risks to it.

The rules on business governance and separation of roles within some business sectors, especially finance, require complete data separation to defend against insider trading and accusations of market manipulation. Network partitions can provide this function too.

By using a network 'sniffer' an attacker can potentially record all of the traffic passing across a segment. The sniffer may be a hardware module or some software installed on a workstation or server as a Trojan to capture data and send it to the attacker, who may be an employee or external to the organisation, for use later. This is likely to include sensitive data, usernames and passwords. If the attacker can see the whole network he can 'sniff' the whole network too. Partitioning a network limits the amount of data that can be seen and makes the job of an attacker much harder. It is also true that partitioning can limit the damage done by malware. The chances are that any infection may be limited to one network partition, limiting the damage done and the effort needed to clean up the system to restore normal operations.

Without network partitions an external attacker who defeats the perimeter security can access any area of the network with little impediment. An internal attacker doesn't even have to beat the defences because they are already on the inside. The decision about how much protection to offer should be made through a risk assessment process, but there are certain common safeguards that should be considered by most organisations.

Any connection to the outside, such as the internet, should be protected by at least one firewall. If there is any other form of remote access, such as dial-up, ADSL or web-based access, then the servers should be located in a DMZ, which sits between two firewalls. Any successful attack on the access point through that external connection does not then immediately grant access to the whole network. It also makes sense to locate the network connection for any WiFi access in the DMZ, because it is so easy to attack.

There are various approaches to partitioning networks, from physical cabling separation, through the use of Virtual Private Networks (VPNs) configured in network hardware or even protocols such as CISCO MPLS. Each has its good and bad points, ranging from strength of security to cost. The appropriate solution will depend on the outcome of risk assessment, risk appetite and budget. A department or site may have an individual Local Area Network (LAN) linked to others via routers to form a Wide Area Network (WAN).

Cryptography in networking

Cryptography is described in more detail in a later section in this chapter, but some basic concepts need to be understood now. There are two common mistakes many people make when they think of cryptography. The first one is that they think it stops people from being able to see your data. This is not the case. Attackers can still see your data, but if you have got the cryptography right it means they can't understand it. The second one is that they think cryptography is only used to provide confidentiality. Once again, this is wrong. The four main uses of cryptography are:

- secrecy – nobody else can see the plaintext;
- data integrity – the data has not been changed, deleted or inserted;
- user verification – this is the person they claim to be;
- non-repudiation – the sender cannot later deny sending the message or its content.

Different forms of cryptographic process can be used and combined into protocols to perform different tasks. For example, Digital Signatures are a form of cryptography and do not normally provide confidentiality; their main function is to provide non-repudiation.

Data travelling across a network is obviously in transit, but do not forget that a network provides access to data that is at rest, on a hard drive or other media. Your architecture must protect both. Good operating systems also use encryption across networks, especially when sending passwords. This feature may not be activated by default; it is always worth checking. This defends against the capture of passwords by attackers with network access.

The most obvious form of cryptography that most people see and use is Secure Sockets Layer (SSL), which provides encryption for websites, especially e-commerce, to protect financial data such as credit card numbers. Its operation is signified by the little yellow padlock symbol in the browser window. The user of the browser does not normally need to do anything other than to check the validity of the SSL certificate to make sure that it belongs to the organisation with whom they want to do business and is valid. All the configuration is done in advance by the operator of the website. When a user connects to the site, their browser and the website set up an SSL channel to protect the data from being read by a third party as it travels across the internet.

In business the increase in mobile working has meant that there has been a steady rise in the need for Virtual Private Networks (VPNs). These are another way of encrypting (protecting) traffic that travels over a public connection, which could be the internet or a dial-up or broadband connection. The common risk with all of these connections is that the data is travelling across a system that is owned and administered by people unknown and therefore not fully trusted by the user. It is also possible for a third party to compromise the channel and eavesdrop traffic in transit. That is why cryptography is used to create a VPN. The data part of the traffic is encrypted before leaving the sender until after it arrives at the receiver, leaving the address part in the clear so that it can be read and routed by the public network.

The system uses VPN client software on the remote system to contact the host server over a public channel. The user has to identify and authenticate themselves in the usual manner. Once the ID&A is complete the host and client agree on a secret key and the encryption process starts. From then on the body of the data is encrypted and protected from eavesdroppers. The concept of the VPN can also be used to separate internal network traffic, as described in the previous section, to ensure it cannot be read by those without a need to know.

Control of third party access

The concept of allowing a third party access to the organisational network is not a new one. Just think of the original uses – a dial-up connection from a supplier, used to support hardware or software remotely. In this day and age it's more likely to be to allow some form of Electronic Data Interchange (EDI) to improve efficiency or speed up business processes. A classic example would be a customer who uses a Just-In-Time approach to manufacturing, placing electronic orders with suppliers for carefully timed deliveries of components.

This link may be over the internet via some kind of VPN or through a private link. There will certainly be a need to partition the network to limit the areas that the third party can access, because of the need to manage risks to information assets. It is another example of the 'need-to-know' principle. They may be a business partner but they do not need to know much about your organisation that isn't in the public domain. There may even be regulatory requirements governing this access (covered in the next section).

The primary concern is to ensure that the access point can only be used by authorised persons or applications from within the third party. Identification and Authentication are still required to stop attacks across the link by third-party staff or anyone who manages to find a way to connect into the link. The standard approach to protecting the link itself is cryptography, such as a VPN, as described in the previous section. A good design will normally have the link to the third party located within a DMZ, protected by a firewall from the outside world and another one that only allows permitted traffic through into the organisation's inner network to access a specified server and vice versa.

Network Usage Policy

The Network Usage Policy document exists to define the purposes for which the network may, and may not, be used. It will also define the individuals and roles who are allowed to use it and the official line on access control. This will include definitions of the user profile for each role – privileges, password lengths and strengths, renewal period, and so on.

Intrusion monitoring and detection

It has already been mentioned that networks are often attacked from the outside by unauthorised users or by authorised users within the organisation attempting to perform tasks for which they are not authorised. It is important that the network has some means of detecting and reporting on these attacks. This is part of the role that is generally referred to as 'Protective Monitoring'.

The first task is to ensure that all relevant log data is recorded securely in such a way that an attacker cannot change or delete the information in order to cover their tracks from investigators and auditors. This can provide evidence of what happened and be used to identify any damage done and how it was achieved. The data must be periodically reviewed in order to identify any unauthorised activity. Log data that is never examined is of very little value and not much of a deterrent.

The second task is to look for patterns of behaviour that indicate some kind of attack. This can be hardware or software based and can provide automated alerts for many of the attack forms. There are several different solutions on the market. Many of them use the SNORT engine, which is a publicly available shareware product. It is signature based and easily updated. Like any kind of product none of them is infallible, but the good ones will detect and stop the vast majority of attacks.

It should be said that this area requires good knowledge and experience if it is to be performed well. There is no substitute for hours spent studying this subject. Courses and external websites can be used to gain knowledge and keep current with new techniques. Know your enemy and his (or her) modus operandi.

Vulnerability analysis and penetration testing

An even more demanding task is that of analysing systems for vulnerabilities and performing penetration tests (pen tests). Only the most skilled and dependable of specialists should be allowed to conduct this kind of work as it is very easy to adversely affect the availability of systems and the data itself if they don't have the right knowledge or tools. There are also significant legal issues to consider before undertaking any form of 'pen testing'. Good 'pen testers' are often considered to be amongst the elite of Information Assurance professionals.

Vulnerability analysis is the process of examining the network for any vulnerabilities that could increase the frequency or impact of any threat. An example would be a modem connected to the network, making it easy for an attacker to find a way in, using war-dialling. Attacks are likely to be much more frequent because a modem such as this is easy to find. This task is best done by someone who knows the network in conjunction with someone who understands security.

Penetration tests are sometimes referred to as 'ethical hacking' because the testers will use many of the techniques that would be used by a hacker in order to identify any weaknesses in the network. Vulnerabilities are often not just weaknesses that allow access to data, but the ability to cause denial of service too. Owing to the possible implications, there is a lot of paperwork to be completed before the work can start, including a detailed briefing document defining:

- the terms of engagement;
- what is in and out of scope for testing;
- acceptable levels of disruption (if any);

- level of social engineering allowed or expected;
- tools and techniques to be used;
- format of reporting and secure deletion of data obtained during the test;
- action upon finding a vulnerability – major and minor;
- use of a non-disclosure agreement.

Anyone who has not specified or managed a pen test before is strongly advised to seek advice and guidance from someone who has.

Secure network management

The basic technical elements for network security have already been discussed so it is time network management was considered from the perspective of the department manager and senior management. The task of managing a network securely is one of the most crucial aspects of IT service delivery. No network means no communications, no security means you are open to loss of data, intellectual property, revenue and reputation. Any one of these can put an organisation out of business; an insecure network can easily cause several of these at once.

Some business sectors require minimum standards through legal and regulatory controls. Others choose to implement them to comply with standards such as ISO 17799/27001. Network management can play a major role in managing risk and improving resilience for Business Continuity.

In order to manage their business effectively any organisation needs to have information about their infrastructure, especially their:

- assets – physical and logical;
- architecture – systems integration and interconnectivity;
- risks – threats, impacts and vulnerabilities;
- countermeasures – logical and physical defences.

In addition, a good management team will understand the:

- business processes that the IT systems support and service;
- organisational policies for IT, quality and conduct of operations;
- procedures or processes for all tasks;
- need for effective communication routes within the IT department and with other departments.

If this information doesn't exist, work will be required to create or develop them in agreement with all the business areas and then to implement and operate them. Ideally this should be done to a recognised framework like the ISO/IEC 27000 series, the IT Infrastructure Library (ITIL), ISO 9001 or the standard for the relevant industry sector.

It is useful to follow the Plan–Do–Check–Act model:

- Plan your actions;
- Do them;

- Check you have done them by auditing;
- Act upon your findings to improve the whole system.

Then go back to Plan and repeat...

Don't forget the principle that management of anything requires metrics; you can't manage effectively what you can't measure – how do you know it is working, or how well? Networks are no different. Decide on how secure it needs to be and how you will know when you achieve it. Monitor and report regularly to justify your budget and team.

The success of GANT has led to the organisation growing in size and the recruitment of a team of wildlife surveyors to look for the toads across the country. These people are out in the field and need remote access to the IT systems for reference and reporting purposes.

In addition, there will be a national campaign to get members of the public to report sightings through a website into which they will enter data. Access to this must be secure enough to stop it acting as the start point for a remote attack, yet allow anyone to interact with it to input valid data.

This requires a new network structure and remote access capability – broadband, dial-up and web-based methods will all be required.

Activity 4.7

One of the directors has been told about the ability to connect into the office from home by a friend in the pub, and wants to be able to do the same for GANT. How would you explain the security issues that surround the use of remote working to him?

Activity 4.8

There are concerns that the network is being accessed by people who do not have the necessary authorisation. How would you identify the right place to install an intrusion detection system and its sensors?

Activity 4.9

GANT has been approached by the directors of the Society for the Listing of Undiscovered Gastropods (SLUG) who are suggesting that their survey teams could work in conjunction with those of GANT to cover more ground. How would you design the security architecture for a data connection between the two organisations?

EXTERNAL SERVICES

LEARNING OUTCOMES

The intention of this section is to provide the reader with an understanding of the security issues surrounding services that use the network, often bought in from external suppliers.

Securing real-time services

The rapid rise in popularity of services such as Instant Messenger (IM) and video conferencing have added another dimension to the challenges facing Information Security managers. There are already examples of IM being used:

- to extract data;
- to insert malware onto networks;
- as a channel for phishing attacks;
- for unauthorised purposes leading to legal action against the perpetrators.

Video conferencing isn't necessarily quite as vulnerable. Many organisations still use separate ISDN or other data connections that are not linked to their data networks. The data can still be the subject of eavesdropping, leading to a loss of confidentiality. Systems using webcams or sharing data connections have the same risks and threats as the data channel and can be used as an easy backdoor into the network if not properly segregated and protected.

Other real-time services, such as ordinary telephony, Voice Over IP (VOIP) and Closed-Circuit TV (CCTV) feeds, are also possible avenues of attack. VOIP is especially vulnerable if it is integrated into a single messaging system. Those with data connections can be used as a route into the organisation's data networks. Ordinary PABX systems can be the subject of various technical attacks (some of which are known, such as phreaking and dial-through fraud), leading to losses in the millions, if they are not configured, protected and monitored effectively. Just because it isn't like other data formats, in documents for example, does not mean it won't be attacked. The enterprising attacker has known for a long time that anything related to telephony is vulnerable to attack. All you have to do is find the right number, dial it and you have a connection.

Quite often attackers will use a tactic called 'war dialling', which is to ring every number the company has and see which ones have a modem attached or which will allow access to the Main Telephone Exchange control system. War dialling can also be a useful tactic for the Security Manager; security auditors have quite often used this technique and found unauthorised modems, connected by users, that the IT department knew nothing about.

Since many of these services are quite new, the technology available to protect them is also new and may not be as mature as products that protect against other threats. That means they may still have weaknesses that can be exploited. Attackers could well target these as being the weakest spot in the defences.

Securing data exchange

The exchange of data over the network needs to be protected against all three threats – Confidentiality, Integrity and Availability. Data must arrive without being altered, deleted or subjected to eavesdropping. The ability to send data whenever required must also be maintained. It doesn't matter what form this data takes, the same principles apply. It is merely the countermeasures used to protect the data that will vary. Cryptography and security protocols can be used to perform this function for data in transit. The key issue is to ensure that all parties protect the data to the same standard. If one does not, then they risk being identified as the easy target and the additional protection at the other locations will count for nothing.

The last point to note is that, once data arrives, it must be checked for any signs of malware or compromise before being allowed access or given any credence as legitimate traffic. This should be conducted in the DMZ, described previously, before passing through into the inner network.

The protection of web services and e-commerce

In business-to-business relationships there is normally a lower degree of risk when Electronic Data Interchange (EDI) occurs. A level of trust is often established by some means before EDI begins. Security architects must remember that the users of web services and e-commerce are often members of the public and so organisations have no control over the configuration and integrity of the PC being used to access the service being provided. It is important therefore to consider the possibility of malware such as infectious Trojans or keyloggers being installed on the user's PC and to design security to protect the servers providing the functionality.

There is also the obvious issue that websites are normally public facing and therefore open to attack by anyone with an internet connection. It is estimated that up to one in three of all websites have been compromised with malware. Protection must be given to stop attackers from extracting data, entering false data and adding their own code to the site, either for propaganda purposes or to add malware that is downloaded by any visitors.

The most obvious form of cryptography that most people see and use is Secure Sockets Layer (SSL) (described earlier in this chapter), which provides encryption for websites, especially e-commerce, to protect financial data such as credit card numbers. When a user connects to the site, their browser and the website set up an SSL channel to protect the data from being read by a third party as it travels across the internet.

In business the increase in mobile working has meant that there has been a steady rise in the need for Virtual Private Networks (VPN), also described earlier in this chapter. These are another way of encrypting (protecting) traffic that travels over a public connection which could be the internet, a dial-up or broadband connection. The common risk with all of these is that the data is travelling across a system that is owned and administered by people unknown and therefore not fully trusted by the user. It is also possible for a third party to compromise the channel and eavesdrop traffic in transit. That is why cryptography is used to create a VPN. The data part of the traffic is encrypted before leaving the sender until after it arrives at the receiver, leaving the address part in the clear so that it can be read and routed by the public network.

The system uses VPN client software on the remote system to contact the host server over a public channel. The user has to identify and authenticate themselves in the usual manner. This is all done in plaintext but once the ID&A is complete the host and client agree on a secret key and the encryption process starts. From then on the body of the data is encrypted and protected from eavesdroppers. The concept of the VPN can also be used to separate internal network traffic, as described in the previous section, to ensure it cannot be read by those without a need to know.

Protection of mobile and telecommuting services

In the modern world, more and more people are spending time out of the office travelling or working from home. This increase has been facilitated by the new technology that allows improved remote access, not just broadband at home but also in hotels, and wireless networking. The mobile phone companies also provide services such as GPRS (GSM Packet Radio Service), 3G, HSDPA (High-Speed Downlink Packet Access) and EDGE (Enhanced Data Rates for GSM Evolution), which use their 2G and 3G infrastructure to provide a high bandwidth connection to the office and the internet.

We have already talked about securing the systems in the office that receive this kind of traffic, so we will concentrate in this section on the elements that are 'out on the road'.

The three main problems facing assurance practitioners here are:

- the connection uses network infrastructure that does not belong to the company, so traffic can be viewed, altered or deleted by an attacker;
- the users take their IT and communications equipment away from company premises, where it is more vulnerable to theft, loss or compromise;
- ensuring that connections are only used by authorised employees.

The first problem can be defended against with encryption. Creating a VPN tunnel from the user device back to the office can defeat all but the most determined attacker if it is implemented properly (as described in a previous section).

The second challenge can be partly safeguarded with encryption to protect data held on devices carried off site. If hardware is stolen the attacker cannot login to the device and read the data, so all they have done is stolen a device to reformat and sell, not valuable company data. The other part of the equation is to make sure that the users have received appropriate security awareness training about mobile working and are issued with good physical locks to secure their equipment. Part of the awareness training should be about working in unsecured environments; who can see your screen and paperwork or overhear your conversations?

The last part is to make sure that any communications ID&A process includes a PIN or token code, and that devices capable of remote communications can have their service disabled quickly. This stops the attacker from being able to access your network and from running up big bills with your service provider.

Secure information exchange with other organisations

We have already described the process of securing a connection to a third-party organisation, but there are more than just the technical issues to consider. We briefly mentioned that there may be regulatory or legal requirements governing data interchange, and now is the time to go into more detail. The main acts to consider in the UK are:

- Data Protection Act (DPA);
- Human Rights Act (HRA);
- Financial Services Act (FSA);
- Official Secrets Act (for government and defence projects) (OSA);
- Markets in Financial Instruments Directive (MiFID);
- Freedom of Information Act (FoIA).

Without doubt, the most important of these is the DPA, This defines very clearly how data is to be protected and used, taking into account the rights of the data subject as defined in the DPA. Other legislation will only relate to the financial industry (e.g. FSA and MiFID), but is very important to them.

When two or more organisations plan to work together, the important start point is for those organisations to agree and sign a protocol that specifies all of these matters as part of a legally binding contract where all parties agree to common standards for the processing and protection of data provided to the others. Each party is then bound under law to a duty of care. All parties are then said to have shown due diligence and have defence in law (and usually the right of redress) against wrongdoings by the other.

The Directors of GANT have decided to open up an e-commerce site to sell toad-related merchandise and host a forum dedicated to amphibians in general. This will be in partnership with several other wildlife groups working with other amphibians native to the UK. The economies of scale have been recognised and welcomed by all parties.

In order to monitor stock levels and pass orders back to the right group for dispatch, there need to be secure links and data sharing agreements created.

Activity 4.10

The Directors want to know how to protect GANT against malware contained in messages posted to the proposed forum. What would you advise them to do?

Activity 4.11

As their advisor on assurance, you need to make sure that GANT don't fall foul of the Data Protection Act when exchanging information with their new partners. What do you suggest to them?

Activity 4.12

Thanks to an unexpected grant, GANT has acquired a video-conferencing system and you have been asked to link it into the network so that anyone can watch the participants of a meeting from their desk. What threats do you think you should protect against?

IT INFRASTRUCTURE

LEARNING OUTCOMES

The intention of this section is to provide the reader with an understanding of the security issues surrounding security of the IT Infrastructure and the content of the associated documentation.

Separation of systems to reduce risk

A simple, yet very effective, way to manage risk and provide assurance is to keep systems separate. Although there are advantages to joined-up systems that share data, it is not always necessary. In some cases it may be decided that the risks outweigh the advantages and it should not be done. An alternative is to allow very limited functionality to pass between systems through an inter-domain connector (IDC) or to allow data to pass only one way, through some form of data diode or specially configured router.

Another advantage is that separate systems are less complex to manage and easier to assess for risk because of the reduced complexity that always increases the possibility of error in IT systems. Increased complexity usually means more cost to implement and support the IT infrastructure. If the functionality cannot be shown to provide a positive business benefit, why do it?

Conformance with security policy, standards and guidelines

There is no point in having standards for the design, implementation and operation of the systems if they are not followed. Having said that, if the procedures are not aligned with the processes and requirements of the business, the staff will not follow them. The same is true of the security policy, standards and guidelines. They have to be aligned to the operational needs of the business – for day-to-day operations and for effective business continuity and disaster recovery. This is a complex subject and one that may need expert advice to get it right. Accreditation to ISO/IEC 27000 series will require that all the relevant controls have been identified, documented, implemented and then followed. Regular internal and external audits will be needed to confirm this. The hierarchy of these documents is as follows.

- The policy defines the overall Information Assurance goals of the organisation and must be supported by the Board and Chief Executive to provide authority.
- The standards define the minimum acceptable criteria for achieving that policy in the key areas (e.g. the control groupings in ISO/IEC 27000 series).
- The guidelines advise how to design and implement workable procedures and countermeasures to meet the standards and enable the business to manage risk.

Access control lists and roles, and control of privileged access

The concept of access control lists and roles has already been mentioned earlier in this book. The learning point here is that there is no point having such controls if access to the ability to update or change those controls is not also protected. An attacker who finds that they cannot access certain material may well turn their attention to finding a way to subvert those controls. The obvious place to start is by seeing if they can grant themselves the necessary privileges perhaps by creating a new account for themselves about which the system administrator may know nothing. Many organisations use extra safeguards for the accounts that can grant these sorts of privileges. There will probably only be one or two accounts with these rights and they often have longer passwords (e.g. 12 characters long instead of 9) to make them even harder for an attacker to try and break.

Principles and requirements for correctness of input and accuracy of stored data

There is no point in having the most secure system in the world if the data it contains is inaccurate and of no use. While stored data can be subverted by attackers and malware, the most common cause is either incorrect user input or errors in software design or coding. One of the main controls in the UK's Data Protection Act, which is mirrored throughout the European Union, is a requirement for data to be accurate. This means it is not just good business practice, it is also the law.

There are several ways to promote data accuracy and they all need to be used in conjunction with each other.

- Make sure the design of the software and database is correct, so that values reflect the right information and relationships have the right meanings.
- Use proven code review techniques when developing and testing the application before it goes live.
- Use defensive coding, which checks for values within acceptable ranges and looks for correct relationships with other fields before accepting an update command to change the database.
- Train the users in how to use the application properly. Make sure they understand the meanings of the fields and their relationships.
- Audit the system regularly to look for anomalies. Automated tools can help this process.
- Have a means whereby it is easy for those who have data in the system to report any errors and have them resolved as soon as possible. Try to identify how the errors occurred and then how to stop them happening again.

Principles of recovery capability, including backup and audit trails

Having produced a means of creating and holding data securely, it is vital to be able to recover it should anything go wrong. Problems can range from the theft of a laptop or the failure of a hard disk through to the entire building being lost to fire. It has been shown many times that any organisation that loses access to its data for more than 10 days is very likely to go out of business. In some cases more than 48 hours is enough to signal the end, or at least invoke severe financial penalties and major loss of goodwill.

It is absolutely essential that backups exist for all data, and not just a current backup. Use of an approach such as the Grandfather-Father-Son (GFS) approach (maintaining at least three generations of the backed-up data) to allow recovery of data back to a previous point in time is highly desirable. There have been occasions where organisations have discovered a piece of malware that has been present for months, quietly changing data values at random. The only way to resolve the issue is to roll back the system to a point in time before the malware was present and rebuild the data from paper records. Without a GFS backup approach this is not possible.

The cause of the risk may be outside your control, and you may not even be able to use your own premises (think of 9/11 in the USA in 2001 or Buncefield in the UK in 2005) but you still have to be able to recover data and operations. Consider a disaster recovery contract or having the ability to relocate the data centre to another company site in times of emergency. Whatever you do, keep a copy of your backup in a secure location off-site. More detail on this aspect of Information Assurance is provided elsewhere in this book.

An audit trail has four main uses:

- where did we get to – what is complete and what transactions do we need to roll back?
- to identify what happened and who did it;
- compliance with standards and legislation and demonstration of due diligence;
- as a deterrent against internal attack.

Collecting and keeping transaction and event logs is often referred to as 'Protective Monitoring', because it is a means of doing all of the above tasks. Treat the logs in the same way as your data backups. With the right tools and training, the audit data can provide powerful insights into what is going on.

Principles of intrusion monitoring and detection methods

Intrusion Detection and Prevention Systems (IDS and IPS) use automated tools to analyse log data, system activity and network traffic in an attempt to identify and, in IPS, to block unauthorised users or malware from causing a security breach. There is so much log data and system activity, especially in large systems, that it is impossible for any one person to monitor it all in real time and uneconomical for any organisation to pay sufficient numbers of people with the right skills to do the work. The only practical solution is automation.

These systems can capture data from network traffic and devices such as routers and firewalls, Network Intrusion Detection Systems (NIDS) and from system hosts' Host Intrusion Detection Systems (HIDS). The analysis is done by either an application or a hardware device, many of them using statistical techniques and SNORT to analyse the data looking for changes in system configuration or operation, or for known types of behaviour, often referred to as a signature.

The problem with these systems is the number of 'false positives' that they often return, especially when first installed. It takes a skilled user to configure them correctly and to educate the system to understand what is, and is not, normal activity. The IPS solutions cause the most problems, because they tend to stop authorised users from working when they block a false positive.

Installation of baseline controls to secure systems and applications, and the dangers of default settings

Baseline controls are standards used to define how systems should be configured and managed. The intention is that any new systems in any location should be built using the settings and guidelines contained in this document. In this case, we are concerned about configurations for Information Assurance.

The contents will include details on:

- which versions of operating systems to use;
- which parts of the operating system to install;
- the patches required;
- additional applications such as anti-virus software, intrusion detection agents, etc.;
- settings for password length, access control lists, etc.;
- network configuration.

Baselines are a good start to implementing security, but there is no 'one size fits all' answer. The configuration for an email server is different from that for a web server, which in turn differs from those for a file and print server. A further danger is that people assume that a machine built to the baseline is secure. The problem with this is that new vulnerabilities and exploits are discovered all the time and new patches are issued for the operating system and applications. The assurance provided by the baseline does not last beyond the first new patch.

Part of the initial default installation process for many software applications and hardware devices is a default password. These are configured on the basis that a password of some sort is better than no password at all. Unfortunately, there are many sites on the internet that list literally hundreds of default passwords. Once an attacker identifies the infrastructure in use he can try the default passwords, which will often give them administrative privileges and provide an excellent basis for an attack. It is most important that all default passwords are changed as soon as the installation is complete. Since they are for administrative use and provide significant administrative rights to the user, that password needs to be longer and stronger than ordinary user ones, making it much harder to break.

Configuration management and operational change control

The topic of configuration management follows on logically from that of baseline controls. It is the process of monitoring and controlling the configuration of devices and documentation within the infrastructure. The configuration documentation should describe the baseline that is in place and it can then be used to identify any changes made.

Change control management requires the effective process of configuration management as an essential element. The documentation can be used to help assess the requirements for changes and the impacts these changes may have before granting approval for the change. It is also important that the documentation is kept up to date to reflect any changes made. The documentation can also be used as part of the auditing process, for quality, assurance and operational purposes.

The protection and promotion of security documentation

If your organisation has any links to third parties or external suppliers, such as managed service providers or outsourced operations, it is very important that they are required to work to the same Information Assurance standards and adopt the same working practices, or at least those that are clearly compatible. If they do not, they may become the weakest link in the chain and can invalidate much of the good work done in-house. The use of working protocol documents and contractual clauses can require them to do so, and allow auditing to ensure compliance. It is becoming more common to see third parties required to have an accreditation such as ISO/IEC 27000 series before they can work for an organisation. This provides a degree of confidence in their assurance, including the quality and content of their documentation.

Having produced a set of security documents it is most important that they are protected against unauthorised access and loss. They may be physical, electronic or both, and all must be safeguarded. The contents of these documents describe how the countermeasures and procedures in place work to protect the assets of the organisation. Knowledge of the content would make life much easier for an attacker to find a vulnerability in the infrastructure and gain access. Access to the documents, physical or logical, must be very strictly controlled and monitored to prevent abuse. It is often worth considering the introduction of a Protective Marking system to allow certain documents to receive extra protection and safe handling.

GANT continues to grow and now has more IT infrastructure than can reasonably be supported in-house. The economics do not justify employing the necessary specialists, yet the skills are required to be available when necessary. The time has come to issue an Invitation To Tender (ITT) to third-party suppliers of IT support and other services to provide managed services and IT support to the organisation.

Activity 4.13

You have been tasked with ensuring that the ITT documentation contains the necessary statement of requirements for Information Assurance and professional standards of work. What would you include?

Activity 4.14

The members of the Board are aware that they ought to have a formally documented Information Assurance policy and supporting documentation, but they are not clear on the structure that it should take. How would you explain to them the purpose of each kind of document and their hierarchy?

> ### Activity 4.15
> Another requirement to be included in the third-party ITT is for the baseline builds for the systems to be implemented and supported as part of the contract. What requirements would you include for the builds, documentation and change control?

IT TESTING, AUDIT AND REVIEW

LEARNING OUTCOMES

The intention of this section is to provide the reader with an understanding of the issues surrounding security of the IT Infrastructure and the content of the associated documentation.

Methods and strategies for security testing systems

Having built what is believed to be a secure system that meets the needs of the business, there is almost always value in proving that the end result is secure. This provides confidence to you and your senior management in both the systems and your abilities to design and implement them.

A single test after completion is not sufficient, however, as threats and business requirements are constantly changing. Tests and reviews should be repeated at periodic intervals to look for any new issues of technology, threat or process that need to be addressed. Some of this requires expert testing by a professional Penetration Test team (as described earlier) and some of it requires a review by a combination of business and security analysts. From time to time the advice of an independent external consultant can help to identify areas that may have been overlooked or about which the internal team have limited knowledge. This should form part of the ongoing risk management process, which exists to manage all risks, including these.

Correct reporting of testing and reviews

The test and review process requires accurate and comprehensive reporting if it is to serve any value. The report must be an open and honest 'warts and all' report that highlights any shortcomings in the security architecture. Any attempt to hide or downplay problems may lead to vulnerabilities being left in place that can be successfully exploited.

As ever, there must be a detailed technical content and an executive summary for those who don't have the time or knowledge to digest the entire report. This summary must contain the 'take-away' messages and important conclusions, along with a brief justification for further action and expenditure. Once again it may be necessary to give this report some level of protective marking to prevent unauthorised access.

Verifying the links between IT and clerical processes

The importance of aligning the Information Security architecture, policy and procedures with the needs of the business and its primary operational processes has already been emphasised in this book on more than one occasion. In the best traditions of the 'Plan-Do-Check-Act' cycle, this is where you should Check that the task has been done properly and that the basis for the original design has not changed since the last review. This check will show if people are following the procedures and that those procedures are correct for the current circumstances. If you find that the procedures are being widely disregarded or side-stepped, it is often a good indication that the design, procedures or both are wrong and changes should be considered.

Principles of monitoring system and network access or usage

We have already described the need to collect event log data from a whole range of systems, appliances and devices, and to monitor the traffic passing over the network and any external data links, such as the internet. There are commercial devices and software applications that can be used to perform this role, automatically processing anything up to hundreds of thousands of events per hour and capturing data for further use later. Many organisations will keep six months of event log data for just such eventualities.

The data that has been collected can be analysed to detect unusual patterns of behaviour, malware and signatures of known attacks. It can also be reviewed forensically to gather evidence of wrongdoing and abuse that can be used in an internal disciplinary case or provided to criminal justice organisations as part of their enquiries. The analysis needs to be performed by well-trained and skilled individuals. The training must not only be in the technical side of recognising unusual activity, but also in how to collect and preserve data in such a way that it is legally admissible in court. This kind of work can be outsourced to specialist third parties by smaller organisations without resources of their own.

The new systems are up and running, supported by the third party. GANT now needs to be able to audit not only the activities of the users, but also the service provided by the third party. This audit is for both the technical services and the quality of service against defined Service Level Agreements (SLAs). It is also important to check that the work done does meet the requirements of the organisation, so some internal auditing must be done.

Activity 4.16
How will you define the content and standard of reporting that you require from your third-party suppliers?

> ### Activity 4.17
> How would you check for alignment between the actual business processes and the Information Security management system?

> ### Activity 4.18
> As part of an in-house exercise, your consultant has recommended that part of it should be the simulation of recovering data from a PC for use in an investigation. How would you plan to do this ?

SYSTEMS DEVELOPMENT AND SUPPORT

LEARNING OUTCOMES

This section outlines the principles behind developing and supporting systems with an appropriate level of assurance.

Security requirement specification

The design of any application, system or network must meet the operational requirements of the users and also be aligned with the Information Security architecture of the organisation as a whole. The security requirement must be part of the overall Statement of Requirements document from which the design is generated. It is most important that the assurance requirements are captured at the start of any project in order to ensure that they are effective and that there is no adverse impact on the project or product from trying to reverse-engineer the assurance requirements later on. Adding them later will almost always add complexity and cost to any project.

Another issue can be attempts by the project team to reduce the assurance requirements to save time and money on the project if there have been cost over-runs or slippage of time scales. The security manager must be ready to defend his requirements but not to be totally inflexible to urgent operational requirements. Just remember to have the project and senior management sign off acceptance of the increased risk that results from any changes.

Security should not be thought of as only being the need to defend against improper access and misuse. It also means:

- defensive coding to make sure that only valid and accurate data is processed by the system;
- proper functional testing to ensure it behaves as expected and within the design criteria;
- methods to back up and secure data against loss or damage;

- adequate assurance of availability;
- compliance with any legal and regulatory requirements;
- security of communications;
- effective auditing of activity.

Security involvement in system and product assessment

All new systems and products should have to go through some form of appropriate acceptance testing before being used in production. It does not matter if they were developed in house or purchased, they should be assessed for acceptable and appropriate levels of security. For example a product bought from a reputable supplier should be given more trust than a piece of freeware written by someone you have never heard of, downloaded from a website.

Every product should be considered for its potential effects on confidentiality, integrity and availability, both directly and indirectly in conjunction with other assets, as part of the risk assessment process. Many organisations maintain a separate test environment that replicates the live systems to allow assessments to be conducted without risk of adverse impact. Another approach is to examine the source code (not always practical) by eye or with automated tools. Use of a malware scanner is always recommended for new code.

Security issues associated with commercial off-the-shelf products

The most obvious threat is of rogue code hidden within an application that performs activity against the best interests of the organisation. It could also be that there are 'bugs' that, while not intentionally malicious, have a serious adverse impact. We mentioned a separate test environment in the previous section and this is why it is important – to help find any such code by identifying its behaviour before it affects production assets. Sometimes unscrupulous people will advertise cheap copies of applications because they have altered the code to include malware. The reduced price means it is more likely to be purchased and their malware installed.

The security issues don't just mean checking for rogue code. It is also important to check that the product is a legal copy and not pirated. Make sure that the supplier is reputable, not some dubious market stall selling cheap copies. Failure to buy genuine copies can leave the organisation open to prosecution under the (UK) Copyrights, Designs & Patents Act of 1988. That can mean financial penalties, impact on operations and loss of reputation.

Importance of links with all business areas

The development process is another area that benefits from contact with all business areas that will be impacted by the new deliverable. All too often it happens that end users are given what the designers thought they wanted, but about which they had never bothered to ask. Consultation from day one has all sorts of benefits. The end users get the deliverable they need with a form of security built in that they can not only live with but see a positive benefit from it being included. Project Managers call this stakeholder management, but it is a powerful tool that should be used by everybody.

A good security manager is in close contact with all his fellow managers throughout the company to ensure open communications and good feedback. It may be that the security team learns something new during the development process that could come in useful in the future. Keeping current with new system technologies and software tools is as important for security architects and managers as maintaining current knowledge of legislation and threats.

Separation of development and live systems

We have already touched on this briefly. The main reason for keeping the live and development systems separate is to protect the live data from any unintended actions that might compromise it. Work to develop new systems and applications almost always contains mistakes in coding or design, sometimes both. That is why functionality and acceptance testing is required. Any attempt to run unproven and incomplete code against a live database could have a major impact on the ability of the organisation to function. The international standard, ISO/IEC 27000 series, contains a requirement to keep these two systems separate, as do some of the regulatory frameworks that exist around the world, especially in the banking and finance industries.

The last issue to consider is that the users may well need additional training before they can use the new systems properly and the development system can be a good place to allow them to make their mistakes, away from the live data. Accidental errors introduced by users is a regular source of issues and during training this can be a more frequent occurrence, because they are less familiar with the system. Training on the development system removes the concerns about errors being introduced and also allows trainees to make mistakes in a safe environment. A script can be used to reset the data to known values for another attempt at the procedure, further testing or the next group of trainees.

Security of acceptance processes and authorisation for use

Once a deliverable, be it hardware, software or both, has completed development and is ready for deployment, it must be tested to make sure it does exactly what the requirements specify as documented in the functional test plan. If the product is an update of an existing product, there must also be regression testing to make sure that no unexpected changes to existing functionality have happened during the update process. This includes testing the security aspects of the product and also ensuring that the testing is conducted securely.

The deliverable(s) must not only work, but do so securely and not have any unintentional adverse impact upon the business processes or other business areas. A risk assessment should have been conducted as part of the design and development life cycle and the forecasts should be checked against actual outcomes of testing. Security testing to consider includes:

- effectiveness of defensive coding;
- protection against malware and code injection through interfaces;
- backup and recovery of data;
- access control;
- auditing and behavioural analysis;
- communications security;
- resilience.

Final Acceptance Testing should be performed by representatives from:

- the project team;
- end users of the deliverable;
- business management;
- the assurance team.

The final authorisation to go live should require sign-off from all of these representatives before it can proceed.

The role of accreditation for new and modified systems

Some organisations, especially in central UK government and the military, have an Accreditor, who is responsible for ensuring that any changes or additions to their Information Systems and networks are of a required standard. This person has to approve the Information Security architecture, policy and procedures before the product(s) can be deployed and used. Normally this process is supported by formal documentation to standards defined in Government documents.

Accreditation can also apply in the business world, especially in Finance and Aviation systems, where systems must be accredited by a regulatory body as being fit for purpose before they can be used. An alternative approach is where a new system needs to be capable of accreditation to a standard such as ISO/IEC 27000 series. It may be that the organisation already has the accreditation, or is working towards it, and wants to ensure that the new system is capable of meeting the required standards for controls and countermeasures so that they will pass audit without remedial action.

The same principle applies to existing systems that are modified or updated. All changes should go through the same review process to make sure that the standards defined when the system was new are being maintained in the latest work. Many organisations also require periodic review and re-accreditation even if there does not appear to have been any change. Sometimes users will make changes in design or working practices without permission, or the environment changes (e.g. new threats and technology). Periodic review will help to identify these and formal processes can then be used to take remedial action.

Change control for software integrity

Any change to a software application, while designed to enhance its functionality, can introduce unintended problems. Every organisation should implement and enforce an effective formal change control process to manage the risks to their information assets and reputation.

The start of the process is the submission of an outline of the proposed changes to a review board, who will assess the benefits against the risks and the work required to achieve the change. One of the members of this change board should be a representative from the assurance team who will determine the risks and any changes to threats and vulnerabilities it may bring about. If the board approves the request they may specify certain conditions and approaches to be used in order to manage the risks. Once the development work is complete, the new version must undergo regression and functionality testing, as described previously.

The process must apply not only to the software or hardware, but also to update documentation that describes its use, function and design. A copy of the new code and accompanying documentation must be lodged in a secure place for business continuity purposes.

Security issues arising from outsourcing software development

The practice of outsourcing is becoming more widespread. It often drives down costs, but it can also introduce new risks to the process. Some of these risks carry security implications, such as the introduction of malicious code, deliberately or accidentally (both have been known to happen), into the deliverable or customer systems during installation.

There is also the risk that there will be a loss of intellectual property or trade secrets through the information that has to be given to the third party that may find its way into the possession of a competitor. A similar risk applies to any data sent to the third party. The laws on the protection of data (see elsewhere in this book) apply to anything sent to a third party as part of the development process.

A further concern is of a legal dispute developing between the customer and supplier. This risk can be managed by having appropriate terms and conditions in the contract, including agreed terms for dispute resolution, possibly by mediation, and the legal system or country in which disputes will be resolved. However the business must realise they are likely to be the biggest losers if a contractual dispute has to be sorted out through the courts. They may not have the system they need to operate effectively. It is always advisable to manage the risks by selecting a supplier that has reached level 5 on the Capability Maturity Model (CMM) for managed organisational processes.

Preventing covert channels, Trojans and rogue code

Mention has already been made of the risks of unwanted code ending up in a product that is being developed or updated. Some kind of methodology should be used to inspect the code in order to identify any such malware. Code should also be developed to a clearly defined set of standards.

For short pieces of code, the code walk-through process is a simple yet effective way of checking for any extraneous lines of software, but for many modern products that are much larger, this is not practical. The testing process will require use of a system that is separated from the live network and replicates it as far as is possible, as previously described. Some kind of automated testing tool could be used, in conjunction with the examination of the resulting data, audit logs and outputs from network analysers, to look for unexpected and abnormal behaviour as part of the testing and acceptance stage of the development life cycle.

This work can be complex and lengthy if the application is large. It should be noted that this is one of the most complex and difficult tasks to perform fully and soon involves very complex mathematics if taken to its fullest extent. There are experts who understand the process, the various tools and their outputs and it may be advisable to involve one of these in this process if the risk of malware and its potential impact is deemed sufficiently high. There are also organisations who run Commercial Licensed Evaluation Facilities ('CLEFs') throughout Europe with the skills and toolsets to do this kind of task on your behalf.

Security patching

It is a fact of life that every software application and operating system contains bugs. The complexity and length of the code makes it impossible to completely test every single execution path through it. These bugs can have different impacts ranging from incorrect values being stored in a database to allowing unauthorised access to the system or network. One way or another, they will have some form of adverse impact on the confidentiality, integrity or availability of the information assets of the organisation.

When bugs are found the supplier will normally issue a patch that can be installed in order to remove the vulnerability. These patches need to be tested and installed at the earliest opportunity. Hackers will also download the patches and attempt to reverse-engineer them in order to exploit the vulnerability if they can. The elapsed time from release of patch to release of exploit is now often measured in days.

Some people argue that patches should not be installed on certified products (see next section) as this changes the code away from the evaluated target. The official advice is that installing a patch to fix a known vulnerability is a much lower risk than that of accidentally introducing another vulnerability at the same time. Patches should always be applied. Having said that, patches should be tested, before they are rolled out, in an environment that is not connected to the live system to make sure they don't have an adverse impact on business functionality.

Use of certified products and systems

There are some industry sectors and circumstances under which it is advisable or even mandatory to use software products (e.g. firewalls), hardware devices (e.g. network switches) and operating systems that have been formally certified as providing a minimum standard of security, safety, reliability or a combination of these. Examples of this might include the nuclear industry, air traffic control systems, finance, government and defence organisations. There may be industry or government requirements for the use of this kind of software or it may just be a requirement defined by the management of the organisation as part of a drive towards higher standards.

Probably the best-known system in use today is the 'Common Criteria' assessment scheme that is recognised internationally as discussed in an earlier chapter. This provides a scale of product assurance, ranging from EAL (Evaluation Assurance Level) 1 to 7; the higher the number the greater the level of assurance. The concept is that an assured product can help to formally reduce risk in a quantifiable way when designing security architectures. The key issue to note is that each product will have a 'security target' of the features and functions that have been assessed. It is very important to make sure that the features you plan to use are included within that target, otherwise the certification is of no value.

Unfortunately the testing process tends to be lengthy and expensive, so a lot of manufacturers don't bother to have their products tested through this scheme. There are now other initiatives, such as the CSIA Claims Tested (CCT) scheme in the UK, designed to provide a minimum standard of assurance, quickly and at minimum cost, that the product has the functionality it claims. This is sufficient for many organisations and helps to meet one of the controls in ISO/IEC 27000 series for use of assured products. Another form of certification applies to encryption products, but that is discussed later in this book.

Use of escrow to reduce risks of loss of source code

If source code has been written or provided by a third-party organisation, the customer is dependent on that supplier for support, updates and changes to their software. There have been cases in the past where a supplier has gone out of business or been sold to a competitor and the end user has been forced to spend considerable sums of money to resolve the problem that poses a threat to their business, especially in getting support if something goes wrong.

One solution to this is escrow. The supplier and customer agree on a neutral third party (often a firm of lawyers or a bank) who will hold a copy of the source code and development materials. There is a legally binding agreement which specifies the circumstances under which the third party will release the material to the customer and ownership passes to them, along with all the relevant rights to use and develop the application further as required. It will often include the circumstances described above and there may be other specific conditions that must be met.

The work that GANT is doing now requires some fairly complex bespoke code to be written, as there aren't any commercial off-the-shelf packages dealing with amphibians. As the Information Assurance representative, you will need to be involved in the design and testing stages of the project to develop and implement the software.

Activity 4.19
You have been asked to suggest selection criteria for a third-party application developer. What would you put forward as mandatory and desirable factors in the selection process from a security perspective?

Activity 4.20
You hear two of the main users of the new application discussing a change they plan to make to the way they input data. What do you tell them they need to do before they go any further with their plans?

Activity 4.21
GANT has been offered a grant from local government towards the costs of the new application in return for helping to meet some of their environmental data reporting requirements to central government. There are some conditions attached, one of which is to use security approved products to protect the data. The management asks you to explain what this means.

THE ROLE OF CRYPTOGRAPHY

LEARNING OUTCOMES

Following study in this area, readers should be able to explain and justify each of the following concepts:

- basic principles of cryptographic theory, techniques and algorithm types, their use in confidentiality and integrity mechanisms and common cryptographic standards;
- general policies for cryptographic use, common key management approaches and requirements for cryptographic controls;

- principles of link, file, end-to-end, and other common encryption models and common Public Key Infrastructures and trust models;
- common practical applications of cryptography – for example, for digital signatures, authentication and confidentiality.

Introduction

Cryptography is a very wide-ranging and potentially detailed area of Information Assurance. No attempt has been made within this chapter to cover the whole topic in depth, as this is better researched from standards and works on the subject – a number of references to such works is given at the end of the chapter.

Concepts of cryptography

Much of what takes place in the context of exchanging information is based on establishing a partnership or chain of trust between two or more parties. If the parties are meeting face-to-face and have already established some form of trust between them, then subsequent transactions should hold no major risks. However, when the parties are separated by some distance they must satisfy themselves that the trust relationship can be maintained.

Specifically, they must usually ensure that with regards to any information which passes between them:

- it is kept secret, assuming that this is a key requirement of the relationship (confidentiality);
- it is not changed by third parties while in transit (integrity);
- the origin of the information is assured (authentication);
- the originator cannot deny having sent the information (non-repudiation).

There are two similar but separate needs to provide confidentiality. The first is to secure information stored in a system against unauthorised access – a process frequently achieved by use of password protection, but occasionally by some form of encryption of the information itself. File or disk encryption are examples of this. The second, dealt with here, is to secure information while in transit between sender and recipient so that unauthorised parties are unable to understand the information even if they are able to intercept it.

Principles of cryptography

In order to provide confidentiality, information or 'plain text' may be encrypted – changed into 'cipher text', so that the original plaintext cannot be read or inferred – and then sent to the recipient who reverses the process by decrypting the message to recover the original plain text.

Cryptography may be used in several ways. Firstly for example it may be used to encrypt information during transfer from one computer to another;

secondly it may be used to encrypt a number files on computer media; and thirdly it may be used to encrypt an entire hard disk drive.

Secret (or symmetric) key cryptography

There are two methods of encrypting information – in the first, information is encrypted effectively a bit at a time (as in binary digit) and each encrypted bit is transmitted to the recipient who decrypts it in real time. An example of this is that of GSM mobile phones in which the encrypted speech or text messages are encrypted in the handset and transmitted to the local base station where decryption takes place. The speech or text is then delivered to the recipient as plain speech or text. This is illustrated in Figure 4.1.

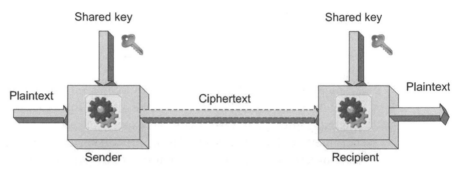

FIGURE 4.1   *Symmetric key encryption*

Encryption which works in this way is referred to as a stream cipher, examples of which are A5/1 and A5/2 used for GSM mobile encryption and RC4 which is implemented as part of the Secure Sockets Layer (SSL) technology which secures many internet e-commerce transactions.[1]

In the second method, information is encrypted in bulk as one or more blocks of data and the entire message is sent to the recipient. Decryption need not be in real time, but may take place sometime later, and is carried out on the entire block of encrypted data. This method of encryption is referred to as a block cipher. Examples of block ciphers are RC4, DES, Triple-DES and AES.

Apart from the information to be encrypted, the processes of encryption or decryption require two things – a computational method known as an algorithm and a key. Algorithms tend to be few in number as only those which deliver strong encryption can be used with any degree of certainty. The weaker algorithms are weeded out by a process of cryptanalysis in which different types of attack are made against the algorithm in order to try to recover the plain text.

The encryption key is kept as a shared secret by both sender and recipient. Keys are simply a string of binary digits or bits and, in general, the greater the key length the stronger the key is. Cryptanalysis attacks on keys generally involve an exhaustive key search or 'brute force' attack in which each possible combination of bits which make up the key are tried in turn. Eventually one will work, and by making the key greater in length, the number of possible permutations will be increased resulting in it taking longer for an attacker to identify the valid key and decrypt the message.

Another consideration is the 'cover time'. This is the minimum time for which the information must remain secret. It follows therefore that if an attacker can recover the key by brute force in less than the cover time, a stronger key is needed. That said, most key lengths in commercial use today are sufficiently strong to withstand all but the most determined attack by a very powerful computer or a large number of smaller syndicated computers as happened with the Data Encryption Standard (DES) some years ago.

DES used a 56-bit key – i.e. 2^{56} possible combinations. This was eventually broken by an exhaustive key search using a purpose-built computer in less than one week. DES security was later improved by tripling the key length to become 'Triple-DES' using a 168-bit key (2^{168} combinations). This has now been largely superseded by the Advanced Encryption Standard (AES), which is based on a block cipher algorithm.

Once the recipient has received the encrypted message, it can be decrypted using the same secret key and the same algorithm as that with which it was originally encrypted, resulting in an exact replica of the original message. This method, known as secret key or private key encryption, is also known as symmetric encryption because it makes use of the same key for both the encryption and decryption processes.

However, as we have seen, the cover time for the information may be critical to the two (or more) parties, and if successive messages are to resist unauthorised interception and decryption by an exhaustive key search, it is vital that the encryption key is changed at intervals – perhaps daily – or even for each successive message.

The problem now is how to pass on the new key to the recipient. Consider for a moment that a 'man-in-the-middle' attack[2] is taking place and that an attacker has managed to recover the message key by exhaustive key search. If the sender included the new key with the message, that key would already be compromised, so another method must be found which will permit the new key to be sent securely.

Public key (or asymmetric) cryptography

This 'key exchange problem' had been a cause of concern for many years. This was solved initially by a UK-based team but only after the formation of a company (RSA Security) was it possible to exploit the technology on a commercial basis.

The end result of solving the key exchange problem is that it is now possible to exchange secret keys between sender and receiver without them being compromised. This applies even if the message itself has been decrypted by an exhaustive key search. At the same time the recipient can be assured that the new key has originated from a trusted source and not from a 'man-in-the-middle' attacker.

In the asymmetric model, there are two entirely different keys known as a public key and a private key, both of which relate to an individual or entity. As the names suggest, the public key is intended to be used by anybody – it is not secret and is shared with anyone who needs to use it. The private key on the other hand **is** intended to be kept secret by its owner. These two keys are produced in the same operation and are mathematically linked, but in such a way that it is virtually impossible[3] to deduce the private key from the public key. Anyone can encrypt data to send to a recipient using the recipient's public key. That data can only be decrypted using the recipient's private key, known only to themselves. This means there is no need to agree and exchange a secret encryption key in advance. A complete stranger can send the recipient a private message. Figure 4.2 illustrates asymmetric key encryption.

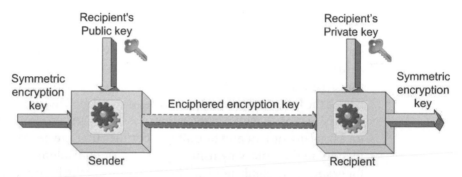

FIGURE 4.2   *Asymmetric key encryption*

Thus the exchange of symmetric keys between sender and recipient is solved – at least in part.

A further problem which still remains is that the recipient requires authentication of the sender to be certain that there is not a 'man-in-the-middle' attack in progress. Public key cryptography works just as well in reverse – if something is encrypted with a sender's private key, then it can be decrypted with his public key. Any recipient who is confident that the public key really does belong to the sender can use this to authenticate the origin of the encrypted symmetric key.

The next issue is one of integrity of the message. Verification of the integrity of a message can be achieved by a process known as 'hashing' – a hash is otherwise referred to as a message digest. A message digest is produced when a message is passed through an algorithm which will always carry out the same action on a message. There is no way to recover the original text from a strong message digest (imagine trying to re-assemble an egg once it has been scrambled).

If a message digest is produced from the original message, encrypted with the sender's private key and sent to the recipient, they will be able to decrypt this encrypted or 'signed' message digest using the sender's public key. They can then produce their own message digest and compare that with the received message digest. If the two are identical, integrity of the message has been proven. Examples of message digest algorithms are MD5 and SHA-1. This is illustrated in Figure 4.3.

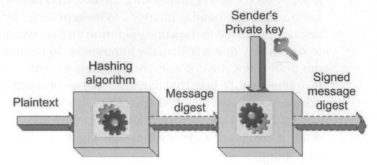

FIGURE 4.3   *Producing a signed message digest*

There remains one more link in the chain – that of authenticating the sender's public key. This can be achieved by the sender obtaining a digital certificate from a certification authority (CA) (for example Verisign) in which the CA certifies that the digital certificate signed with their private key authenticates the individual's or other entity's public key. This equates more or less to the situation in which a notary witnesses the written signature of a person on a legal document and by doing so certifies that the person has proved his identity to the notary by using a passport or equivalent identity document for example. It establishes trust in the identity of the holder of the certificate.

Most or all of the above components comprise what is generally referred to as a Public Key Infrastructure (PKI), and can be accommodated in a single transaction which might contain:

- the message, encrypted with a symmetric key, providing confidentiality of the information to be transmitted;
- the symmetric key itself, encrypted with the recipient's public key, providing confidentiality of the message key;
- the message digest, encrypted with the sender's private key, providing an integrity check on the encrypted message, an authentication check on the sender and non-repudiation of the information transmitted;
- optionally, a digital certificate, providing authentication of the sender and non-repudiation of the message sent.

Figure 4.4 illustrates how message integrity is verified.

One question which is frequently asked is 'If asymmetric key cryptography does not suffer from key distribution problems, why not use that all the time?'

The answer is quite straightforward. Symmetric key cryptography can be processed very quickly, especially if implemented in dedicated hardware. Asymmetric key cryptography on the other hand uses complex and repetitive mathematics to encrypt and decrypt information and this takes much longer to carry out, especially on computer systems with relatively slow processing capability. Asymmetric key cryptography is therefore used for encrypting and

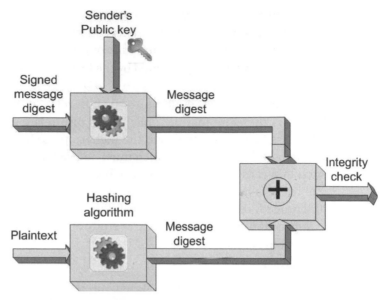

FIGURE 4.4   *Verifying message integrity*

decrypting shorter items of information – such as keys and message digests as discussed, leaving symmetric key cryptography to encrypt and decrypt larger volumes of information.

Pretty Good Privacy

The need for reliable, available encryption prompted an American, Phil Zimmermann, to develop Pretty Good Privacy (PGP) in the late 1980s. It contained all the elements described above – symmetric keys to encrypt information and asymmetric keys to secure the symmetric keys and to sign message digests. It also included the ability to encrypt files on disk and to exchange secure email messages.

PGP is now available commercially in a number of forms and it also provides for digital certificates, but, instead of relying on certification authorities, PGP operates a so-called 'web of trust', which is ideally suited to small networks of users. In this model, each user acts as a CA for other users whom he trusts. By extension therefore if someone trusts this user, they will also inherit his trust of the other users.

General policies for cryptography

Policies for the use of cryptography will be largely based on the results of risk assessments (see earlier chapter), to a certain extent on legal requirements such as data protection and on regulatory requirements which may be sector-specific, for example in financial services.

Policies must take into consideration:

- the method of storage of information;
- the method of transmission of information;

- the required cover time for the information;
- the relative strength of the encryption algorithms and key sizes – when offset against the cost and time of processing;
- the relative risks presented by the loss of confidentiality or integrity of information;
- the laws of the countries in which it will be used.

It follows therefore that the policies will also relate closely to an information classification scheme, and the higher up the hierarchy, the greater the strength of the encryption which must be used. Policies will also determine such things as the frequency at which keys must be changed and how (and where) keys are stored and managed, which in turn will involve processes and procedures, roles and responsibilities and segregation of duties.

Suggestions for further reading or study on the subject of cryptography are given at the end of the book.

If we consider GANT's situation there is a great deal of information contained in the computer system which could cause problems if it were to fall into the wrong hands. As we have seen in Chapter 1, there are two areas of particular interest.

(i) Information is currently kept openly on the GANT website which identifies the locations where the Natterjack toad breeds and lives, which could be of interest to property developers.

(ii) Financial information about the members' fees and grants provided is also kept on GANT's computer and, while disclosure of this information itself might not be a major issue, it could render members and sponsors vulnerable to intimidation, as some of their personal details (aside from those that they wish to be made public) might be openly available.

At the same time, GANT does need to publicise its work through its website, and clearly there must be some form of segregation of information which is available through this – keeping the public information openly available – while securing the confidential information and allowing bona fide members to access it through secure means.

It is also necessary from time to time for members (especially committee members) to exchange this information electronically.

Activity 4.22

Describe the steps GANT might take in order to protect its databases from unauthorised access and alteration beyond those afforded by simple password protection of the user area on their computer system.

Suggest how a commercial product such as PGP might be introduced in order to secure sensitive information passing between GANT committee members.

TRAINING

Protecting the organisation's information is not usually at the top of most managers' priorities. They are more likely to be concentrating on immediate pressures like hitting targets or meeting deadlines. They may not have considered how reliant they are on their Information Systems to help them achieve these goals or whether these systems are vulnerable. Too often, the need to secure data properly is only brought to one's attention after it is lost or becomes corrupted. Ensuring that users therefore understand their assurance responsibilities, and are aware of the risks to their Information Systems, is a key security control.

LEARNING OUTCOMES

The intention of this section is to provide the reader with the basic knowledge needed to develop assurance training initiatives within an enterprise. Following study in this area, the reader should be able not only to explain and justify the main concepts but also to develop a high-level approach and draft documents to meet the general requirements in the areas of:

- purpose and role of assurance training;
- approaches to training and promoting awareness;
- available training materials;
- sources of information for training material.

Purpose and role of security training

Organisations need both their staff and any third parties accessing their information to comply with the Information Assurance policies and procedures in order to reduce the likelihood of assurance issues. Providing appropriate assurance training will help individuals to understand their assurance responsibilities, how the enterprise's information assets can be put at risk and how this can be avoided. Enterprises that do not implement awareness and training initiatives are more likely to experience security-related issues. Assurance training is, in relative terms, a low-cost assurance control that can create a positive and lasting change in users' behaviour.

By understanding the risks, your users are more likely to remember what they need to do to protect the organisation's information and the systems containing it. For example, most people would realise that leaving their wallet on display in an unlocked car could attract an opportunist thief. They would certainly have a personal appreciation of the loss and inconvenience caused by its theft. However, they might not equate the loss of information assets in quite the same way. They also might not be aware that disclosure of sensitive information could lead to a breach of current Data Protection legislation or that not following a set procedure, such as a data backup, could result in a severe financial loss to the enterprise.

Anyone with access to the enterprise's Information Systems should receive some form of Information Assurance education and training. The level of training that they may need can vary with their role, but it should be sufficient to ensure that they can carry out essential assurance procedures and have sufficient understanding of the correct use of their Information Systems. It should always include awareness of the Acceptable Use Policy, no matter who they are.

The key messages, tone and approach of an assurance training or awareness programme must be relevant to the intended audience and consistent with the values and goals of the enterprise. Messages may contain common themes but the language and delivery should be tailored to suit the audience. Therefore, when developing assurance training, thought should be given to the messages to be conveyed and what needs to be achieved. It should consider the following questions:

- What does this group of people need to know?
- Why do they need to know it?
- What is their current understanding?
- What should they think and do after the messages have been delivered?

Do use language that they will understand and avoid jargon. Examples and case studies will need to convey 'real-life scenarios' and be appropriate to them. Security incidents that may have occurred previously within the enterprise or within other similar organisations are always useful to get the message home.

Assurance awareness and training should be seen as a continuous process rather than as a once-only exercise. Its overall objective is to reduce Information Assurance risk by developing a positive security culture. This is achieved by increasing the level of understanding about Information Assurance and explaining to users what is expected of them to protect the organisation's information assets.

Approaches to training and promoting awareness

There are two broad approaches to improving levels of knowledge; firstly, through specific Information Assurance training, and secondly, through raising awareness of Information Assurance. Training tends to be focused and addresses specific issues. Its primary aim is to achieve within the user a certain level of competence in a given area. Awareness is more general and aims to create a change in user behaviour and influence the perception of risk.

Individual campaigns should be developed to target particular areas for improvement, cater for the various types of audiences or to cover some specific assurance matters. Effective campaigns need to be meaningful to their audience to result in a long-lasting change in user behaviour and should concentrate on what an individual can do to improve assurance.

As with other assurance activities, it is important to gain sponsorship from the senior management of the enterprise. If senior management are seen to value and support positive security behaviour, then line management and general staff members are more likely to adopt similar behaviour themselves. Without senior sponsorship, line managers may be reluctant to release staff members to take part in the campaign or communicate the need for assurance to them. In turn, staff members may not take the campaign seriously as they may not have been given sufficient time and support to be involved, nor may they appreciate the importance of assurance within their roles as this may not have been communicated to them.

An awareness campaign or assurance training programme should be developed as a formal project with agreed objectives so that it can be delivered efficiently and measured for success. It is important to concentrate on the assurance issues that are relevant to the enterprise and not about what the hot topics are within the industry.

The issues that will be addressed by the project and the training messages should be identified. Each training message should explain the assurance issue and what can be done to address it. If users do not understand what the problem is and what is expected of them to help address it, then they are less likely to adopt the desired behaviour. Constant repetition of the same messages or information presented in a dull manner will create user disinterest. Some issues like password sharing are perennial problems, but it is important to try and deliver them each time in a fresh way.

The type of approach adopted will be constrained by a number of factors including the size of the enterprise, its culture, available funds and either the scale or the scope of the campaign. If the organisation has a press office, communications specialist or perhaps a training department, then try and involve them as they should be able to provide guidance and advice on a suitable approach.

Timing is everything. To get the best attention from the target audience, schedule campaigns to fit in with working schedules and enterprise priorities. Avoid busy times such as year-end accounting, month ends, peak sales periods or peak holiday periods.

Available training materials

There is a variety of methods and materials that can be used to support awareness and training campaigns. Choice is usually constrained by budgets and the size and culture of the organisation.

Face-to-face presentations are effective as the participant is able to interact directly with the trainer but they can be resource intensive, especially if many people need to be trained. External training courses can be used to cover specialist topics. If there are sufficient numbers it is sometimes more cost effective to get an external trainer to carry out the training course on the premises. As an alternative, courses or workshops could be developed in-house. Messages can then be tailored to each audience and the sessions repeated many times over at little or no extra cost. Face-to-face training will take staff members away from their normal activities for periods of time, so this approach could meet with resistance from line managers unless support is gained from senior management.

Training videos and DVDs can deliver a message that is consistent through-out the organisation and have the benefit of being easily transportable. This could work out as a reasonably low-cost option if it is needed to be viewed by users across many office locations, branches, retail outlets or homes. They are less personal than face-to-face training and it is less easy to track who has viewed or completed the training. They can sometimes be costly to pro-duce and they are not always easily adapted if circumstances or technology change. There are companies that provide off-the-shelf training videos cov-ering subjects that may be appropriate to the enterprise or which may be adapted. With this approach there are potential issues over access to the necessary DVD- or video-playing equipment and often a loss of the actual media.

Computer-based training (CBT) provides a similar solution to videos and DVDs but can be more interactive and have the advantage of being delivered directly to the user's desktop, minimising their time spent away from the workplace. Obviously, they are only relevant to people who use or have access to a PC workstation as part of their job function. Most CBT packages are able to offer a tracking system to record attendance and any scores from tests. Again external companies may be able to provide an off-the-shelf solution at a reasonable cost. In some instances a CBT module can be used for an initial Information Assurance campaign and then included as part of an induction course to ensure new personnel understand the assurance culture and requirements of the enterprise when they start.

Electronic formats such as workstation screen savers and emails can also be a useful way to deliver important or timely assurance messages straight to the desktop. Many organisations have intranets and these can also be used effectively and at low cost to convey training and awareness messages. There are a numberof external companies that produce awareness material again at low cost that can be adapted for use on intranet sites. The distribution may be quick and easy but electronic methods rely on the end user choosing to access and read the information. Systems for the effective management of not only assurance policies, but any other policy too, are now available and gaining in popularity. These can include asking the reader a number of pertinent questions before allowing them sign as having understood the policy.

There are numerous visual aids that can be used to convey assurance messages. These include paper-based media such as posters, leaflets, book-lets, brochures and reference cards. They are relatively low cost to produce and can be effective. However, there is no guarantee they will actually reach your intended audience so they need to be supported by other methods. For example, posters can reinforce the messages delivered within a CBT module or a face-to-face training session. Leaflets or postcards could be sent by the director responsible for Information Assurance by contacting all department managers and asking them to get their staff members to read them. Finally, most people enjoy being given a small gift so personalised items such as pens, mouse mats, puzzles or stress balls can play a part in delivering key Information Assurance messages.

Measurement of success is a difficult area. A test or quiz at the end of a face-to-face training session, video, DVD or CBT module can gauge to some degree how much the participant has learnt. It can also provide a record that the participant has successfully completed the course for either regulatory, administrative or diligence purposes. Effective assurance training should attempt to deliver a positive change in user behaviour which will lead to a reduction in losses from assurance incidents and reduce risk, but it is often difficult to properly quantify and measure has much value has been gained by the organisation. However, compared with other control methods, awareness is a relatively low-cost control and even a minor change in behaviour will far outweigh the costs of any investment.

Sources of information for training material

As the approach and content of a training or awareness programme needs to be tailored to the requirements of the enterprise it is necessary to do a certain amount of research in selecting appropriate material. Specialist training organisations can help to source information and help to tailor an approach but there are many other sources of information many of which are online.

Within the UK the various government departments give advice to individuals and organisations on how to protect their information, provide warnings of potential threats and offer news about Information Assurance problems. The European Network and Information Security Agency (ENISA) is a European Union initiative that has produced user guides on how to raise Information Assurance awareness. These are also available in French, German and Spanish. The Americans also have a non-regulatory Federal agency – the National Institute for Standards and Technology (NIST) – which provides advice on assurance training.

Some government organisations provide specialist training. The UK Cabinet Office have an Infosec Training Paths and Competencies (ITPC) scheme, which offers qualifications that accredit skill for Information Assurance specialists and contractors working in central government, the police and other areas of government.

Information can also be gained through industry conferences and seminars. These can be a useful source of information as the issues discussed tend to be current and topical. They also provide an opportunity to network with industry peers who are generally facing similar challenges. Some conferences are run by vendors and may be free to attend. Trade bodies are also able to provide industry specific content.

Industry-based magazines and publications often provide many useful articles and features on a wide range of Information Assurance matters. There are numerous online newsgroups and bulletin boards that can provide relevant information. Organisations such as the SANS Institute (Sysadmin, Audit, Network, Security) share good security practice and provide a wealth of information, quite often at no cost.

> Last month Dr Peabody left some papers containing details of some of the members on a bus. Fortunately they were handed in to the bus company who were able to return them. There was also an attempted break-in to the office a while ago where a small amount of money was taken, which caused a lot of disruption as membership papers were strewn over the floor by the thieves as they were looking for cash. Ms Jackson is concerned that the level of assurance training within GANT is not high and needs to be improved as a priority especially concerning the protection of members' information.

Activity 4.23

(i) What would you include in an initial awareness campaign and why?

(ii) What methods would you use to get your message across?

PHYSICAL AND ENVIRONMENTAL SECURITY

There is a need for Information Security managers to have a good appreciation of associated physical security issues so that they can make sure there is a seamless Information Assurance management system across the whole organisation.

LEARNING OUTCOMES

Following study in this area, the reader should be able to define and explain each of the following terms and be able to describe their appropriate use as applicable.

General controls

There are three principal types of control that are available to the security manager. Each has its place and role to play and, when used in conjunction with one another, can supplement and enhance the overall assurance of an organisation significantly and effectively. However, if they are used inappropriately or without due consideration, they can actually end up reducing overall assurance by providing a loophole, weak link or back door into a secure environment. The old adage that a chain is only as strong as its weakest link is still very true.

Physical security

Physical security relies on the presence or otherwise of physical limitations to the activities a criminal or other unauthorised person might wish to carry out. The origins of such security are almost as old as man himself – ancient earth-works such as Maiden Castle in Dorset are evidence of an era when man had to protect himself from fellow man and indeed probably from the animal world too to some extent. The high ramparts of earth were later replaced by stone ramparts of castles which were also supplemented by moats and the like.

Today these are replaced by walls, fences and other obstacles that can prevent, or at least make it very difficult for, an intruder gaining access. Locks on doors of varying degrees of sophistication do the same job – provided the door itself is strong enough. There have been instances where very expensive digital or combination locks have been put on doors which themselves could be lifted off the hinges or simply forced open by battering the hinges off their mountings.

It is usual for physical security to be the first line of defence in many organisations. Stopping people from entering the building, or at least having a reception area where they are 'detained' until suitable authority or other arrangements are made, is the usual first point of security. However, these are only useful and successful if the reception is properly manned and that it 'guards' the only entrance into the building. Fire escapes, back doors left open for those escaping the office for a breath of fresh air and other similar entrances must also be suitably protected. For the more adventurous, climbing walls and fences to gain access to roof lights, upper floor windows or stairs is also a source of a security risk that must be assessed and managed.

On the smaller scale once inside a building the use of locks for offices, server rooms and other sensitive areas is again commonplace. Locks on filing cabinets, desks and other document storage facilities are also commonplace and entirely suitable as one layer of security whilst accepting that they will not deter for long the most determined criminal.

Technical security

Technical security is the general term used for any security measure that employs technology in some way. This is usually related to computers and the software techniques that can be employed but it could equally apply to technical locks using tokens or finger prints, to hardware through the 'locking' or disabling of ports or to some other technological solution for a specific application.

One of the main concerns about such measures is the ease with which they can be overcome. Some are undoubtedly very difficult to circumvent and, in the case of encryption for example and as discussed earlier, the better encryption techniques are essentially uncrackable in any real sense of the word. There have been instances though where electronic locks have been used that, when there was a power failure, were left in a 'safe state' of unlocked hence providing no protection at all. It has been acknowledged that some of the early attempts at technological security measures using tokens were less than successful when it was found that any credit card with a security strip could be used to operate the lock rather than just the authorised one.

Things have got better and there is now a wide array of security measures that can be taken by security managers. The use of a device or system that has been independently checked by some authority, such as the British Government's certified products schemes (Security Equipment Assessment Panel, SEAP), provides a significant increase in the level of assurance provided by the technological device. The use of cryptography as a means of protecting valuable or sensitive information either in storage or in transit has developed very significantly and is now widely available to anyone who has a need for its use. The use of the Secure Sockets Layer (SSL) in electronic transactions on the internet is a good example where some complex cryptographic systems have been made to work in a very simple and straightforward way to the benefit of the general public.

Also in this category the use of electronic door locks, swipe card readers and the like can be included. These technical devices are more secure than their basic mechanical counterparts but may still suffer from similar problems. Tailgating – the art of following a legitimate entrant into a building very closely before the door has had time to close again – is a well-known issue. The provision of individual 'pods' with automated doors allowing only one person in at a time, can counteract this problem. Once inside, if a visitor is left to wander the building unaccompanied, this then presents further security issues.

Procedural security

Procedural security covers the rules, regulations and policies that an organisation puts in place to help reduce the risk of issues arising. They could for example include clauses in employment contracts that legally bind employees to obeying the system security policy or other appropriate rules and regulations. Whilst in itself this doesn't prevent problems happening, it can make them less attractive to staff if they know they could be disciplined for contravening the rules. As a matter of interest, this has now begun to happen, with several members of staff from different organisations, in both the public and private sectors, being dismissed for breaking such polices.

This sort of measure would also cover the correct vetting of staff before they are employed to ensure they don't have any convictions or other incidents in their background that might mean they are unsuitable for employment in a specific area. The induction training or probation period of employment might be another way of ensuring staff are fully aware of their responsibilities as soon as they join an organisation. Setting standard ways of doing particular tasks associated with information might also be applicable. If for example there must always be two people present when the safe is opened or two people have to confirm the destruction of highly classified material, this too would be a procedural measure.

Overall it is a layered approach to assurance that provides the best solution. This means that all three types of security are used in varying degrees to protect the organisation's information assets. A set of controls need to be implemented effectively such as:

- controls getting into the site (procedural and physical);
- further checks for specific high-risk buildings (procedural, physical and technical);
- specific logons to computer systems containing or processing classified data (technical and procedural);
- a set of well-drafted and effectively policed policies of which staff are well aware and have signed contracts to that effect (procedural).

This combination will provide a high level of assurance and should prevent most incidents happening.

Protection of equipment

To take the idea of different types of control a little further, we might consider the threat of equipment being stolen or taken off site by unauthorised staff. Another possible scenario is the loss of the use of some critical equipment, such as filtration units or air conditioning units becoming ineffective through fault, power failure or other cause.

If it is clear from the business impact analysis that the consequences of these problems would be significant to the organisation in some way, perhaps loss of revenue, loss of credibility, reputational losses or equivalent, then it may be decided that there should be some measure taken to reduce the impact or perhaps even remove the cause of such a problem. This might mean marking all equipment in some way to lessen the attractiveness of equipment to potential theft from either staff or outsiders. Alternatively it might be deemed appropriate to have a stand-by power-generator connected through an Uninterruptible Power Supply (UPS) so that if the mains power fails then the generator automatically cuts in to maintain the supply. This is frequently used for such systems as air traffic control computers, hospital life support systems and critical financial and manufacturing systems.

Simply having appropriate maintenance contracts and service level agreements with realistic timings for the provision of an engineer, for example, are further ways that can be used to enhance the security of the assets with which we are concerned. Provision of alternative power or data supplies is an approach that can achieve the necessary level of service provision, but it will come as no surprise to say that all these come at a price. Sometimes that price will be too great and the organisation may have to accept a lower level of support or a longer period of downtime before a remedy is in place. Realistic assessment of the risk and its impact on the organisation is the key.

As an example, when undertaking a full risk assessment for a public body, each section was asked to define how long they could survive (continue to operate effectively) if all the computers were unavailable. Some sections mentioned minutes up to a couple of hours whilst other could survive perhaps a day. In the personnel department though, they were quite happy to work on for up to a month because much of what they were doing at that time was paper-based. It wasn't until the staff needed paying that the computer systems were critical and so this meant the acceptable downtime could be as long as several weeks but might only be a couple of days if it was coming up to pay day.

How critical elements of any system can be protected is very much determined by physical and technical options. The main power supply to a building might be the only one. If an over-enthusiastic road worker digs up and breaks the cable with his excavator when putting in a new drain, it might take some days for that to be repaired. Would it be appropriate for the organisation housed in the building to go to the not-inconsiderable expense of putting in a secondary backup supply either in the form of a second cable or a standby generator? Probably not in the case of GANT but it might well be if the organisation is a high-street bank with millions of transactions to be dealt with each day.

Inside a building the protection of cables and similar equipment can be equally important. It is not unknown for an ordinary mains electricity socket in the hallways or passageways of buildings to be used for network equipment. If the cleaner decides to use that socket to plug in a vacuum cleaner, significant problems could arise. Some companies wire their buildings with two or more separate circuits: one for critical electrical equipment like computers; one for other electrical equipment that can be unavailable during an electrical supply outage without serious impact on the business; one for normal lighting circuit, desk-lamps and the like; one for emergency lighting in case of fire, power outage and the like. To do this is not cheap but will provide a high level of availability if the circuits are properly used. Often different coloured or different types of sockets are used to prevent the wrong things being plugged into each circuit.

Activity 4.24

Looking at the records and information held by GANT, suggest how long these sections of the group might be able to continue operating effectively if they lost their main computer system which contains all their details.

(i)   Membership secretary;

(ii) general enquiries on the Natterjack toad breeding ground details;

(iii) forthcoming planning application where there was interest in the toads;

(iv) financial information.

Suggest factors that might affect the time scale.

Need for processes to handle intruder alerts, etc.

For each of the three types of control mentioned above there may be one of three uses: preventative action, detective action or reactive action. These three uses can apply equally to each of the three types in so far as it is possible to use the different controls in different ways.

For example, physical security is mainly intended for use as a preventative control – to stop unauthorised people getting into a building, for example. However, it is also possible to use such controls as detective controls – intruder alarms for example – and, although perhaps not so desirable, to use them as reactive controls such as electrified fences such that a potential intruder is 'rewarded' for their trouble by being detected, arrested and therefore prevented perhaps from trying it again.

Similarly, technical controlscan be used in three ways and anti-virus software is an example where in fact the same system can be used in all three. The software tries to prevent any malware being loaded on a computer system (preventative), will routinely run checks to ensure there is none installed (detective) and then provides a system for virus removal should something get through (reactive).

An example of procedural controlsmight be a non-disclosure agreement to protect the intellectual property rights of an organisation. This is designed to prevent unauthorised disclosure by warning of the consequences if such an event takes place and advising staff that they should not release such information without authority (preventative). It might include details of the measures taken to prevent such disclosure including numbering of copies, limited and controlled distribution on signature, etc. (detective). It then might include details of the possible consequences which can be used in the event of a breach – dismissal, legal action or similar (reactive).

Clearly there needs to be a combination of controls to provide an effective coverage. The tools used to prevent incidents can and do fail and so a 'backup' system to detect such events and the potential consequences of such a breach must also be in place. It is no use, for example, having an intruder detection system installed if the system is not monitored routinely and effectively at all times. The five minutes when the security guard pops out to make a cup of tea is inevitably going to be the moment when an intruder makes their entrance.

Clearly there is also a link between the differing types of controls and their uses. The procedures may define the technological protection measures that are used behind some physical barrier. All these need not only to be present but also to be consistent and appropriate. It is pointless protecting information assets with very expensive disaster recovery plans including hot backup sites, for example, if the information is not critical to the organisation and work can continue more or less as normal for a few days without great inconvenience. Once again this is back to the risk assessment, business impact analysis and cost benefit analysis to determine what is appropriate and necessary in any given situation.

When staff leave the employment of an organisation, how they are looked after during the interval between being told they are no longer required and actually leaving the buildings can also be a tricky period. If the separation is not voluntary, in other words the staff member has been told to leave, there is every likelihood that they might try to leave with either some valuable asset of the company or having done something to some asset of the company.

Once again there are stories of disgruntled employees putting malware onto computer systems that run after the employee has departed, of deleting or copying important files in the interval between being sacked and actually leaving, and so on. It is now common practice, and often laid down in the personnel department's procedures, that such soon-to-be-ex-employees should be escorted off the premises and be told there that their personal belongings will be forwarded to them shortly. The removal of their access to all systems including doors and computers, the changing of passwords or codes to which they have had access all have to happen in a similar time frame if the security of the organisation is not to be compromised. It is always worth considering how you would do this if the person to be sacked is your senior, or only, system administrator.

Clear screen and desk policy

With so much data processing now being completed on computer systems, it is inevitable that there will be times when computers are left unattended with sensitive information displayed on the screen. It may be for a short period whilst the staff member collects a cup of coffee but should they then get called away or the fire alarm goes off, the information might be displayed for some time. With the increasing use of open-plan offices where the screens of fellow workers are easily visible to anyone wandering by, it becomes all the more important to protect that information. It may be reasonable to assume that all those walking the floors of such offices are legitimate members of staff with not only a right to be there but suitable authority to see such sensitive information. In other circumstances though, it may be less certain who those wandering by might be.

The use of third-party companies to carry out routine tasks, often some of the more menial including cleaning, presents further issues to the security manager. The supplying company may use staff who have little security clearance and yet they may be free to enter all offices or working areas more or less unsupervised and, whilst there, can gain access to the unlocked filing cabinet, logged-on computers and papers left lying around or in rubbish bins.

In one government department the decision was taken, due to the sensitivity of most of the information they process, to prevent anyone who was not suitably authorised even entering the building. Instead they established a visitors' centre where guests could be hosted and meetings could take place outside the confines of the main building. However, even in this climate of protection for their information, a clear screen policy is enforced to avoid those without a need to know getting to see information they shouldn't.

There has to be an acceptable compromise here. If the time default of the clear screen is set too short it becomes a real annoyance to workers who continually have to enter their password to re-access their computers, whilst if it is too long a period, too much damage could be done by inappropriate people seeing sensitive information. Nevertheless, a suitable time for the screen to be cleared by a standard screen-saver system should be determined and on almost all occasions employed on every computer without allowing the users the option of turning it off. It may simply be better to ensure all users lock their keyboards and invoke the screen-saver whenever they leave their desk, relying on the automated system as a fallback system only.

'If a cluttered desk is the sign of a cluttered mind, what is the significance of a clean desk?' goes the quotation from Laurence J. Peter, a US educator and writer who died in 1988. A tidy or clean desk might be more pleasing to the eye, easier to work at and have all sorts of other benefits but most importantly it allows those items which are sensitive or valuable in some way to be properly looked after. If a desk is cluttered, sensitive documents may well become covered by other papers. Then, when the owner of the desk takes a quick look before leaving the desk for a while, they don't see the potential security breach hidden on the desk.

This is all the more important at the end of a day's work. It is then that a clear desk is much easier to check for important documents that should be locked away. This does include documents which might in many circumstances not be regarded as sensitive. Perhaps a directory of all the staff is left out as it is considered not to be very sensitive. However, if the policy of the organisation is to use something akin to an individual's name as their logon name for the computer systems, as can be very common, this document becomes very helpful to a potential hacker. This could be the contract cleaner who has time to try their hand at getting into the system whilst ostensibly cleaning up each night. All they then need is to watch the unwary user typing in their password when they are working late one night and the potential hacker has all they need to hack into the system and do whatever takes their fancy!

Activity 4.25

The study in which the GANT secretary works is as cluttered as any one might have seen. There are piles of paper and books everywhere with filing cabinets left open and windows unlocked. She argues that no one would be interested in her study and, anyway, if she can't find anything how would anyone else.

Suggest three reasons, with some justification, as to why she should consider the implications of a clear desk policy.

Suggest why other security measures might be appropriate and how she might achieve a secure working environment.

Moving property on and off site

The control of an organisation's property both on and off site is another area of critical interest to those concerned with assurance. Apocryphal stories abound, along with the genuine ones, of laptops left here and there, pictures of new models of car being released to the press before the official launch by the use of camera-phones, CDs being lost in the post, classified rubbish being found at the roadside, a salesman being sacked and taking the company's database of clients with him and so on. These are just a very small sample of the more recent incidents but not long ago there were similar stories about thieves backing lorries into offices and removing all the computers, all the memory chips being stolen out of office computer systems by cleaners and valuable stock items, jewels for example, have been the target of crime almost since the beginning of the consumer society.

The way in which property is securely moved around is very dependent on the nature of the property and its value both intrinsically and to business operations. It might be a very cheap item but if it takes a while to find a replacement and have it delivered from the other side of the world, its loss could be critical to the continued business operations of the organisation.

There are some fairly obvious ways of reducing such risks. Firstly marking all assets with an indelible mark that uniquely identifies it is a good start. This then allows a full inventory of all assets to be taken and maintained. As equipment is exchanged for newer items, then the register must be maintained. Only allowing those with the appropriate authority and skills to move equipment around is another useful control. This is especially pertinent to technical equipment such as computers and photocopiers. These often need specialist skills or resources in order to set them to work effectively after the move and anyway may require additional work such as extra power points to make the move possible. When such an item is moved it should be automatic that the asset register is updated with the new location so that the next time the service engineer arrives, he can be directed to the right office.

Taking equipment off site should also be controlled. The idea of a staff member being able to remove from an organisation's site a laptop containing all the details of the customers of that organisation without any control suggests that the organisation is not too concerned about their customers and that the organisation may be out of business before too long. Clearly laptops and the like are essential tools for the mobile staff member but the control of the information it contains and to which it might give access is also very important. Limiting the facility to take copies of company databases, controlling access to company intranets when accessing the network from off site and other similar controls can be very useful.

Laying down clear procedures to which staff members must sign up concerning how they use the equipment, where it must be stored when not in use and the like is another area where assurance and good practice coincide. The added concerns of the health and safety aspects of the use of company equipment at home and elsewhere are further issues, outside the scope of this book, which must be considered and to wrap all these up in one well-drafted policy for the use of such equipment can be very effective.

This needs to extend to all equipment and access to any asset, information or otherwise, of the organisation. Rules governing the use of mobile telephones are now fairly widespread within many organisations, both private and public sector, controlling their use inside buildings. Indeed it is becoming more common for all mobile phones to have to be surrendered before entering buildings where commercial or very sensitive information might be visible to the casual visitor. It was the lack of such a control that allowed the pictures of a new car to find their way onto the internet long before the official launch of the vehicle.

Overall the world of information is now a very mobile one where we expect to be able to gain access to almost any information relevant to our work or daily lives effectively at anytime, anywhere on a variety of media types. Whilst technology is rapidly allowing this to happen, it is less clear how the assurance world is keeping pace. Whilst significant advances in assurance have been evident in recent years, there is still a long way to go. Dealing with the compromise that is inevitable between full and effective assurance and the availability of information as, when and wherever we might need it is still a difficult judgement call.

Procedures for secure disposal

The disposal of equipment or other information assets that are no longer required has often been another source of good stories: the confidential files being found in second-hand filing cabinets; the valuable or sensitive files found on hard disks in computers that have been sent for disposal but found their way into the second-hand market; the classified waste bags found on open rubbish tips and so on. Having procedures that ensure that any filing cabinet, desk drawer or other container is properly checked by two competent people before it is allowed off site is a good start but there are more issues to consider.

Policies and procedures for the secure disposal of any piece of equipment or other asset, including waste paper, are crucial. Simply writing a policy is not really enough. A recent study by an academic institution into files found on the hard drives of used computers showed that many of the computers had been passed over to a contractor for disposal. It was then assumed by the organisation that everything would be OK. What they failed to do was check on what the contractor actually did with such things. Selling them on an auction site on the internet is not uncommon and if the asset is more valuable, a nicely specified laptop for example, then the temptation to make a little extra money out of the contract is very strong.

A contractor engaged to remove classified wastefrom an office brought a very smart, well-secured vehicle to collect the waste documents but, instead of taking them for secure destruction as expected, the driver simply dumped the sacks of waste in open rubbish skips where anyone could open them and take the contents. It is the responsibility of the organisation, whose information assets have been sent for disposal, to follow a contract through to ensure all is well and the contractor is actually doing as expected.

Electronic mediaare a particular problem. It is often assumed that simply pressing the delete key on a computer will remove the information completely from the system and that is unfortunately very far from the truth. The way data is stored and used on a computer means that destroying it is not like taking a paper file out of the drawer and shredding its contents in a decent cross-cut shredder. That will make reconstitution of the information on paper virtually impossible. With a computer the data is retained long after the delete key is pressed. There are a numberof ways to completely delete the information including writing random data to the same data store a number of times, physically destroying the media itself – cutting-up or shredding hard drives, for example – but most need some special technical equipment or knowledge. Thus it is again important that the assurance professional is ready and able to call in specialist advice and guidance when necessary to ensure appropriate measures are taken.

Security requirements in delivery and loading areas

Delivery and loading areas are often remote from the main buildings of organisations. This brings with it additional security issues that must be addressed. Many of the biggest raids in the UK have been at least initiated by attacking the staff in the receipt or dispatch area of a warehouse or factory. It is common for those working in such areas to have lower security clearances than other members of staff, reflecting their lack of access to critical business information. This may be short-sighted. If those responsible for the receipt and dispatch of goods are regarded as the last check before sending items for disposal, then they need to be cleared appropriately since potentially they will have access to a lot of business critical information. If the goods dealt with are assets of the company, new computers for example, then they need as much protection in the receipt and dispatch areas as they receive in all other parts of the organisation. Simply the sight of heaps of polystyrene, plastic and cardboard can indicate the arrival of a new batch of desktops which could encourage thieves to take a closer look.

Indeed it might be suggested that they need even more protection since it would be easy for an unscrupulous worker receiving such items to misappropriate them declaring they had not been received, were damaged on receipt or use some other explanation for their absence. In a similar way, if old items of IT equipment are to be dispatched for secure disposal via a contractor, it would not be difficult for the devious worker to devise a means by which some of those goods never reach the appropriate destination but are sent off for sale on the internet or local car boot sale. It is believed that this is a fairly common example of company information being released inappropriately.

DISASTER RECOVERY AND BUSINESS CONTINUITY MANAGEMENT

Even in the best-prepared organisations, problems will arise. Hopefully these problems will have been anticipated in some way and preparations will have been made to deal with them. This section of the book looks at what the security manager needs to understand in order to deal effectively with the inevitable problems that can, and most likely will, arise.

LEARNING OUTCOMES

Following study in this area, the reader should be able to define and explain each of the following terms and be able to describe their appropriate use as applicable.

Relationship between BCP and DR

A Business Continuity Plan (BCP) is, as the name suggests, all about maintaining the continuity of business operations. Problems will always occur in any organisation no matter how well run it might be and these problems will adversely affect the operational capability in some way. It might be something seemingly very simple such as the main printer running out of toner through to something much more serious such as a power outage. In either case the situation will be made much more acceptable to both users and senior managers if someone has thought through what might happen and put in place some tried and tested plans to deal with it. Maintaining normal operations as effectively as possible whilst resolving the issue is the approach that must be taken.

There is a second issue. In an ideal world, if concern over the assurance of information is very high the way to achieve the 'ultimate secure environment' is to lock all information in a large safe and lock the door. This would have the effect of ensuring that no one would be able to access the information inappropriately but would have the seemingly disastrous result of making the information virtually impossible to use. The solution is therefore clearly some form of compromise which is, as mentioned earlier, what Information Assurance is all about. The availability of information is critical and business continuity planning is part of that mechanism to allow operations to continue come what may.

Clearly there may be times when the problem that has arisen is so major or significant that normal operations are damaged or disrupted beyond reasonable or rapid repair. This is when disaster recovery (DR) takes over and plans for dealing with the most major of issues is a key area of Information Assurance. This deals with having to do things in a significantly different manner as a result of some very major problem. It might be short term or long term before 'normal operations' are restored. Indeed it may be that the normal operations are never restored in which case the DR plan may become the new 'normal operations'.

Naturally, as we have learnt earlier in this book, the keys to planning of this sort are the risk assessment and business impact analysis (BIA). It is possible to consider major disaster recovery plans involving hot, warm or cold backup sites, significant investment and major planning and testing but if the anticipated problem is only going to happen once in a hundred years, and only then as a result of some event so significant that half the western world has been thrown into uproar and disarray, then it is probably not sensible to expend significant amounts on a disaster recovery plan – unless you are the organisation that is required to deal with that situation of course!

The degree to which a DR plan is developed has to depend entirely on the BIA. If the impact of any specific or general event is so severe as to significantly increase the likelihood of the organisation not being able to operate effectively ever again, then this must be anticipated and appropriate plans developed. On the other hand if the event is likely to cause minor disruption and can be dealt with in the first few hours of the situation to get back to normal, significant investment is possibly not required. There is though another factor to consider. If this seemingly minor event occurs each week, then the cumulative effect of the event may raise its importance and impact and, therefore, the likely acceptable expense on its BCP.

A key difference between BCP and DR is the scale of the plans invoked in any specific situation. If the plan calls for minor adjustments to normal working practices or, at the most, a comparatively small change in normal operations, then this should form part of the BCP. If on the other hand the plan requires whole-scale evacuation, major changes to the way things are normally done or a prolonged period of major disruption, then this is classed as DR. There is also a clear link to financial consequences as well, both in terms of the disruption to operations and the cost of the implementation of the plans.

The last line in the syllabus covers the distinction between DR and BCP in each operational environment. It is critical that each of these aspects is considered and processes, safeguards, provisions and other activities are based securely on the risk assessment and the consequential BIA. Inevitably this will mean that some organisations place great emphasis on the DR side of their planning whilst others might choose effectively to ignore that and deal only with the BCP side. Whilst at first glance this may seem foolhardy, it may actually be the most sensible way of dealing with the issue in the most cost-effective manner.

It may be, for example, that a business concludes that the only real risk to its continued operation in the medium term – the area covered by DR for example – might be that there is a major disruption of all services in the office block in which they operate. However, if those services are commonplace, water, telephones, electricity, computers, etc., and there are many similar establishments within an appropriate distance that could provide these facilities, then it may be entirely acceptable simply to ensure that all records are duplicated and maintained in secure storage somewhere else without the need for a DR plan that is any more complicated.

On the other hand, in a business driven by the rapid turnover of cash as a result, say, of retail e-sales, a short-term loss of its website could mean a major downturn in productivity and hence finance. In this case the emphasis might need to be on very significant BCP and DR planning if they are to be able to cope with any eventuality. The operational environment in which the company works must be one of the most important factors to consider when looking at the possible outlay on DR and BCP.

Approaches to writing plans and implementing plans

There are a variety of ways in which BCP and DR plans can be developed, some more effective than others, but the most effective is very often simply the one that works for the organisation itself. The first step will be to ensure that the risk assessment has been completed effectively, considering all those 'unlikely' events. It is not necessary to consider all possible events but more the consequences of the event. For example, there are a number of potential events that could make a building unavailable – bomb, flood, fire, aircraft crash, building decay, animal infestation, power outages disrupting supplies for lifts, doors, lighting, etc. Some of these may not affect your building but a neighbouring one, with the same consequences. All these will result in similar outcomes with only slightly different impacts, one of which might be the duration of the disruption.

Nevertheless the plans can be developed to deal with all these eventualities by addressing what to do if the building is unavailable for a significant period. It is also where the procedures for implementation become significant. As a result of the specific event occurring, those in charge would need to decide which aspects if any of the disaster recovery plan should be implemented and to what degree. This will be determined by the magnitude of the problem, the anticipated duration of the problem and the impact on normal business operations.

It is often good practice to involve a number of key staff members in a workshop to determine what would really have a major effect on their work. It is sometimes overlooked that the supply of a seemingly minor part of the business process could have a major impact by disrupting several other aspects of the operations. This may have been done at the original risk assessment but a slightly different approach may be required in order to consider these more unlikely and perhaps fanciful events.

It is often questioned how far this fanciful suggestion of events should be taken. There is no rule but what is clear is that in the recent past some organisations have been caught out by not going far enough. When the World Trade Center in America was first attacked in February 1993 with bombs placed in the underground car park, more than 50 per cent of the companies working in the building at the time never traded effectively again. This was the result of the building being declared unsafe and hence closed to all access until a full building survey had been completed – an activity that took several months. The main problem for the companies involved was the loss of access to vital records, notably those pertaining to cash-flow.

The lack of access is a major issue often overlooked. It is often the case that the lack of access is caused by a problem elsewhere – in the building next door or perhaps some distance away. The need for security cordons of varying sizes, up to some kilometres in certain circumstances, means that the drafting of BCP plans must consider who else is in the neighbourhood and the possible consequences of their presence. Those working near the Buncefield oil deport in the UK should have considered the possibility of an incident affecting them at least, even if they hadn't expected the major events that actually transpired in December 2005.

What is important though is to keep a sense of perspective. A very experienced member from the Institute of Advanced Motorists used to say to potential members that one should never be surprised by anything that happens on the road – expect the unexpected. This was until he talked to a fellow driver who had experienced a Boeing 747 jumbo jet trying to land in front of him on the A4 road out of London instead of the main runway at Heathrow Airport. Perhaps that is beyond reasonable expectation. That an aeroplane could 'fall out of the sky' onto any specific location is possible but there are clearly places where this is far more likely – under the main flight paths into and out of major airports for example. So do we ignore this threat elsewhere? Since it is likely that the business impact will be high, then it is worthy of further consideration. But we do need to consider the likelihood and therefore come up with a reasonable assessment of the risk and then consider appropriate countermeasures.

Implementing these plans also requires some considerable and detailed planning. Simply issuing a document to all staff and assuming that is good enough would be naive. The implementation needs to be accompanied by a significant awareness and education programme to ensure that all staff end up being fully aware of the plans, as they affect them, and what actions they need to take in the event of an issue arising. It is almost inevitable that staff will say they will check on the details 'tomorrow' which, almost as inevitably, will be too late.

The need for documentation, maintenance and testing

Documentation is vital and can be the difference between a successful conclusion to an event and a disaster. It is vital because everyone involved with and affected by the event must have the same understanding and expectation of the response. If anyone 'does their own thing' it is likely to cause even more problems and possibly counteract the good work being done by others. Advice can be sought from the professionals in this area who will help to draft and test documentation and plans for organisations particularly where the issues are complex or likely to prove expensive. Even for the less grand requirements, professional advice at the start can help to ensure the development is on a firm footing.

Just documenting the expected actions and procedures though is not enough. If the documents are not available to those who need them, at the time they need them, they are almost worthless. It is clearly not sensible, for example, to have all the documents stored in a nice secure place in the office if one of the potential events is a lack of access to the office. Giving them to key staff members to look after at home is a better idea unless that staff member is critical to the emergency actions and they happen to be on leave when the event happens. There is also the concern about the overall security of the plans which may well be commercially sensitive, for example. Once again there needs to be the compromise between confidentiality and availability.

Maintenance of the plans is another area that can cause problems. Organisations have in the past spent considerable amounts of time and effort getting the plans written and checked in preparation for some significant potential problem such as the Millennium Bug. They then leave the plans on the shelf for the next few years without further attention. The plans are not used in anger and so they become invalid through lack of attention and maintenance. Then, when they are required again, the plans don't work properly and are likely to cause more problems than they solve.

Contracts for the provision of a disaster recovery facility are now commonplace with companies offering standardised facilities of desks, chairs, computers, printers, telephones, faxes, etc. that can be made available at very short notice (usually within a matter of hours) and configured quite quickly (usually within about 24 hours) to emulate the normal working environment in which a company is used to operating. The investment in such a provision must be made after completing and accepting the findings of the BIA in order to justify the expenditure.

Routines for testing and checking the details of the plans must be comprehensive but again there is a need for a reality check. To close a factory even for a day could have very significant implications for the company concerned and, whilst it might provide an excellent test of the BCP, may actually do more harm than good to the profitability of the company.

Testing can be carried out in a variety of ways. The usual first step is to do a desk check of the plans. This involves the key people sitting round a desk pretending to do the activities required of them in the plans. This will often sort out the major issues with plans and will enable updating and checking to be completed. As a result of this and the appropriate updates the next stage might be to do a limited walkthrough of all the parts of the plans but in manageable chunks. We are all familiar with the fire drills that are required for organisations large and small. This type of practice for similar incidents – chemical spills, power outages, bombs, etc. – can provide a good reality check. Is it really possible to evacuate a 15-storey building with no power for the lifts or main lights within the stipulated time in the event of a fire? What happens if one of the staircases is not available? This also will raise further issues as well as acting as a reminder for staff of the existence of the emergency plans.

The next step may be a full-scale enactment of the plans. This can be critical if the testing so far has only been carried out in parts. When checking the plans for one organisation based in a three-storey building it became clear that each floor was expected to evacuate to a specific building in the neighbourhood in the event of a major incident. This was fine until it was recognised that each of the three floors was expected to go to the same building but that it was not large enough to accommodate all the occupants of all three floors simultaneously. One floor at a time was fine, but not all three.

If the full enactment is to be effective it needs significant planning and must be co-ordinated by a central control organisation, often called the incident room or war room, who in reality would also control the implementation of the BCP or DR plan. Often such facilities are set up and maintained in case of an emergency but clearly they need to be somewhere that is likely to be available in the event of the most serious event. Housing them in the basement of the main building is fine provided that the unavailability of the building is not one of the major incidents being considered.

The reality may well be that this central control facility may need to be set up wherever is available in the event of an incident. It may therefore be more practical to consider temporary facilities and to define the essential requirements in terms of communications, office space and the like. Then having all the necessary information readily available in a portable format should provide the necessary resilience. Identifying a number of potential facilities in other sites belonging to the organisation, sister organisations or publicly available facilities such as community halls, sports centres or the like might be considered prudent. Clearly it is critical that assuming such facilities would be made available is not sensible. A short discussion of the facilities with the management would ensure they would be compliant with a request should the appropriate situation ever arise.

It is often considered appropriate to simulate possible emergencies in some way. One way to do this is to use the 'brown envelope' technique. This entails setting up a scenario of a major incident and then drafting a number of instructions or information sheets given or sent out to relevant staff in 'brown envelopes'. The relevant staff members are instructed to open the envelope at the appropriate time and to take the necessary actions in accordance with the information supplied. This could be to make a telephone call, to invoke a particular element of a plan or some other action including reacting in some specific manner. The control of this exercise must be outside and independent from the 'normal' control of the incident in order to ensure it is as realistic as possible and engenders the correct responses from the incident management team.

This technique can be used to test the plans for one specific location or area of an organisation, or indeed for the whole organisation if it is deemed appropriate and necessary. It may be that the co-ordination of actions in a significant number of locations (shops or branches located all over the country or similar) may require the whole organisation, or at least a major part of it, to participate in this level of testing. This may need to be done over a weekend, for example, when the normal work is unlikely to be severely affected. To try and run such a major exercise during normal operations may be deemed too expensive or difficult to do without seriously affecting normal operations. It is also important to pick a suitable time from the business perspective. Choosing the busy season or at the financial year-end is unlikely to result in wholehearted buy-in to the tests and so will reduce their effectiveness. Nevertheless, whether it is a small-scale trial of the plans in one location or a full-scale whole-organisational simulation, it is critical that the exercise properly tests the appropriateness, effectiveness and comprehensiveness of the overall planning.

Need for links to managed service provision and outsourcing

Any plans for dealing with emergencies must naturally cover those services supplied by third parties as well as those the organisation itself carries out. Naturally this must start with the contract which has to include some mention of the expected level of service provision in the event of an emergency. It would not be helpful if the telephone contractor said that it would take three days to enable the telephones in the incident room in the event of an emergency, for example.

All contractors must then be closely involved with the development and testing of any set of BCP or DR plans. The services they provide may be critical to the overall success of the DR and may be essential in dealing with minor incidents as part of the BCP. Indeed it may be that, as part of the contract, the responsibility for the management and resolution of minor incidents as part of the BCP could be passed over to the supplier. It would naturally be prudent to check that their plans work and are consistent with those of the client organisation.

Where managed services are under consideration, the contracts must provide the facility to ensure these services will continue to be provided under the changed circumstances of the DR or BCP. Whilst it may not be feasible to envisage all circumstances that might arise and hence ensure every angle is covered, it should be possible to ensure that changes to the contract don't require lengthy procurement processes that will take longer to sort out than the original problem.

Need for secure off-site storage of vital material

As already mentioned, the access to BCP and DR plans is critical. It is useless to spend a lot of time and money on developing and testing the plans if they are not available at the crucial time. It is critical that the plans are available to those who need them whenever and wherever they are. They must always be consistent – everybody has the same and latest version – and they must be in a usable format. It is inevitable that there will be a significant quantity of personal data in the plans – contact details for all the key players and indeed possibly for all staff may have to be included. The requirements of the Data Protection Act must be acknowledged.

In the past there have been 'war chests' containing all the plans, contact details and the like for the management of a possible situation. These had to be stored somewhere and it would be the responsibility of one or more people to take the chest to an appropriate location when required. It has been known for key individuals to have to store these chests at home as being the place least likely to suffer a major incident.

With the more modern technology now available, a better solution might be to provide them to key people on an encrypted memory stick in a format that requires no major application to read them such as Adobe Acrobat Reader™ – the small application could be on the stick too. This could be used anywhere there is a computer with an internet connection (now an acceptably common requirement) and, with a simple piece of software, when accessed it could be made to check a central repository for the latest version. This meets many of the issues raised above including the issue of security, particularly if the stick is securely locked in some way in case it should fall into the wrong hands.

The alternative is to find somewhere secure to store all the plans that is always going to be accessible in the event of a problem at the main building. This may prove problematic. A sister organisation or perhaps another branch of the same company might be an appropriate place but it is more likely to be geography dependent than anything else. There are accepted distances for the cordons that might affect the accessibility to a building. It is important to take these sorts of distances into account when deciding where the most appropriate storage location might be. Naturally, among the possible events leading to the use of the BCP or DR plans, a terrorist incident or fire will be one of the major factors to consider. The Buncefield and World Trade Center incidents may make people think again about the impact of other businesses in the locality and consequently where an appropriate place might be to store the emergency plans safely.

It might also be necessary to consider how critical information or other assets might need to be stored elsewhere to enable 'normal business' to be maintained. This might mean taking backup tapes from computer systems off site each night to ensure their availability or could entail having a secure store of critical supplies (maybe drugs for a hospital for example) some-where appropriately available. Yet again it is important to have reality checks on these types of stores. It could end up with a complete ready-use store else-where, which in turn means further BCP issues, more expense and ultimately distracting the organisation from their main business activities.

Need to involve personnel, suppliers and IT systems providers

It is vital, naturally, that all staff, full and part time, temporary and permanent, must be fully aware of the workings of the BCP and DR plans as all the staff are affected by them. This may also impact visitors to the site but this may be best dealt with by the host staff member being responsible for the security of their guest. The requirement for an ongoing education and training programme is clear but again this must be tempered against the risk and compared with the BIA. It is good practice to ensure there is an induction course covering all the basic requirements and perhaps highlighting the individual's responsibility in the event of an incident. This could then be supported by a series of 'exercises', reminder sessions, updated leaflet or email distributions and the like.

The extent of such a programme of education and training must always consider the other key players namely suppliers, outsource companies and the like. Staff who routinely work within the establishment of the client, manning an IT helpdesk or other such facility for example, must be involved and actively engaged in a manner that doesn't affect their productivity but equally helps to ensure they do not become a liability. In the event of a fire, the first question asked by the arriving fire-fighters will be, 'Is anyone inside?' Unless an unequivocal 'No' is given in response, their first efforts will be targeted at getting the people out. If only part of the organisation has any method of recording those who are working in a building it will be very difficult to ensure that a full picture of the evacuation is available. This in turn could not only compromise the safety of the fire-fighters unnecessarily but could also affect the impact of the fire-fighting efforts to reduce the damage caused.

When it comes to DR, the need for suppliers of crucial services to be involved is also paramount. Their responsibility should be towards their client but it may take a second place if the operational effectiveness of the company itself is in danger. The joint understanding of client and supplier is then all the more critical. How this is dealt with in a contractual manner will be determined by issues and requirements outside the scope of this book. Nonetheless, it is critical that those who have to manage and work with the contracts on a day-to-day basis must understand the detail of how any SLA will work in the event of a major problem arising.

On these occasions, IT companies are always the first ones that come to mind but it must be remembered that all the other suppliers ranging from telecommunications and mail through food and stationery supply to cleaning and waste disposal services must be considered as well. Whilst not all of these may need to be dealt with within the first 24 hours of an incident, it is highly likely that they will have to be dealt with within a fairly short period of time of an ongoing problem. Workers in a new building used as a DR site will still need to be fed and watered, supplied with paper and have the waste paper cleared.

Relationship with security incident management

Incident management is the term used to describe the work done to deal with the incident itself. It is usual to have a team specifically trained and ready for this work since it is often quite technical. There are often legal aspects to consider too – if the building is the site of a crime then the police will close it to all and may impound anything contained in the vicinity. Forensic readiness is the work of ensuring that when an incident takes place crucial evidence in the form of temporary files on a computer, fingerprints (electronic or human), logs and a wealth of other materials are not destroyed whether intentionally (by the perpetrator) or accidentally (by turning off a PC or server or walking through a crime scene in dirty boots).

Once again planning is the key and it is vital that due consideration is given to all the materials (information, tapes, etc.) that will be required to maintain business as usual and/or to activate a DR site. Where these materials are stored has been mentioned earlier but it is worth considering the possible eventuality that there is no access at all under any circumstances to 'normal business information'.

The relationship between the teams responsible for dealing with the incident, the BCP and the DR plan must be a very close one. There is a wide range of overlapping areas and as such there must be no chance of anything being missed. It is more likely that doing it twice is a better option than running the risk of it not being done at all. Clearly there are issues in many areas here and once again it is at the planning stage that these must be talked through and worked out in such a way as to be applicable in any circumstances. Table-top walkthroughs often bowl out problems in this area when one team can say, '. . . and then I would do this' and another team can say, '. . . but we would have done that already'. Or, 'You can't do that because we will have already . . .'.

One of the most difficult areas to work through is that of prioritisation. It might be very important for the business to continue in certain areas but, if the incident management team wants to seal off a specific location, it may not be possible to get the necessary information or equipment to continue. Someone needs to be in a position of authority to make the necessary and, most importantly, timely decisions.

National and international standards

When the syllabus for this exam was devised and this book was envisaged, a specific decision was taken not to follow or use any one standard. The reason for this was to ensure that the resulting qualification was as generic and applicable around the world as possible. It is for that reason that little mention has been made to specific standards although there are many that could have been covered.

In the case of BCP and DR, there are a number of standards in the UK and elsewhere in the world that cover some or most aspects of the management of BCP and DR. BS25999-1 is the British Standard on Business Continuity Management but there are a number of other documents that would provide useful information: Publicly Available Specification 77 (PAS77) – IT Service Continuity Management, the ITIL guide on service management best practice now produced by the IT Service Management Forum and ISO/IEC 27000 series of Information Security Management standards to name the more significant ones. In addition, the Business Continuity Institute produces its own guidelines which are an excellent source of information. The reader would be well advised to consult the appropriate documentation that is available to ensure that what they implement in this area is based on good practice and therefore likely to be successful. The real problem with this area of Information Assurance is that, like a teabag, one is never going to know how good it is until it is put into hot water!

INVESTIGATIONS AND FORENSICS

We have already mentioned that, even in organisations with very effective governance, there will be occasions on which it is necessary to investigate activity and use forensic techniques to discover and preserve evidence for later use. Some of this has already been described in previous sections and the reader will be referred back to that material where appropriate. The reader is advised to read the section on 'Security incident management' in Chapter 3 if you have not already done so. Much of the knowledge for this section is described in that material.

LEARNING OUTCOMES

Following study in this area, the reader should be able to define and explain each of the following terms and processes and be able to describe their appropriate use as applicable.

Common processes, tools and techniques for conducting investigations

In Chapter 1 we described the reasons why organisations must develop policy, processes and procedures (Developing policies, standards, procedures and guidelines internally and with third parties).

These reasons include the need to be ready to investigate incidents and possible criminal offences. Although the events that initiate this kind of response may vary greatly, the response itself will often be very similar in nature. It is important that the process has been developed and checked with a specialist in this area before it is used. The response needs to be prompt, appropriate and valid. Any mistake can render the findings inadmissible in a court or employment tribunal. It is no use bringing in law enforcement agencies if the evidence has already been contaminated beyond usability.

It is also vital that, when an investigation starts, the incident team consults senior management to decide whether the organisation intends to prosecute (e.g. if the organisation has been hacked or suffered a loss) as this determines whether or not to involve criminal justice agencies and the level of effort required in gathering the evidence, for example getting external specialists on site to image drives for evidence.

Legal and regulatory guidelines

In Chapter 1 (Relationship with corporate governance and related areas of risk management) we described the greatly increased legal and regulatory requirements that have been introduced in many jurisdictions worldwide for Corporate Governance and accountability. Part of this requires the ability to investigate incidents and attribute responsibility to an individual.

More importantly, the investigation must be conducted in a manner that preserves the evidence in a form that is compliant with legal procedures. This is outlined in the section on 'Legal and regulatory guidelines affecting conduct and standards of evidence' in Chapter 3 and the section 'Collection of admissible evidence' in the same chapter describes the challenges in collecting and preserving the evidence.

Part of the section on 'Relationship with security incident management' in this chapter explains the need to practise incident response and investigations to help identify any flaws in the plans. Time spent planning, training and practising is very rarely wasted.

One final tip: whatever you do, make sure you understand the Rules of Evidence for the jurisdiction that you are in and do not break the chain of custody for your evidence.

Need for relations with law enforcement

Chapter 1 has a section on 'The role of Information Security in counter hi-tech and other crime' explaining that there are times when it may be necessary to engage with specialist law enforcement organisations who work in the computer crime area or those working to protect what is often generically called the Critical National Infrastructure of a country. There may be agencies, such as the Centre for the Protection of National Infrastructure (CPNI) in the UK and the Department for Homeland Security (DHS) in America, who wish to work with your organisation to help improve the level of security if it is considered important to the 'national interest'. This includes utility and communications companies, among others.

There are also various emergency response teams, such as CERT in America, GOVCERT in the UK and the Forum for Incident Response and Security Teams (FIRST). Find their websites and read their guidance documents for much valuable information.

The section on 'Working with law enforcement organisations' in Chapter 3 describes the mandatory requirement in the UK to report certain crimes or activities to law enforcement agencies. Don't forget that this also applies to anything found in your systems; for example, if a member of staff is suspected of offences involving child pornography using office IT and there are suspicious files.

The law enforcement agencies often have specialist staff who can offer advice and guidance to any organisation that feels at risk from logical or physical attacks. It is always worth contacting them for any material they can provide.

Issues when buying in forensic and investigative support from third parties

Some organisations choose to outsource forensics and investigations to a third party. This may be because they are too small to have their own skills in-house, it may be because it is not considered to be a major risk or for any one of a number of other reasons. The section on 'Security issues when procuring forensic services and support from third parties' in Chapter 3 highlights the assurance issues concerning confidentiality and non-disclosure when using a third party.

One area we have not addressed is that of timeliness. In order to preserve evidence, devices must not be used, even if it is a critical server or business asset, until forensically investigated. That means that any evidence must be collected as soon as possible to allow a prompt return to normal operations.

It is most important to gain agreement and support from senior management in advance as to the method by which third-party support is procured, how any such work is to be done and the means by which their help should be invoked. There isn't time to identify possible suppliers, go out to tender, negotiate terms and schedule the work. Incident response needs to be very prompt. A framework agreement is required.

Companies that do decide to have their own in-house resources must make sure that the products and skills they acquire are sufficient for the task and will provide legally admissible evidence. There are well-known products with a very good reputation and there are others that make bold claims but don't meet the standard. It is important to do your homework before buying goods or services.

Once you have them, make sure that assets and skills are tested and updated regularly to make sure they are ready when actually needed. One simple mistake can invalidate everything else you do correctly.

Conclusion

We have tried throughout this book to give the reader enough information to help them to reach a level of understanding and knowledge that will prove to be an excellent basis for taking the ISEB's Information Security Management Principles foundation examination. We have also tried to provide a general grounding to any interested reader in the fundamentals of the subject. It is not intended that this should be the only book that is required if you are to take up a role in Information Assurance – far from it – but we do hope that it whets your appetite for the immensely complex and interesting field of Information Management and its assurance.

Those who choose to go on to more demanding and detailed areas of study or employment will find a vast array of texts available which cover any one or more of the areas in this book in much more detail. If your interest is less detailed, then we hope we have given you enough information to allow you to make appropriate decisions on your activities, further study, preparations and possible careers in Information Assurance. Those who have responsibility for all or some of the aspects covered here may well find it useful as an introduction which will help to sell the concepts to senior managers.

In all your work, we wish you well and hope that all your preparations prevent the worst happening – that is the best we can offer you.

Sample Questions

1. Symmetric key encryption systems are those in which:
    a. sender and recipient have completely unrelated encryption and decryption keys;
    b. sender and recipient both share the same encryption and decryption keys;
    c. sender and recipient have different but mathematically related encryption and decryption keys.
2. Production of a message digest enables the recipient to:
    a. verify the integrity of the message content and authenticate the sender;
    b. verify the integrity of the message content only;
    c. authenticate the sender only.

3. Asymmetric key encryption is not generally used for encrypting large messages because:

   a. it only works on very short message lengths;

   b. it is less secure that symmetric key encryption;

   c. it takes much longer to carry out the encryption and decryption processes.

4. What is the main purpose of assurance training?

   a. To prevent incidents from occurring.

   b. To ensure the organisation complies with legislation.

   c. To make people aware of their assurance responsibilities.

   d. To ensure that management objectives are achieved.

5. Assurance training should focus on which of the following?

   a. Topical assurance issues.

   b. Assurance issues that are relevant to the organisation.

   c. Organisational structures and management structures.

   d. All security issues.

6. Which of the user groups below should receive security training?

   a. All users of the organisation's Information Systems.

   b. Senior management.

   c. End users within the organisation.

   d. All technical and administration staff.

7. What are the three main types of controls that can be used to protect information?

   a. Confidentiality, integrity and availability.

   b. Vulnerability, risk and threat.

   c. Detective, reactive and preventative.

   d. Physical, technical and procedural.

8. What are the different ways in which controls can be used?

   a. Confidentiality, integrity and availability.

   b. Vulnerability, risk and threat.

   c. Detective, reactive and preventative.

   d. Physical, technical and procedural.

9. What is considered the most effective approach to security?

   a. Have as much security as the organisation can afford.

   b. Only use those securities measures that are absolutely essential.

   c. Only use security measures that provide the best possible assurance available in that field.

   d. A layered approach with a combination of different measures for different risks.

10. A clear desk policy would be regarded as which type of security measure?
    a. Procedural.
    b. Technical.
    c. Physical.
    d. None of these three.
11. Which of the following describes an appropriate manner for the effective deletion of information from a computer system?
    a. Pressing the delete key several times.
    b. Checking to ensure the directory no longer contains an entry for the files.
    c. Writing random data to the same data file for at least seven cycles.
    d. There is no effective way of ensuring effective data deletion from computer systems.

Pointers for activities in the chapter

Activity 4.1

The important thing to remember is the need to balance the risk of malware against the costs of purchasing and implementing countermeasures. A good base set of recommendations would be as follows.

- Have a combination anti-virus and personal firewall program on each PC that has a connection to the Internet or is networked to another computer that does. Choose a product that will also restrict the executables that will run on that computer to a known list of authorised products.

- Change all the default settings in operating systems, applications and browsers, for example passwords, configurations, open ports, etc. to make it harder for malware to compromise the computer.

- Apply patches to the operating system and applications promptly.

- Educate users about the threat and some of the tactics used.

- Have a backup policy, do it regularly and then test it.

- Consider a firewall with intrusion detection or prevention capability for a network connected to the Internet.

Activity 4.2

The need for Information Assurance is not intuitive. People need to be made aware of the risks and threats, together with some basic guidance on what to do. Make sure that the following are in place:

- security policy document, defining what to do;

- relevant terms and conditions in contracts of employment;

- a clear and easy-to-follow Acceptable Use Policy;

- material for assurance awareness training;

- code of conduct for staff and volunteers.

The organisation is starting to grow and now is the time to define the Information Assurance culture that will be of great benefit to GANT in the years to come.

Activity 4.3

Remember that transferring the work to a third party does not absolve GANT from responsibility for the assurance of their data. GANT is as culpable as the third party if a breach occurs and GANT can be shown not to have exercised their duty of care, often known as due diligence, in ensuring that the third party:

- was aware of its obligations;
- implemented and maintained appropriate countermeasures;
- submitted to periodic compliance audits.

Activity 4.4

The policy document needs to include a specification for access control and minimum requirements for Identification and Authentication:

- for users in the office;
- for any remote access users.

This should take into account any data from risk assessments performed for GANT.

The documents should also define requirements for:

- separation of roles and responsibilities – for example users and administrators;
- implementation of user groups based on roles, often grouped by job function;
- enrolment of new users and deletion access rights of those who leave.

Activity 4.5

The first task is to identify all repositories of data and work outwards to identify the means by which they are accessed internally and externally (if any).

The next task is to decide how to manage the risks each of these means of access brings to GANT.

Activity 4.6

Suggested steps in the process:

- Decide how to identify and value assets for Confidentiality, Integrity and Availability.
- Identify different kinds of media and suitable labelling and protection strategies for them.
- Decide on an appropriate labelling system for the assets, for example
  - Highly confidential
  - Confidential
  - Sensitive – environmental.
- Identify the assets using the guidelines defined.
- Label the assets and implement any other countermeasures required.

Activity 4.7

Start by explaining that it is like putting a door with a lock in what is currently a solid wall round the systems of GANT. It allows access to people who have the right key, but that lock can also picked by a skilful attacker.

It is also worth explaining that it is possible for sensitive data to end up being saved on the home PC, which is not as well protected as the office systems and therefore is a weak spot vulnerable to attack. A network usage policy or technology (or both) needs putting in place to ensure that this does not happen.

Another important point is to explain that the connection can be eaves-dropped, just like a telephone conversation, and the data passing backwards and forwards can be copied. That might include usernames and passwords. A means of protecting the traffic and login data must be put in place, preferably involving some kind of one-time password system such as a token.

Activity 4.8

The first thing to recognise is that this is usually a job for an expert and so consider asking for some outside help or training. Like a firewall, these are tricky systems to configure properly and are of little value unless working properly. Once you have the data, you then need to be able to understand what it is telling you.

The most important thing is to identify what is and is not allowed to happen on the network and define these as rules in the IDS. The second thing is to identify the points in the network where monitoring is best used. Obvious locations are any connection to external networks and the internet and any point used to separate networks, where an attacker might be trying to gain access to a partitioned area containing sensitive data.

Activity 4.9

Actions include the following.

- Identifying the most cost-effective means of linking the two organisations, depending on the number of users, volume of data and the frequency with which the connection will be used. The options include dial-up, ADSL (broadband), VPN and leased line.

- Deciding how to secure the connection:
  - How should each user Identify and Authenticate themselves to the other organisation?
  - What kind of protection does the data travelling across the connection need?
  - What kind of data sharing protocol is needed for legal purposes (e.g. Data Protection Act)?

Activity 4.10

The forum will have the same kind of threats as email and websites, in that it is possible to hide malware in the messages and it is also possible for an attacker to try and take control of the website itself, to hide malware in the code for the pages. You recommend that the forum should not be made available without appropriate countermeasures being in place to screen any postings to it for malware. You recommend that specialist advice be sought from an expert in this field.

Activity 4.11

The DPA can be complex to understand. It is important to read through all the material, work out which parts apply to GANT and its partners and then write a protocol to govern the data sharing with the third parties. Get the document checked by a lawyer who has knowledge of the DPA before using it.

Activity 4.12

The video conferencing system will provide an easy access route into the GANT data network unless careful thought is given to the protection of the link. The protocols allowed through from the system must be tightly controlled and the link may need monitoring with an Intrusion Detection or Prevention system of some sort to defeat attempts to hack into the network.

Activity 4.13

The ITT documentation should make sure that the invitees are aware of:

- the levels of Confidentiality, Integrity and Availability required for GANT assets;
- any legal requirements, such as the Data Protection Act, that will apply;
- any in-house standards for Information Security, such as ISO 27001, to which the supplier must adhere;
- the requirement for the successful bidder to sign a formally binding contract and data protocol for any GANT data for which they may be responsible;
- their duty of care towards GANT assets in general;
- their agreement to no-notice compliance audits by GANT or their appointed auditors.

Activity 4.14

Your description should include the following hierarchy:

(i)   Policy – one-page document signed by the chief executive, requiring everyone to take Information Assurance seriously because it is everyone's responsibility.

(ii) Standards – defining what is acceptable in terms of Information Assurance design and implementation.

(iii) Procedures – The operating instructions to ensure compliance with policy and standards. The 'how-to' documents.

(iv) Guidelines – documents that clarify any complex areas and processes, such as risk management.

Activity 4.15

The baseline documentation should consist of a specification for each type of workstation or server, listing at least:

- minimum required version and patch level of operating system;
- components of the operating system to be installed and their configuration;
- standard access control lists and privileges for default user accounts;
- lists of applications to install, the components of them to use and their configuration;
- any specific security countermeasures or configurations to be loaded and implemented;
- network addressing format and type (DNS, DHCP, static IP, etc.);
- backup strategy for data.

The documentation to be provided for each system should detail the physical and logical build state, hardware serial numbers and location. These documents will form the reference point for the change control process.

Activity 4.16

The report's specification must include:

- a requirement for data that provides evidence of performance against SLAs;
- time scales for reporting and regular deadlines to ensure timeliness of reports;
- standards for reporting incidents;

- escalation procedures for both parties;
- any level of Protective Marking for such a potentially sensitive document.

Activity 4.17

The internal audit process will require the checking of the use of the controls and policies against actual practice. A good tip is to pick a process and follow it through from start to finish, talking to people who actually use it regularly, and also looking at audit and event data to make sure that all the elements agree.

Activity 4.18

The most important point is to be able to follow the guidelines for the collection of evidence in such a way that it is admissible in a court or tribunal. These are contained in guidance issued by the Association of Chief Police Officers in the UK. The process often requires some specialist hardware and software.

For a small organisation like GANT, probably the most important part of the plan is to state that you would bring in an external consultant with specialist knowledge in how to do this or have a contract in place with an organisation that can do it for you.

Another important aspect is to make sure you know the activities about which you are legally required to notify the police:

- suspected paedophile images or activity;
- terrorism;
- danger to life of an individual.

Activity 4.19

There is a series of mandatory and desirable criteria, which should be listed in the Invitation to Tender (ITT) document. Tenderers should be required to answer all these questions as part of their initial submissions:

Mandatory

- Supplier to agree to no-notice quality and assurance audits by GANT.
- All source code and development material to be placed in escrow in case of business failure by the supplier.
- All staff who will work on the project have been vetted for honesty and reliability.
- Supplier agrees to sign a legally binding data sharing protocol as part of the contract.
- Supplier has suitable indemnity insurance.

- Supplier to provide three referees for previous work of this type.

- Deliverable product and all outputs capable of being inspected by standard malware scanners.

Desirable

- Supplier has achieved level 5 on the Capability Maturity Model (CMM) scheme.

- Supplier has achieved a quality accreditation such as ISO 9001.

- Supplier is accredited to ISO/IEC 27000 series for Information Security.

Activity 4.20

Before any kind of change can be made the suggested modification must be formally reviewed and approved by a Change Management Team. This is in order to protect the existing information assets and business processes against any adverse impact to service delivery.

If the request is approved the users will be asked to help design the change. The work will be done on the development system by the developers and then the users will be asked to test the new and existing functionality to make sure there are no unexpected results.

Having said all this, in a properly configured Information Security architecture, the users would not have the necessary privileges or access to the development tools and source code to make changes. They would have to go to the development and system administration teams.

Activity 4.21

There are several rating and assessment schemes for the security of IT products. The level of product accreditation required is proportional to the impact on GANT and the toads themselves if there was an issue with the information assets. It is not anticipated that a high level of accreditation will be required in this instance.

The second point to note is that, while the level of assurance goes up from using such products, the range of choice goes down and the price often goes up. This is because not all manufacturers go through the assessment process and those that do need to recoup the costs involved. It may be that an unacceptable proportion of the grant would be consumed by the assured products and not the application, but only a quick review of the requirements and available products would confirm this.

The final point to make is that one should never rely on the claims of the supplier to have met a particular standard. This should always be verified with the organisation that performed the assessment and the website for that particular standard to make sure that they are listed as having passed.

Activity 4.22

Possible solutions for database protection could include:

- two-factor authentication;
- encryption of the database;
- audit trail of changes list.

Possible uses of a commercial product would need to take into account:

- key management;
- key escrow;
- use of digital signatures on emails.

Activity 4.23

(i) The initial training campaign should focus on confidentiality of information generally. All staff should understand the importance of protecting members' information and the possible threats to the organisation in terms of sabotage, theft, etc. Specific training should be given to any staff handling personal records so that they can understand their specific responsibilities in protecting this type of information. The types of messages that could be included are:

- responsibilities when handling information about people;
- enterprise's requirements for handling information especially about people;
- the importance of password protection and maintaining a clear desk policy;
- protection for information that has to be taken out of the office.

(ii) Face-to-face training would be the preferred option as the enterprise is small probably with one-to-one training within the UK with Dr Peabody and any other staff handling membership or other confidential information. Producing an induction pack could ensure that any new personnel are made aware of their assurance responsibilities. Producing some posters to be put on the wall to remind people to be careful about protecting GANT information.

Activity 4.24

Without detailed knowledge it is difficult to guess how long each section could survive but it might be reasonable for the following.

(i) Membership details. It is unlikely that any details about the membership would be required urgently and so it might be appropriate for this section to talk of a week being an acceptable period. There could be some events that make this time scale too long. For example if the annual conference is coming up, then it might make the information much more important and in the last few days before the issue of the routine newsletter fairly critical if the newsletter is to get out on time. There would of course also be the discussion around how important the newsletter was – would it matter if it was issued a few days later?

(ii) Natterjack toad breeding ground details. Once again this information might not be terribly important in general and so an interruption to availability of a few days or perhaps even weeks might not be a problem. If a high-profile, very significant planning application was coming to the final stages of a court action though with the final court case pending in a few days time, this too might alter things. It might not be feasible or financially acceptable though to have special measures in place for such an event and they would have to accept the higher risk to that information.

(iii) Forthcoming planning application where there was interest in the toads. It may be that the details of this application are held on paper in which case there would be no problem but if emails, copies of letters or other related documentation was held on the computer once again this could be critical at certain times.

(iv) Financial information. The general running of a group like this would not entail significant financial work at any time except perhaps at the financial year-end when the Charities Commission or taxman require financial information to be presented for inspection. This might again alter the requirements enough to warrant some additional measures being put in place.

A full business impact analysis would determine the overall level of risk and specific areas where special measures might be needed. This would then provide the necessary justification for the senior staff to decide on the appropriate measures to be taken.

Activity 4.25

The first requirement would be to carry out a risk analysis. This would determine what the real risks to the information are likely to be. Considering such threats as those posed by visitors, cleaning staff, temporary staff members as potential information thieves would help determine the likelihood of the risk. This assessment would also need to consider who might be interested in obtaining the information and to what lengths they might be prepared to go in order to obtain it.

Considering how well the information is currently recorded (catalogued in some way), which would allow regular checks of the information to ensure there have been no losses or compromises, would provide information on the weaknesses and vulnerabilities. Keeping records of copies taken of documents and their distribution would be useful. An information asset register might be the starting point for a more orderly control of information.

Locking drawers, cabinets and filing facilities would clearly be a good start but the full risk analysis would be a better start and this must be done as a result of the business impact analysis which would then provide the justification for such action and expenditure if required.

Answers to sample questions

1. The correct answer is b.
2. The correct answer is a.
3. The correct answer is c.
4. The correct answer is c.
5. The correct answer is b.
6. The correct answer is a.
7. The correct answer is d.
8. The correct answer is c.
9. The correct answer is d.
10. The correct answer is a.
11. The correct answer is c.

NOTES

1 GSM encryption can also be thought of as 'link' encryption, as only the connection between the handset and the base station is encrypted. Secure telephones which also use stream ciphers encrypt the entire connection from handset to handset and are therefore said to perform 'end-to-end' encryption.

2 In which an attacker has succeeded in inserting himself between the true sender and recipient, and looks to each exactly like the other.

3 Virtually impossible in this context means virtually impossible to most of us. It should be assumed that the security agencies of major governments will have the method, means and motivation to recover private keys.

REFERENCES AND FURTHER READING

There are numerous books and papers on cryptography and it is impossible to list them all here. Instead we have identified some of the key publications and websites dealing with the topic.

One of the most illuminating introductions to cryptography is '*Cryptography. A Very Short Introduction*' by Professors Fred Piper and Sean Murphy of Royal Holloway, University of London.

A rather heavier tome is '*The Code Breakers*' by David Kahn, which was originally published in 1967, so does not contain information on more recent developments in cryptography, but remains an excellent reference work covering the history of cryptography and that of cryptanalysis, especially during the First and Second World Wars.

Another highly readable book, '*The Code Book*' by Simon Singh, was serialised on television and contains a ten-stage cryptography challenge.

Finally, for those who wish to explore present-day cryptography in greater detail, there is RSA Security's *Official Guide to Cryptography*.

Publications

Anderson, R. (2001) *Security Engineering*. John Wiley & Sons. ISBN 0471389226.

Beker, H. and Piper, F. (1982) *Cipher Systems*. Van Nostrand. ISBN 0442306083.

Bernstein, P.L. (1996, 1998) *Against the Gods*. John Wiley & Sons, Inc. ISBN 0471 295639.

Burnett, S. and Paine, S. (2001) *RSA Security's Official Guide to Cryptography*. McGraw-Hill. ISBN 007213139X.

Diffie, W. and Hellman, M.E. (1976) New directions in cryptography. *IEEE Trans. Inform. Theory*, 22(6), 644–654, http://www.cs.jhu.edu/~rubin/courses/sp03/papers/diffie.hellman.pdf.

Diffie, W. and Landau, S. (1998) *Privacy on the Line*. MIT Press. ISBN 0262041677.

Ford, W. and Baum, M.S. (1997) *Secure Electronic Commerce*. Prentice Hall. ISBN 0134763424.

Kahn, D. (1967) *The Codebreakers*. Scribner. ISBN 0684831309.

Menzies, A.J., van Oorschot, P.C. and Vanstone, S.A. (1996) *Handbook of Applied Cryptography*. CRC Press. ISBN 0849385237 (see also under websites).

Piper, F and Murphy, S. (2002) *Cryptography. A Very Short Introduction*. Oxford University Press. ISBN 0192803158.

Rivest, R.L., Shamir, A. and Adleman, L. (1978) A method for obtaining digital signatures and public-key cryptosystems. *Commun. ACM*, 21, 120–126, http://people.csail.mit.edu/rivest/RivestShamirAdleman-AMethodForObtainingDigitalSignaturesAndPublicKeyCryptosystems.pdf.

Salkind, N.J. (2004) *Statistics for People Who (Think They) Hate Statistics*. SAGE Publications. ISBN 0761 92776X.

Schneier, B. (1995) *Applied Cryptography*. John Wiley & Sons. ISBN 0471117099.

Singh, S. (1999) *The Code Book*. Fourth Estate. ISBN 1857028791.

Smith, R.E. (1997) *Internet Cryptography*. Addison Wesley. ISBN 0201924803.

Websites

The Handbook of Applied Cryptography website (from which it is possible to download the book in pdf format)
http://www.cacr.math.uwaterloo.ca/hac/
RSA Security Labs website with amongst other things a cryptography FAQ in the 'Historical' tab, http://www.rsa.com/rsalabs
The US National Institute of Standards (NIST) cryptography website, http://csrc.nist.gov/

Index